Palgrave Macmillan Studies in Banking and Financial Institutions

Series Editor
Philip Molyneux
University of Sharjah
Sharjah, United Arab Emirates

The Palgrave Macmillan Studies in Banking and Financial Institutions series is international in orientation and includes studies of banking systems in particular countries or regions as well as contemporary themes such as Islamic Banking, Financial Exclusion, Mergers and Acquisitions, Risk Management, and IT in Banking. The books focus on research and practice and include up to date and innovative studies that cover issues which impact banking systems globally.

More information about this series at
http://www.palgrave.com/gp/series/14678

Andrada Bilan • Hans Degryse •
Kuchulain O'Flynn • Steven Ongena

Banking and Financial Markets

How Banks and Financial Technology Are Reshaping Financial Markets

palgrave
macmillan

Andrada Bilan
Department of Banking and Finance
University of Zurich
Zürich, Switzerland

Hans Degryse
Faculty of Economics and Business
Katholieke University of Leuven
Leuven, Belgium

Kuchulain O'Flynn
Department of Banking and Finance
University of Zurich
Zürich, Switzerland

Steven Ongena
Department of Banking and Finance
University of Zurich
Zürich, Switzerland

ISSN 2523-336X ISSN 2523-3378 (electronic)
Palgrave Macmillan Studies in Banking and Financial Institutions
ISBN 978-3-030-26843-5 ISBN 978-3-030-26844-2 (eBook)
https://doi.org/10.1007/978-3-030-26844-2

Cover illustration: Credit Easyturn / E+ / Getty

This Palgrave Macmillan imprint is published by the registered company Springer Nature Switzerland AG.
The registered company address is: Gewerbestrasse 11, 6330 Cham, Switzerland

Contents

1 Introduction 1

2 Securitization and Lending 5

3 Interest Rate Risk 31

4 Credit Risk 61

5 Collateral and Lending 105

6 Global Banking 133

7 FinTech and the Future of Banking 179

8 Conclusion 201

References 205

Index 219

List of Figures

Fig. 4.1 CDS Contract Payment Diagram
Note: This figure illustrates the payment structure of a CDS contract. A protection buyer (buyer of the CDS) makes periodic payments (CDS spread) to the protection seller (seller of the CDS). The protection seller pays the buyer a protection value if a "credit event" occurs. The definition of a "credit event" depends on the standardized contract used, which is determined based on the domicile country of the underlying reference entity 64

Fig. 4.2 CDS credit events and bankruptcy law
Note: This figure illustrates the two conditions for the positive and negative effects of CDS on an underlying firm to be felt. The first is the ability to restructure a company under the domicile country's law. The second condition only plays a role if the first condition is met. The second condition is that the CDS contract type should not pay out when the underlying debt is restructured. If restructuring is not permitted under law, then the CDS contract type is irrelevant and the firms have no incentive to strategically default (as they will be liquidated). However, the incentive for empty creditors to push a firm into bankruptcy remains. If restructuring is permitted and defined as a credit event, in this context, CDS has no effect on the underlying firm. Finally, if restructuring is permitted and not defined as a credit event, then CDS acts as a commitment device as well as increases the probability of default through the effect of empty creditors 83

Fig. 6.1 Stylized global banking system diagram
Note: This stylized diagram of the global banking system includes the mechanisms which the global banking literature seeks to understand. Here, blue represents effects originating in the home country banks or the foreign affiliates of these banks. Green represents the same for foreign banks or local affiliates of foreign banks. The yellow arrows represent the global interbank market where home banks lend to other local banks, foreign banks, and local affiliates of foreign banks. An inward transmission of monetary policy is represented as follows: the arrows from the foreign central bank, Central Bank F, to the affiliate of the home bank, Affiliate of Bank H, and the foreign bank, Bank F, represent the transmission of monetary policy through these banks. These banks then transmit this foreign monetary policy to Non-Bank Borrowers in the home country, in green. This is done directly through cross-border flows (the curved arrows) or through home banks, Bank H, or local affiliates of foreign banks, Affiliate of Bank F. The diagram also shows the outward transmission of the monetary policy. This follows a similar path as the inward transmission but where the monetary policy originates from the home central bank, Central Bank H. The dashed vertical line depicts the boarded between the home country and the foreign country. The area around this dashed line represents the friction of foreign exchange. Finally, the lightning bolts represent shocks to the foreign bank, blue, or the home bank, green. Here "shocks" can either be shocks to the assets of these banks or changes in macroprudential policy 136
Fig. 6.2 Stylized global banking system diagram-Interbank Integration
Note: See Fig. 6.1 for a description of the mechanisms depicted. The bold parts are the mechanisms considered in this section; the opaque parts are not considered 144
Fig. 6.3 Stylized global banking system diagram-Banking Affiliates
Note: See Fig. 6.1 for a description of the mechanisms depicted. The bold parts are the mechanisms considered in this section; the opaque parts are not considered 150
Fig. 6.4 Stylized Global Banking System Diagram-Global Banks-Local Funding Shocks
Note: See Fig. 6.1 for a description of the mechanisms depicted. The bold parts are the mechanisms considered in this section; the opaque parts are not considered 153

Fig. 6.5 Stylized Global Banking System Diagram-Inward Transmission
Note: See Fig. 6.1 for a description of the mechanisms depicted. The bold parts are the mechanisms considered in this section; the opaque parts are not considered 155

Fig. 6.6 Stylized Global Banking System Diagram-Outward Transmission
Note: See Fig. 6.1 for a description of the mechanisms depicted. The bold parts are the mechanisms considered in this section; the opaque parts are not considered 161

Fig. 6.7 Stylized Global Banking System Diagram-Macroprudential Regulation
Note: See Fig. 6.1 for a description of the mechanisms depicted. The bold parts are the mechanisms considered in this section; the opaque parts are not considered 165

Fig. 7.1 The evolution of financial services
Note: Source: IMF (2019) This figure outlines the needs of consumers for financial services, disaggregated by traditional and fintech services 180

List of Tables

Table 2.1	Securitization and lending	7
Table 3.1	Interest rate risk	56
Table 4.1	Credit risk	95
Table 5.1	Collateral and lending	107
Table 6.1	Global banking	168
Table 7.1	Fintech and lending	182

CHAPTER 1

Introduction

The traditional role of a bank is to transfer funds from savers to investors, engaging in maturity transformation, screening for borrower risk, and monitoring for borrower effort in doing so. Until not so long ago, a traditional loan contract included as salient dimensions its amount, the interest rate, its expected credit risk, the required collateral, and the currency in which the loan was granted, all "wrapped" up in a singular way of the bank-firm engagement that occurred mainly through the loan officer. However, the scope of the modern banking industry today is much broader, offering a range of sophisticated financial products, a wider geography-including exposure to countries with various currencies, regulation, and monetary policy regimes-and an increased reliance on financial innovation and technology.

The new bank business models have had repercussions for the traditional loan contract and ways of doing business as well. In particular, the main components and risks of a loan contract can now be altered and hedged on the market, by means of securitization, interest rate swaps, credit default swaps, and foreign exchange transactions. Securitized loans can often be pledged as collateral, thus facilitating new lending. And the lending technology is evolving from one-to-one dialogues between a loan officer and a borrower, at a bank branch, towards more informationally neutral technologies such as peer-to-peer lending or crowd funding.

This book outlines in detail this transition from traditional to modern banking. In six different chapters, we explore the effects of increased finan-

A. Bilan et al., *Banking and Financial Markets*, Palgrave Macmillan Studies in Banking and Financial Institutions,
https://doi.org/10.1007/978-3-030-26844-2_1

cial sophistication on a particular dimension of the loan contract: amount, interest rate, credit risk, collateral, currency, and lending technology. We evaluate the economic benefits and costs of this new financial ecosystem, by relying on recent empirical research in banking and finance.

In Chap. 2, we address the impact on the **loan amount** that the phenomenon of loan securitization has had. Securitization implies that financial intermediaries that grant illiquid loans subsequently pool them together, diversifying risks and converting them into liquid assets or asset-backed securities (ABSs). These assets are then sold to outside investors, in exchange for wholesale funding. While the largest share of ABSs cover home mortgage loans, other types of loans have also been securitized, including automobile credit, student loans, or corporate loans.

A liquid market for securitized assets has recognized benefits for the banking industry, such as improving risk-sharing and reducing banks' cost of capital. The volume of credit to both households and firms should increase as a result. However, the global financial crisis of 2007-2009 started in the securitized subprime mortgage market, which collapsed after having accumulated unmanageable amounts of risks. The academic literature has since sought to understand this fact. The explanations advanced include market imperfections such as increased informational frictions or banks' search for yield. Chapter 2 reviews the theories and estimates put forward in the recent banking literature, to quantify these benefits and costs of securitization on the volume and the quality of credit.

In Chap. 3, we study how modern finance has affected the **interest rates** charged on loans, by enabling banks to hedge interest rates. In an interest rate swap, banks exchange floating for fixed interest rates, against a fee. Financial intermediation often exposes banks to interest rate risks by creating mismatches in the maturity structure and repricing terms of their assets and liabilities. To reduce these risks, banks use two types of risk management practices: on-balance sheet and off-balance sheet risk management. Through on-balance sheet risk management, banks actively seek to match the maturities of their assets and liabilities. This chapter is concerned with off-balance sheet risk management, which occurs when banks trade derivatives in order to hedge interest rate risk.

The ability to use swaps to hedge against interest rate risks improves the intermediation efficiency of banks, as it allows them to take on more credit risk. However, the flip side is that hedging activities might also make banks' lending policies less sensitive to changes in monetary policy. Understanding to what extent hedging affects the transmission of monetary policy is crucial for both market players and regulators. Chapter 3 reviews the existing evidence and points towards areas where the interaction between hedging activities and credit is still to be researched.

Chapter 4 discusses how banks these days can trade away **credit risk** (i.e., the risk that the loan amount will not be returned due to borrower financial distress), by using the Credit Default Swaps (CDS) market. This is an over-the-counter market, where a limited number of large investment banks create markets for buyers and sellers of credit risk, such as banks, insurance companies, and mutual funds. Banks trade in the CDS market for two reasons: to hedge existing credit exposures and to speculate on credit risk. We review recent academic contributions that have sought to explore the interaction between CDS and credit markets, mainly through banks participation in both.

Empirical evidence shows that when liquidity in the CDS market improves, banks use more swaps to hedge risky credit exposures. This enables banks to engage in risk shifting and free up bank capital. Both effects increase bank credit supply. However, allowing banks to trade in both markets also generate negative externalities. Because banks become "empty" creditors when they hedge loan exposures with CDS, accessing bank credit ex ante might become more difficult or more expensive for companies that are referenced in the CDS market. Finally, trading in the CDS derivatives might also suffer if banks trade on private information, which they acquire by forming relationships with borrowers. Chapter 4 assesses the empirical relevance of these hypotheses.

Chapter 5 reviews the different forms of **collateral** pledged in bank loans and their role in easing transactions. The primary reason for the use of collateral when banks grant loans is to reduce the effects of information asymmetry between the bank and its borrower. In this case, the collateral is usually made up of the borrowers' tangible assets which the bank can take possession of in case of default. At the core, banks offer different collateral menus to screen for borrower risk: the lower the probability to default on a loan, the more substantial the collateral the entrepreneur is willing to pledge. Further, the collateral attached to a loan provides an incentive for the bank to more diligently monitor the borrower. This, in turn, increases the likelihood that the project is successful. Recently, also intangible assets (e.g., intellectual property rights) have been pledged as collateral and have improved access to credit markets. In Chap. 5, we assess the empirical importance of real estate and movable and intangible collateral for loans to households and firms.

Chapter 6 concerns the **currency** in which the loan amount is denominated. When banks conduct business globally, both their sources of funding, as well as their volumes of credit, can be expressed in a foreign currency. Therefore, in addition to supply and demand shocks at home, global banks are also exposed to economic fluctuations in foreign exchange markets. Typically, banks hedge this risk ex ante by engaging in cross-currency FX swaps. These swaps are simultaneous spot purchases and forward sales of foreign currency, at the prevailing FX forward rates. However, changes in the forward rates will still affect bank lending decisions, because they affect the cost of hedging of new loans. Increases in forward FX rates will make lending in the foreign currency less attractive, with the reverse being true for domestically headquartered banks. Moreover, trading frictions and the liquidity of FX markets will also determine the price and the availability of a hedge, with a direct impact on the relative cost of lending in foreign markets. In Chap. 6, we review recent empirical evidence linking the functioning of the FX market to bank lending activity.

In Chap. 7, we address the role of Fintech platforms, which are innovations to the **lending technology** characterized by dynamiting traditional customer relationships. Banks gather hard and soft information on their borrowers, by establishing relationships in which they screen and monitor their borrowers. This can have both negative effects-when the bank charges excessive interest rates due to informational rents-and positive effects-by guaranteeing access to credit to relationship borrowers, even in times of distress. These two sides of bank-customer interactions are under challenge by FinTech. A range of innovative platforms, including payment service providers, aggregators and robo advisors, and peer-to-peer lenders have the potential to interfere with these traditional links.

On the one hand, the increased competition that FinTech brings might reduce excessive bank rents. For example, peer-to-peer lending provides a direct alternative to retail banking, with the potential to increase affordable credit to small businesses. On the other hand, while FinTech might decrease transaction costs and borrower choice, it might lead to less relationship lending in the economy. This could hurt bank profitability, but, more importantly, it could also hurt access to credit, particularly in downturns, when stable credit is needed the most. Chapter 7 reviews recent academic and policy thinking on how FinTech might affect the creation of value within the bank-borrower relationship.

CHAPTER 2

Securitization and Lending

While securitization dates back to the seventeenth and the eighteenth century in Holland (Goetzmann and Rouwenhorst 2008), its massive usage is a relatively recent development in credit markets. Securitization implies that financial intermediaries that grant illiquid loans subsequently pool them together, diversifying risks and converting the loans into liquid assets or asset-backed securities (ABSs). These assets are then sold to outside investors, in exchange for wholesale funding. While the largest share of asset-backed securities cover individual mortgage loans, other types of loans can also be securitized (including automobile credit, student loans, or corporate loans).

At the end of 2007, the US-securitized mortgage loan market reached \$6.42 trillion (Loutskina 2011). A liquid market for securitized assets has recognized benefits for credit markets, such as improving risk-sharing and reducing banks' cost of capital (Pennacchi 1988). Credit to both households and firms should grow as a result. However, the global financial crisis of 2007-2009 uncovered ways in which the process of securitization could also hurt lending. It is well understood that the crisis started in the securitized subprime loan market, which collapsed after having accumulated unmanageable amounts of risks. This prompted both researchers in finance and policymakers to seek a better understanding of the benefits but also the vulnerabilities of the markets for asset-backed securities. Below, we review some of the recent empirical literature addressing this need. As with the remaining chapters, we first review the main data sources

A. Bilan et al., *Banking and Financial Markets*, Palgrave Macmillan Studies in Banking and Financial Institutions,
https://doi.org/10.1007/978-3-030-26844-2_2

used by empirical researchers studying securitization and then we discuss the most common methodologies employed, before presenting selected contributions. Table 2.1 offers a compact overview of the papers reviewed.

2.1 Data

Without aiming to be exhaustive, we go over some of the main sources of data that are used in this literature. Most of the data sets have a panel structure, with a time and a cross-section dimension, typically across banks, firms, or loans. To study the banking market, researchers usually employ bank financial indicators containing information extracted from balance sheets and income statements. Such financial data is available either through regulatory reports (e.g., the Federal Reserve's Report of Condition and Income or "call reports") or from private data providers (such as SNL Financial). Indicators for the intensity of securitization can be obtained from private data provider Dealogic, which reports banks' involvement in different types of securitized assets (mortgages, corporate loans, covered bonds) or from rating agencies such as Moody's. Trading data involving asset-backed commercial paper or bonds can be found either in trade repositories, such as the Depository Trust and Clearing Corporation (DTCC), or by approaching the dealer banks that make markets for these products.

For loan-level analyses, the source of data depends on the type of credit product concerned. Most of the empirical research on mortgage lending has focused on the US market, where data is available either from the Home Mortgage Disclosure Act (HMDA) or the First American CoreLogic LoanPerformance databases. Detailed information is available, including mortgage rates, loan size, maturity, year of origination, contract types (hybrid, fixed-rate, adjustable rate), default information, as well as borrower characteristics (credit scores, debt-to-income ratios) and loan application status (denied, approved, originated). Data aggregated at ZIP code level is also available from Equifax, another data provider that maintains consumer credit history and related indicators on US households. Equifax provides annual aggregated data for outstanding credit and amounts in default, broken down by type of loan: mortgages, home equity lines, credit card debt, auto loans, student loans, and consumer loans.

Loan-level data on corporate credit has come from a variety of sources. In the US, the most widely used data source is the syndicated loan market

Table 2.1 Securitization and lending

Paper	*Research question*	*Data*	*Methodology*	*Main findings*
Loutskina (JFE, 2011)	*Does securitization change bank liquidity management?*	Bank financial statements extracted from the Federal Reserve call reports in a long-term panel (1976 to 2007)	**Correlations:** between the intensity of securitization and bank on-balance sheet liquidity indicators. Enhances with difference-in-differences specifications around regulatory interventions	From 1976 to 2007, as banks' ability to securitize loans has increased, the percentage of total assets held as liquid securities decreased on average by 7.33 percentage points
Maddaloni and Peydró (RFS, 2011)	*Does securitization impact the transmission of monetary policy or of banking regulation?*	European data from the Bank Lending Survey (BLS) on bank self-reported lending volumes across countries	**Exogenous Variation** in monetary policy driven by the fact that the Euro-wide target rate is relatively orthogonal to the individual countries' macroeconomic conditions	Low monetary policy short-term interest rates soften lending standards for both firms and households, which is amplified by high securitization activity
Acharya et al. (JFE, 2013)		Moody's rating reports on conduits with information on sponsors, type, assets, guarantees, and ratings; ABCP transactions collected by the Depository Trust and Clearing Corporation (DTCC); bank financial data from Bankscope	**Correlations and cross-sectional variation** across banks with different levels of capital and different exposures to losses on conduits	Increasing conduit exposure from 0% to 100% of bank equity reduced the bank's stock return during a three-day event window at the beginning of the financial crisis by 1.1%

(continued)

Table 2.1 (continued)

Paper	*Research question*	*Data*	*Methodology*	*Main findings*
Demyanyk and van Hemert (RFS, 2011)	*Was lax screening by banks a reason for the distress in subprime mortgages that led to the 2007-2009 financial crisis?*	Loan-level data on half of all US subprime mortgage contracts and characteristics from LoanPerformance, originated over 2001 to 2007	**Proportional odds duration models,** estimating the probability of default on a loan controlling for observables	Adjusting for observed characteristics and macroeconomic conditions, loan quality deteriorated progressively between 2001 and 2007, but this was masked by a simultaneous boom in house prices
Mian and Sufi (QJE, 2009)		Data on mortgage lending activity from Equifax with information on volumes and defaults at the level of US ZIP codes; new mortgage lending collected through the Home Mortgage Disclosure Act (HMDA) and aggregated at ZIP code	**Correlations,** across priors derived from theoretical predictions and using microdata	Over 2002 to 2005, subprime US ZIP codes experience an increase in mortgage credit twice as large as prime ZIP codes, while their income growth is negative. Simultaneously, subprime securitization increases. From 2006, defaults are three times as large in subprime ZIP codes
Keys et al. (QJE, Keys et al. (2010))		Individual data on US mortgage lending from LoanPerformance, over 2001 to 2006	**Regression discontinuity** around the credit score which serves as securitization threshold for mortgage loans	Doubling the likelihood of securitization on otherwise similar loans is associated with a 10%-25% increase in the likelihood of default. This can be attributed to lax bank screening at loan origination

Purnanandam (RFS, 2010)		Loan-level mortgages collected through the Home Mortgage Disclosure Act (HMDA) and bank financial characteristics from the Federal Reserve call reports	**Difference-in-differences**, exploiting the intensity of securitization across different banks subject to a liquidity shock on securitized assets	Banks with higher rates of securitization prior to the 2007 liquidity shock have significantly higher rates of defaults on entire loan portfolios afterwards. Therefore, lax screening incentives were prevalent, and not limited to narrow credit score segments
Benmelech et al. (JFE, 2012)	*Does credit-risk transfer lead to lax credit standards in corporate lending?*	Loan-level data on the US syndicated loan market and collateralized loan obligations (CLOs) loan portfolios from Creditflux	**Difference-in-differences**, comparing the performance of securitized syndicated loans with non-securitized syndicated loans	No evidence that securitized corporate loans were riskier than similar loans that were not securitized between 1997 and 2007
Albertazzi et al. (WP, 2016)		Loan-level data from the Bank of Italy Credit Register and Supervisory Records on the entire population of firms borrowing from Italian banks over the years 2002-2007	**Joint estimation** of the probability of securitization and default on the sample of loans	The tests confirm the presence of adverse selection, reject the presence of moral hazard, and show that the negative effect of adverse selection is more than accounted for by positive selection on observables at the time of loan origination

(continued)

Table 2.1 (continued)

Paper	*Research question*	*Data*	*Methodology*	*Main findings*
Carbo-Valverde et al. (JFS, 2015)	*Are other modalities of credit-risk transfer of mortgage loans less vulnerable to lax screening?*	Firm and bank financials from Amadeus as well as securitization information from Dealogic	**Simultaneous estimation** of credit supply and demand from firm financials; correlations between the estimate of credit constraints and the degree of securitization at bank level	Different types of securitization generate different effects: one standard deviation in securitization activity during a crisis implies a 1.2% positive impact on loan supply when securitization is achieved through covered bonds, compared to a negative impact of ?2.4% in the case of asset-backed securitization
Gorton and Metrick (JFE, 2012)	*Are securitized markets vulnerable to runs?*	Securitized bonds from the dealer banks, covering non-subprime credit products such as credit cards, student loans, auto loans, and commercial mortgage-based securities, enhanced with indicators of subprime distress (the ABX index) and bank counterparty risk (the Libor-OIS spread)	**Correlational evidence**, horseracing the Libor-OIS spread versus the ABX index to explain contagion from the subprime to the non-subprime market segments	The Libor-OIS index is significant when explaining spreads, repo rates, and haircuts on the four classes of non-subprime bonds, which suggests that the perceptions of bank counterparty risk increased consistently with a run on banks

available from Thomson Reuters' Dealscan database, although information on securitized loans is also available from other providers such as Creditex. In Europe, loan-level data is held by the credit registers of national central banks and they include all bank-firm lending above a certain threshold. As in the case of mortgages, these data sets offer an array of characteristics on the loan itself (maturity, interest rate, performance) or on the borrower. Finally, information on bank lending behaviour is sometimes available also from surveys (an example being the Bank Lending Survey carried out by the Eurosystem).

In addition, in many empirical analyses, credit data is supplemented with firm financial information, generally available either from Compustat (worldwide) or from Bureau van Dijk and Moody's Analytics (European), and financial market indicators.

2.2 Methodology

The empirical literature investigating the relationships between securitization and bank lending uses extensively panel data econometrics. In general, the research design seeks to establish causality between securitization and the functioning of credit markets.

One way to take a stab at establishing causality is to exploit cross-sectional heterogeneity between subjects along theoretical priors. At a country level, for example, Maddaloni and Peydró (2011) investigate whether monetary policy has a larger impact on lending standards in countries with a higher intensity of securitization. Or, at a bank level, Loutskina (2011) studies whether banks with a higher share of loans that can be securitized have lower holdings of liquid assets. Acharya et al. (2013) investigate whether banks with lower levels of regulated capital engage more intensely in securitization. Gorton and Metrick (2012) exploit cross-sectional heterogeneity among several prime and subprime products. Then they study the time dimension to establish that distress in the subprime market preceded the prime market in the run-up to the financial crisis. Finally, at loan level, Benmelech et al. (2012) and Albertazzi et al. (2016) argue that securitization does not negatively impact all credit markets, by showing that corporate loans that were securitized did not underperform similar loans which had not been securitized. All these studies exploit correlations in the variables of interest at an individual-time dimension, allowing researchers to saturate the models with controls at the same level of detail, but also with fixed effects along each of the two dimensions.

However, while many times a useful tool, correlational evidence is vulnerable to endogeneity. In the cross-sectional dimension, banks able to use securitization might be different from banks that are not. Or, securitized loans might be different from non-securitized loans, along dimensions that are unobservable to the econometrician. In the time series dimension, there might be macroeconomic factors and policies with a heterogeneous impact on lending, which might correlate with the intensity of securitization. For example, increasing house prices or extending government guarantees might lead to the securitization of riskier loans. Finally, observed loan volumes and spreads are the equilibrium result of transactions between banks and borrowers, and, as such, they are subject to the simultaneity between supply and demand.

The literature has addressed these issues in several ways. The recent availability of banking microdata allowed researchers to construct increasingly homogeneous samples, thereby comparing individuals with similar characteristics, within the same product or geographical market segment (Albertazzi et al. 2016; Benmelech et al. 2012; Mian and Sufi 2009; Demyanyk and Van Hemert 2009). Other studies relied on established empirical techniques that specifically tackle endogeneity, such as difference-in-differences or regression discontinuity designs (Purnanandam 2010; Keys et al. 2010). And, even when detailed microdata has not always been available, simultaneous estimation has helped researchers disentangle supply and demand (Carbo-Valverde et al. 2015).

Below, we review these contributions in detail.

2.3 Securitization and Bank Business Models

The possibility to engage in loan securitization has changed the way banks do business. The impact has been either direct, by altering bank management decisions, or indirect, as securitization affected the transmission of monetary policy or of bank regulations. Below, we review some empirical contributions that have documented these changes.

The conventional benefits of securitization are put to the test in Loutskina (2011). The author uses bank balance sheets and income statements extracted from the Federal Reserve call reports to study how securitization changes bank liquidity and funding management. Relying on panel data analysis conducted over 30 years (1976 to 2007), this study documents that securitization indeed reduces banks' needs to hold liquid assets. In turn, this increases banks' ability to extend credit. The reason is clear: loans that are long term and illiquid can now be sold in the market in exchange for new liquidity. Banks, thus, adapt their business from holding loans on balance sheet up to maturity to selling them to outside investors.

To capture this effect empirically, Loutskina (2011) constructs an index measuring the potential liquidity of each bank's portfolio. More precisely, this is a weighted average of a bank's potential to securitize its own loans, based on the shares of loans of the same type already securitized on the market. She then finds that the index is inversely correlated with the banks' holdings of liquid assets, measured as the share of marketable assets and federal funds sold to total assets. Further tests conducted around regulatory changes affecting liquidity for securitized assets confirm that this market offers a substitute to bank on-balance sheet liquidity.

But securitization can also have indirect effects on the banking market. These stem from its interaction with monetary policy or bank regulation. In this sense, Maddaloni and Peydró (2011) show that while low monetary policy interest rates lead to a softening in bank lending standards, the effect can be magnified by securitization.

That an expansionary monetary policy might spur risk-taking in lending by banks has been recognized in the banking literature as the "risk-taking channel of monetary policy". Agency problems in banking-due to bailouts and liquidity assistance-mean that low interest rates may induce banks to soften their lending standards by improving banks' liquidity (Allen and Gale 2009) and net worth (Adrian and Shin 2010). Moreover, low interest rates make riskless assets less attractive and may lead to a search-for-yield by financial intermediaries (Rajan 2006).

Above, we discussed how the possibility to securitize loans improves bank liquidity. But this behaviour could prove excessive during a monetary expansion. In addition, loan securitization is one other way of creating assets that yield attractive returns for investors. As a result, while expansionary monetary policy alone could lead to softer lending standards, securitization may further amplify this phenomenon. To investigate this channel, Maddaloni and Peydró (2011) use European data from the

Bank Lending Survey (BLS), covering Euro-area countries.[1] The authors assemble survey data from 12 countries which were in the European Monetary Union between 2002:Q4 to 2008:Q3.[2]

Directly assessing the effects of monetary policy on bank lending standards can lead to biased estimates, because both tend to be endogenously determined, together with local economic conditions. However, the authors argue, this is less a concern in the Euro-area. Here, monetary policy rates are set by the Governing Council of the European Central Bank (ECB) and are identical across countries, while there are significant differences in terms of GDP and inflation. Based on this observation, the authors devise an identification strategy which exploits cross-country variation in monetary policy conditions across Euro-area countries.

A first empirical specification investigates the effect of a low monetary policy rate on lending standards:

$$LS_{t,i} = \alpha_i + \nu_t + \beta STrate_{t-1,i} + \gamma LTrate_{t-1,i} + \delta Controls_{t-1,i} + \epsilon_{t,i} \tag{2.1}$$

where $LS_{t,i}$ is the net percentage of banks that report having tightened credit standards in quarter t and country i. $STrate_{t-1,i}$ captures the local effect of monetary policy conditions, proxied by Taylor rule residuals. The residuals are country-specific and are obtained by regressing the EONIA rate on local GDP growth and inflation.[3] A positive residual indicates contractionary monetary policy (or high short-term monetary policy rates), while negative residuals proxy for expansive monetary conditions (low rates). The main macroeconomic controls include the ten-year government bond interest rates, as well as GDP and inflation rates for each Euro-area country. Country and time fixed effects control for all unobservable, time-invariant local conditions and, respectively, all unobservable but time-varying shocks that affect monetary policy and lending standards.

A second specification measures whether the effect of an expansionary monetary policy is amplified when securitization activities intensify, by

[1] Jiménez et al. (2014) and Ioannidou et al. (2014) already provide empirical evidence for the existence of the risk-taking channel of monetary policy.

[2] The 12 countries are Austria, Belgium, France, Finland, Germany, Greece, Ireland, Italy, Luxembourg, the Netherlands, Portugal, and Spain.

[3] The EONIA rate is the Euro OverNight Index Average, the short-term rate on the interbank market targeted by European monetary policy.

interacting the short-term rates with indicators for securitization. Here, as well, the authors rely on cross-country variation in securitization practices and regulation. To measure securitization activity, they use the ratio between the volume of all the issuances of asset-backed and mortgage-backed securities in each quarter and country (as reported by Dealogic), normalized by GDP.

$$LS_{t,i} = \alpha_i + \nu_t + \beta STrate_{t-1,i} + \zeta Securitization_{t-1,i} + \theta(STrate * Securitization)_{t-1,i} + \gamma LTrate_{t-1,i} + \delta Controls_{t-1,i} + \epsilon_{t,i} \quad (2.2)$$

The results confirm that low monetary policy short-term interest rates soften lending standards for both firms and households. And, crucially, this softening is amplified by high securitization activity, especially in the case of mortgages (the θ coefficient on the interaction between securitization and short-term rates is positive and statistically significant).

Aside from its interaction with monetary policy, securitization may also dilute banking regulation if, for example, it affects how banks respond to capital requirements. Acharya et al. (2013) argue that, prior to the financial crisis, commercial banks relied on securitization in order to circumvent regulatory capital constraints.

Because securitization transfers loan exposures from the banking sector to outside investors in exchange for cash, banks can use it to reduce their capital requirements (i.e., the level of capital that they have to hold against risky assets). Focusing on the asset-backed commercial paper (ABCP) market prior to 2007, Acharya et al. (2013) show that some banks use heavily this product, but without adequately transferring the underlying risk. As a result, these banks are in a vulnerable position when the crisis starts. Below, we first describe the most relevant institutional features of the ABCP market and then we review the empirical methods employed by the authors.

In the run-up to the financial crisis, banks set up new institutions, called "conduits", which were meant to purchase medium to long-term assets from the balance sheet of the originating bank. The conduits securitized the assets, and financed them by issuing short-term ABCP to investors. These conduits were risky: if the value of the assets in their portfolio deteriorated, the conduits might not raise enough cash to refinance maturing commercial paper (hence, they were vulnerable to "rollover risk").

However, many of the investors in ABCP at the time were money market funds, who preferred safe assets. To attract these investors, banks insured the assets with explicit guarantees. The guarantees were structured in a way that the investors got paid off even if the conduit's cash flow was insufficient to satisfy all claims. Crucially, in spite of the guarantees, banks relying on this type of securitization could reduce significantly regulatory capital requirements. In some cases, this reduction was down to at most a tenth of the capital required to back on-balance sheets assets.

As a result, banks retained most of the credit risk even after securitizing the loans. At the beginning of the financial crisis, when the value of the assets of the conduits suffers a negative shock,[4] losses to outside investors are actually very small. But the impact on banks is negative and large, because they held the financial responsibility of the conduits and had previously committed to repaying maturing ABCPs at par to investors because of the guarantees.

To document these events empirically, Acharya et al. (2013) use comprehensive panel data. The main data source is rating reports for all 938 conduits rated by Moody's Investors Service from January 2001 to December 2009, containing data on conduit sponsor, type, assets, and guarantees. This is enhanced with Moody's Weekly Announcement Reports of rating downgrades on the conduits, from January 2007 to December 2008. In addition, the authors access a proprietary data set on all US ABCP transactions between January 2007 and February 2008, collected by the Depository Trust and Clearing Corporation (DTCC). Finally, they include bank financial data from Bankscope and bank share prices, which are publicly available.

The empirical analysis follows three steps. An initial descriptive analysis shows that the majority of conduits were sponsored by commercial banks and were structured with liquidity guarantees which permitted capital reductions. Within this set of banks, the paper shows, capital-constrained commercial banks were more likely to sponsor conduits. The authors use panel regressions in order to assess the relation between bank exposure to ABCP (measured as the ratio of ABCP relative to bank equity) and bank

[4] In July 2007, ABCP outstanding amounted to $ 1.3 trillion. But, on 9 August 2007, the French bank BNP Paribas halts withdrawals from three funds invested in mortgage-backed securities due to losses from the underlying assets. This has a profound impact on the ABCP market, which experiences the equivalent of a banking run with outstanding volumes dropping to $ 833 billion in December 2007.

capital:

$$Exposure_{it} = \alpha_i + \delta_t + \beta CapitalRatio_{it} + \gamma X_{it} + \epsilon_{it} \quad (2.3)$$

where $Exposure_{it}$ measures the ABCP exposure of bank i at time t, $CapitalRatio_{it}$ is the capital ratio of bank i at time t, α_i are bank fixed effects, δ_t are time fixed effects, and X_{it} are controls for time-varying bank characteristics (size, return on assets and short-term debt, deposits, and loans, each as a share of assets). Bank capital is measured both as economic capital (book equity to assets) and regulatory capital (Tier 1 regulatory capital to risk-weighted assets). Economic capital is included because regulatory capital is vulnerable to reverse causality. If banks had already engaged in securitization in order to arrive at their existing capital ratios, then, in equilibrium, the econometrician would only observe relatively larger levels of regulated capital. In this case, economic capital might provide a better measure of capital constraints than regulatory capital, as the former is not monitored by bank supervisors.

A second specification measures whether, ex post, when asset quality deteriorates, conduits experience a run from their short-term credit providers, leading to lower ABCP issuance and higher spreads. To do this, the paper exploits cross-sectional variation in the strength of the guarantee: while some guarantees cover completely credit and liquidity risks, others are weaker. The analysis focuses on the period of four months before and after the start of the financial crisis on August 9, 2007, as follows:

$$y_{it} = \alpha + \beta_j Guarantee_{ij} + \gamma_j After_t Guarantee_{ij} + \delta After_t + \epsilon_{it} \quad (2.4)$$

where y_{it} is either the natural logarithm of the face value of ABCP outstanding of conduit i in week t or the overnight ABCP spread over the federal funds rate on new issues by conduit i on day t. $Guarantee_{ij}$ is an indicator variable for guarantee of type j of conduit i and $After_t$ is an indicator variable that equals one after the start of the crisis. Additional specifications include time fixed effects, conduit fixed effects and sponsor-time fixed effects. If the financial crisis made investors increasingly concerned about conduit risks, then conduits with weaker guarantees should have a lower performance and less ability to roll over maturing assets (γ_j should be stronger for relatively weaker guarantees).

Thus, for conduits that are fully guaranteed, no realized losses should be passed to investors. In exchange, banks with greater exposure to these conduits should experience a negative shock, as they would have to absorb the losses on conduit assets. To verify whether this was indeed the case, a final specification tests whether these banks experience lower stock returns, in an event study around August 9, 2007. The baseline specification is:

$$R_i = \alpha + \beta ConduitExposure_i + \gamma X_i + \epsilon_i \tag{2.5}$$

where R_i is the cumulative equity return of bank i, computed over the three-day period from August 8 to 10, 2007. $ConduitExposure_i$ is bank i's conduit exposure relative to equity in January 2007, and X_i are bank characteristics. Consistent with the hypothesis, we would expect a negative β.

The estimations show that, first, banks that are more capital constrained have larger ABCP exposures. Second, when asset quality deteriorates at the beginning of the financial crisis, ABCPs with weaker guarantees experience larger investor outflows. And, third, banks highly exposed to conduits appear to be the main losers from the underperformance of the conduits: an increase in conduit exposure from 0% to 100% of bank equity reduces the stock return during the three-day event window by 1.1%.

2.4 Types of Securitization and Asymmetric Information

The previous section discussed how, prior to 2007, the market for securitized assets increased significantly, with positive effects on lending volumes but also negative effects on risk-taking. In this section, we review the literature exploring the reasons for the increased risk-taking. While this effect could simply be the direct consequence of a shift in the distribution of new borrowers, when supply increases sufficiently to satisfy a credit demand of lower quality, this section shows how securitization could also increase informational frictions in the credit market.

In their traditional role as financial intermediaries, banks should reduce information asymmetries between lenders and borrowers. But securitization changes this traditional lending market from an "originate-to-hold" to an "originate-to-distribute" model (Purnanandam 2010). When the originator of a loan holds it to maturity, they have incentives to select the loans that perform best. This is done by both ex ante screening the borrowers and by monitoring them ex post (Pennacchi 1988; Gorton and

Pennacchi 1995; Petersen and Rajan 1994; Parlour and Plantin 2008; Holmstrom and Tirole 1997; Diamond and Rajan 2005). But if banks offload the loans shortly after origination by securitizing them, then their screening efforts might be reduced. In fact, if screening is costly and loans can be easily securitized, banks are likely to only screen borrowers for hard information. This is information that can easily be observed by outside investors and contracted upon. Any soft information that might predict the future performance of a loan, but it is costly to process and, unobservable to outsiders (such as indicators of the future income capacity of the borrowers, or the diligence with which they prepared their application and its quality), could be overlooked.

The empirical evidence suggests that securitization did increase informational asymmetries, but this effect was limited to the subprime lending market. Researchers have sought to explain the increased risk-taking in this market segment by looking for causal evidence of, first, an increase in bank credit supply, and second, of a simultaneous reduction in screening efforts. Below, we review this evidence. Then, we go through studies involving other types of lending (credit to large corporations and to small businesses) or other forms of securitization (covered bonds), and show that these markets appear less vulnerable to informational frictions.

2.4.1 Subprime Mortgage Lending

Among the first studies exploring the reasons for the boom and bust behaviour of the securitized mortgage market in the run-up to the financial crisis are Demyanyk and Van Hemert (2009) and Mian and Sufi (2009).

Demyanyk and Van Hemert (2009) use loan-level data on subprime mortgages from LoanPerformance and document a decrease in loan quality in this market segment between 2001 to 2007. They employ proportional odds duration models, estimating the probability of first-time delinquency on a subprime mortgage loan as a function of loan characteristics, borrower characteristics, macroeconomic conditions, and origination year effects. The evidence is consistent with a sustained increase in risk-taking in this market. Conditional on observables, loan quality deteriorates monotonically between 2001 and 2007, but it is masked by the simultaneous appreciation in house prices. As house prices start to decline in 2006, poor loan quality materializes into realized defaults in 2006 and 2007.

But what is the driver behind this increased risk-taking in mortgage lending? Is it demand or supply driven? And how is it linked to securitization? These questions are hard to address in the context of the Demyanyk and Van Hemert (2009) study, as they employ no control group. Other lending segments might have behaved similarly. Mian and Sufi (2009) take the investigation one step further and show that the increased underperformance was supply driven and specific to the securitized subprime mortgage sector. They employ data on lending activity at the level of US ZIP codes, by combining Equifax information on outstanding credit and defaults with new mortgage lending from the HMDA data set.

Moreover, their work sheds light onto how microdata is necessary for the researcher to choose between competing theoretical explanations. In this case, the expansion in mortgage credit since 2000 could have been caused by two factors. On the one hand, the expansion could have been demand based if the income prospects of subprime borrowers had improved over the same period. On the other hand, it could be that lenders increased their supply of credit, expecting to immediately offload the risk by securitizing the loans. To investigate this empirically, the authors start the analysis at US county level. County-level trends are consistent with the income-based hypothesis: income growth is stronger in counties with a higher share of subprime consumers during 2002 to 2005. However, this correlation could be spurious if the growth in incomes was concentrated among the prime segments of the population. And, indeed, looking at a ZIP code level, the data supports the alternative hypothesis: during the same period, subprime borrowers experience negative income growth. This suggests that borrower income growth is unlikely to have been the driver of subprime mortgage growth.

The authors then employ several empirical tests and provide evidence consistent with a supply-level hypothesis. First, they use loan applications to document that credit constraints relax disproportionately for subprime ZIP codes over the period 2002 to 2005. Second, they argue that this fact is positively correlated with the expansion of subprime mortgage securitization. Third, they find that the increase in the rate of securitization is much stronger in subprime ZIP codes compared to prime ZIP codes during the same period. And, fourth, they study the evolution of default rates and find that these increase significantly more from 2005 to 2007 in ZIP codes that experience an increase in the fraction of mortgages sold in securitizations over the previous years.

Up to this point, the empirical evidence points to simultaneous risk-taking by banks and intensifying securitization over the years running up to the financial crisis. However, a causal interpretation is still difficult to pin down. Subsequent contributions tackle causality and investigate further the underlying economic mechanisms explaining how securitization could have led to deteriorating lending standards.

Keys et al. (2010) use a regression discontinuity set-up to establish causality between securitization and decreased loan performance. Their theoretical premise is that the ease of securitization reduced the incentives of financial intermediaries to carefully screen borrowers in the run-up to the crisis. The authors focus on subprime mortgage lending and use individual data on mortgages from LoanPerformance, over the period January 2001 to December 2006.

The endogeneity challenge is solved by focusing the analysis around a specific threshold in mortgage borrowers' credit scores. This approach induces exogenous variation in the probability of securitizing a loan. The threshold is based on governmental guidelines, advising against lending to borrowers with a credit score below a fixed level.[5] While the rule was intended for lenders, investors purchasing the asset-backed securities also adhered to it. As a result, loans made to borrowers with a credit score just above this threshold had a higher unconditional likelihood of being securitized, as opposed to loans made to borrowers just below the threshold.

The premise is that the discontinuity in the likelihood of securitization induces a discontinuity in banks' screening incentives. When deciding whether to grant a loan, banks use both hard information and soft information. But if they later plan on selling the loan, banks will be compensated based on the hard information acquired and not on the soft information. Since acquiring soft information at the start of a lending relationship is costly and there is little benefit to it if the loan is meant to be securitized, banks might expend less effort when screening loans that can be easily securitized. To test this hypothesis, Keys et al. (2010) use the specification below, in a two-step approach. First, they test whether there is a discontinuity in the number of loans securitized, above and below the fixed credit score threshold. They collapse the loan data by credit score *i*

[5] Government-sponsored enterprises, Fannie Mae and Freddie Mac, all recommended not to lend to borrowers with credit scores lower than 620.

and estimate:

$$Y_i = \alpha + \beta T_i + \theta f(CreditScore_i) + \delta T_i f(CreditScore_i) + \epsilon_i \quad (2.6)$$

where Y_i is the number of loans at each level of the credit score i, T_i is an indicator that takes value 1 if the credit score is larger than the threshold and 0 otherwise, and ϵ_i is a zero-mean error term. $f(CreditScore)$ and $Tf(CreditScore)$ are flexible polynomials, aiming to fit the empirical distribution of the data as closely as possible. β represents the size of the discontinuity and is estimated by the difference in these two smoothed functions, evaluated at the cut-off.

Second, the authors evaluate the performance of the loans by examining their realized default probability, up to 15 months after origination. If lenders screened with the same intensity all loans around the threshold-loans which should be similar in terms of hard information-then the two groups of loans should have equal default probabilities. For this purpose, the variable Y_i in equation (2) becomes the dollar-weighted share of loans defaulted within 10 to 15 months of origination. β measures the change in the default rate at the threshold.

The first set of estimations show that loans with a similar risk profile but which are just above the threshold have more than double the likelihood of becoming securitized with respect to loans just below the threshold. The second set of results show that doubling the likelihood of securitization on otherwise similar loans is associated with a 10%-25% increase in defaults. The paper argues that this jump represents the negative effect that securitization has on bank screening incentives.

Purnanandam (2010) complements these findings by showing that the softening in screening standards was not limited to a segment of borrower FICO scores, but that banks highly involved in securitization activities did not actively screen entire loan portfolios. Here, the unit of analysis is the bank. The author combines banking characteristics extracted from the Federal Reserve call reports with loan-level information from the HDMA database. The tested hypothesis is that banks with differential involvement in securitization, but otherwise identical, put less effort into screening their borrowers for soft information. The identification relies on the liquidity shock that affected the secondary mortgage market in 2007, whose effects are tested on a matched sample of banks. This sudden dry-up of liquidity for securitized assets meant that banks had to keep most of their loans on their balance sheets. The author then compares observed defaults on mortgage loans granted by banks highly exposed to securitization versus lowly exposed banks in a difference-in-differences set-up:

$$default_{it} = \mu_i + \beta_1 after_t + \beta_2 after_t presec_i + \beta_3 after_t premortgage_i + \sum_{k=1}^{K} \alpha_k X_{it} + \epsilon_{it} \tag{2.7}$$

where the dependent variable measures the default rate of the mortgage portfolio of bank i in quarter t, μ_i are bank fixed effects, and X_{it} are time-varying bank characteristics. The coefficient on the $after_t$ variable captures the time trend in the default rate before and after the mortgage crisis. β_2 measures the change in default rate for banks that originated loans primarily to sell them to third parties, relative to the corresponding change for banks that originated loans primarily to retain them on their own balance sheets. Finally, the second interaction term controls for time-varying bank involvement in mortgage lending, so as to isolate the effect of β_2 from changes in the overall lending portfolios of banks.

The regression is estimated on a matched sample of banks that differ in their securitization activities, but that otherwise granted mortgages to observationally equivalent borrowers, in similar geographical areas and at similar rates. A statistically and economically significant positive β_2 suggests that loans made by banks active in securitization were of inferior quality. These banks, stuck with the loans on their balance sheet after the shock, experience disproportionately higher borrower defaults. Using a matched sample of banks mitigates concerns that the effect might be due to observable differences in the quality of the loans and suggests that results are rather consistent with the hypothesis of diluted screening incentives for treated banks.

2.4.2 *Corporate Lending*

Most of the loan-level empirical evidence points to decreasing lending standards and excessive risk in the subprime mortgage market, caused by the possibility to securitize loans. However, more recent analyses in other lending segments-corporate lending-or other types of securitization-covered bonds-offer a different picture. Based on these findings, adverse selection does not appear to be a necessary consequence of securitization.

Benmelech et al. (2012) show that securitization was not associated with riskier lending in the US corporate loan market prior to the financial crisis. They assemble loan-level information on syndicated loans from Dealscan and Creditflux matched with firm financial information extracted from Compustat over 1997 to 2007. Because syndicated loans are large ($522 million, on average) only parts of them are typically securitized.

To identify loans that were at least partially intended for securitization, the authors use a public list of lenders at the time of syndication. In addition, they construct a control sample of unsecuritized loans. Because banks' soft information is unobservable, the authors use as a proxy the ex post performance on the loans, controlling for observables at the time of origination. Performance is assessed across the two types of loans, using several measures (secondary market loan prices, credit ratings, the spreads on credit default swaps, implied probabilities of default based on accounting information, as well as violations of loan covenants). The detail of the data allows estimation at loan level and with fixed effects for the lead bank in the syndicate. This removes a possible source of selection bias in the sample which could occur if, for instance, unsecuritized loans were issued by banks with relatively weaker screening capabilities. Thus, a dummy on the securitized loans, in this sample, measures the marginal effect of securitization on loan performance, among the loans originated by a given bank. The specifications are further saturated with year and industry fixed effects.

The estimations show that securitized syndicated loans did not perform worse than other syndicated but unsecuritized loans. One possible explanation is related to the size of syndicated loans. Because several lenders are involved in a syndicate, if the remaining lenders are able to compensate for weak screening and monitoring from the party engaged in securitization, then there might not be a drop in loan quality.

Importantly, this improved performance of securitized business loans with respect to subprime mortgages does not appear to be restricted to the syndicated US market. Using different data and a new empirical approach, Albertazzi et al. (2016) find only a limited role of asymmetric information in the securitization of SME loans. Here, the authors seek to separate adverse selection from moral hazard. Their conclusions show that, while there is a certain degree of adverse selection in the market, it is dominated by positive selection on observables at loan origination. Therefore, overall, securitized loans actually tend to perform better than the non-securitized ones.

The study adapts the methodology proposed by Chiappori and Salanié (2000) of testing for asymmetric information in insurance contracts. For securitized loans, this means jointly estimating a model for the probability of a loan being involved in a securitization deal and one for the probability that the loan deteriorates. The analysis uses loan-level data from the Bank of Italy Credit Register and Supervisory Records on the entire population of firms borrowing from Italian banks over the years 2002-2007. The data includes information on the performance of both securitized and non-securitized loans until 2011, as well as bank and firm financial characteristics.

Albertazzi et al. (2016) argue that securitization is affected by asymmetric information if, accounting for a set of characteristics observable to investors, there is positive correlation between the securitization of loans and the probability that these loans deteriorate into non-performing. Specifically, the probability of securitization and deterioration of a loan granted to firm f by bank b at time t can be assumed to depend on a set of characteristics, θ, which represent the information set of the investors in ABS:

$$Prob(Securitization_{fbt} = 1|\theta_{fbt}) = F_S(\eta\theta_{fbt} + \epsilon_{fbt})$$

$$Prob(Deterioration_{fbt} = 1|\theta_{fbt}) = F_D(\eta'\theta_{fbt} + \epsilon'_{fbt})$$

where the functions F can be linear probability models, logit or probit and ϵ_{fbt} and ϵ'_{fbt} are the error terms. The correlation between the error terms provides a test of the presence of information asymmetries.

$$H_0(1) : Corr(\epsilon_{fbt}, \epsilon'_{fbt}) > 0 \quad (2.8)$$

Using firms with multiple bank relationships, the authors propose an empirical test to distinguish between adverse selection and moral hazard. The premise is that adverse selection will affect all financiers in a similar manner. Ex ante, a weak firm is more likely to default on all exposures, not only on the exposure being securitized. However, the incidence of moral hazard due to the lack of monitoring will have a larger negative effect on the lender's own exposure. To disentangle the two effects, the authors decompose the error terms, ϵ_{fbt} and ϵ'_{fbt}, into two components:

firm-time fixed effects (α_{ft} and α'_{ft}) and the remaining errors, μ_{fbt} and μ'_{fbt}.

Testing for adverse selection comes down to assessing the correlation between the coefficients on the firm-time fixed effects:

$$H_0(2) : Corr(\alpha_{ft}, \alpha'_{ft}) > 0 \tag{2.9}$$

Under the null hypothesis, there is positive correlation between the securitization of the loans and the probability that they deteriorated into non-performance due to unobservable firm heterogeneity.

To test for moral hazard, one needs to analyse the behaviour of the remaining residuals:

$$H_0(3) : Corr(\mu_{fbt}, \mu'_{fbt}) > 0 \tag{2.10}$$

If true, then there is positive correlation between the securitization of the loans and the probability that they deteriorated into non-performing due to any remaining unobservable bank-firm-specific heterogeneity. Such evidence would be consistent with the existence of moral hazard.

Albertazzi et al. (2016) find that $H_0(1)$ holds, suggesting the presence of asymmetries of information. Subsequently, $H_0(2)$ holds, while $H_0(3)$ can be rejected, suggesting that these asymmetries of information result from adverse selection, and not from moral hazard. However, they go on to show that the negative effect of adverse selection is dominated by positive selection on observables, at the time of securitizing the loans. As a result, overall, securitized SME loans perform better than the unsecuritized ones.

2.4.3 *Covered Bonds*

In addition to asset-backed securities, where banks typically sell the loans to outside investors, a different type of securitization has developed in recent years, particularly in Europe. It is the case of covered bonds. While in the case of asset-backed securities, the whole credit risk is sold to outsiders, banks issue covered bonds, typically backed by mortgage lending, in order to obtain external funding. As a result, the mortgages are retained on banks' balance sheets and only their interest rate risk is transferred to outside investors. Carbo-Valverde et al. (2015) show that this difference in risk transfer reassures the markets that banks maintain intact their screening and monitoring activities. As a result, banks are able to issue covered bonds also in a crisis, and this sustains their lending activity.

In their investigation, the authors use panel data on firm and bank financials, as well as securitization information from Dealogic, allowing them to identify the type of securitization banks specialize in. The firm-level information includes the names of the banks with whom the firm operates, offering the possibility to match bank and firm data. Carbo-Valverde et al. (2015) first identify credit constrained firms by relying on an econometric model for markets in disequilibrium as in Maddala and Nelson (1974). The model requires separate estimates of the demand and the supply of credit. The demand for credit is modelled as a function of financial variables such as firm activity, size, other sources of finance, and the cost of bank credit. Credit supply depends on the firm's potential collateral, proxied by tangible assets, and on default risk. For each firm, the model then predicts the probability that loan demand exceeds credit supply, which allows the authors to classify firms in function of the intensity of credit rationing they suffer.

The subsequent analysis separates the effects of securitization in good versus bad times. Firms that borrow from banks that are more involved in securitization in good times have lower credit constraints, irrespective of whether this securitization is achieved through asset-backed securities (ABSs) or covered bonds. However, in a crisis, this only remains the case for covered bonds. Banks relying on asset-backed securities reduce credit supply as market liquidity disappears for this type of securitization.

2.5 Securitization and Financial Stability

Because securitized markets have developed in close connection to the banking system, another important question is whether these markets are also susceptible to the main vulnerability of banks: the risk of an inefficient run. A bank run occurs when multiple investors suddenly decide to withdraw from a certain financial product precipitating a loss in its value, even though it would have been efficient to remain invested. The reason is typically the lack of confidence, and the run manifests itself as contagion, from the "bad" to the "good" market. Gorton and Metrick (2012) document such a run in the sale and repurchase market (the "repo" market), where banks typically exchange securitized assets for funding from outside investors. Contagion affected the less- risky, non-subprime assets in this market as it spread from the securitized subprime mortgage market.

Diamond and Dybvig (1983) already showed that traditional banking systems are vulnerable to runs. When depositors jointly lose confidence in a bank's capacity to guarantee their return on investment, they rush to withdraw their savings from the banks. This can trigger a run. While most of the runs on traditional banking in advanced countries ended with the introduction of deposit insurance, parts of the banking business remain susceptible to similar runs. Gorton and Metrick (2012) explain how the repo market suffered from this vulnerability, which materialized in the withdrawal of investors from repo agreements.

Repo agreements are established between banks looking for funds and typically institutional investors. The transactions are securitized, frequently with securitized bonds: the investors buy the asset as collateral from the bank and, at the same time, the bank agrees to repurchase the asset at some later time, for a set price. The difference between the sale price and the repurchase price is the repo rate. Typically, the value of the collateral contracted upon is lower than the value of the securitized assets, with the difference being the "haircut". If the bank defaults on the promise to repurchase the collateral, then the investor has the right to terminate the agreement and keep the collateral.

The chapter argues that securitized banking was at the heart of the financial crisis because it triggered a run on the repo market. As explained earlier in this chapter, subprime housing assets were the first to enter distress, but the crisis spread to non-subprime assets that had no direct connection to housing through the repo market. The deterioration in the subprime sector increased the uncertainty about bank solvency and counterparty risk. This affected the repo markets for all types of collateral, as investors lost confidence in banks' ability to repurchase the assets pledged. As a result, both repo rates and haircuts increased, amplifying the pressure on banks. This progressive deterioration led to a generalized withdrawal of repo funding, very similar to a traditional banking run.

Consistent with the run view of the financial market, Gorton and Metrick (2012) assemble different data sets, enabling them to track how stress in the subprime housing market first affected indicators of bank health and, subsequently, the non-subprime securitized market. They collect a main data set with information on 392 securitized bonds, from the dealer banks, covering non-subprime credit products such as credit cards, student loans, auto loans, and commercial mortgage-based securities. The data set contains spreads on the bonds, as well as repo rates and haircuts. To proxy for fundamentals in subprime market, the authors use the ABX index, a synthetic tradable index that references 20 equally weighted subprime mortgage-backed securities. Finally, the indicator for bank counterparty risk is the three-month LIBOR-OIS, which is the spread between the rate charged for unsecured interbank borrowing (LIBOR) and the rate on an overnight interest swap (OIS), exchanging a floating Fed fund rate for a fixed rate, both with a maturity of three months.

The empirical analysis starts with two stylized facts. First, the ABX index initially indicates a deteriorating subprime market in early 2007. This has a direct impact on banks, which held many of the securitized assets and mortgages on their balance sheets. Second, this leads to tensions in the interbank markets in mid-2007, which is reflected in an increase in the LIBOR-OIS spread.

The timing of these events is key to identifying whether the repo market indeed propagated tensions from the subprime to the prime markets. If there was contagion from the repo market, then the measure of counterparty risk, the LIBOR-OIS spread in this case, should have explanatory power for the spreads of non-subprime securitized assets which were used as collateral in the repo market. If, however, non-subprime assets were directly affected by risks in the subprime class-a scenario without contagion-then the ABX index should be the most important factor explaining changes in non-subprime spreads.

To disentangle one alternative explanation from another, the authors run the following specification on the four non-subprime categories of securitized bonds (credit cards, auto loans, student loans, and commercial mortgage-backed securities):

$$\Delta Y_{i,t} = a_1 + b_1 \Delta ABX_t + b_2 \Delta LibOis_t + b_3 \Delta X_t + \epsilon_{i,t} \tag{2.11}$$

where the $Y_{i,t}$ is, in turn, the weekly spread, the repo rate and the repo haircut on bond i at time t. ABX_t is a vector of the last four observations of the ABX spread, $LibOis_t$ is a vector of the last four observations of the LIBOR-OIS spread, and X_{it} is a vector of financial controls, including the ten-year Treasury rate, the returns on the S&P index, the VIX index, the slope of the yield curve, and the overnight swap spread. Because spreads are more similar to unit root prices than to independently and identically distributed returns, all variables are included in first differences.

The results from the main specification consistently show that the LIBOR-OIS variables are jointly significant when explaining spreads, repo rates, and haircuts on the four classes of non-subprime bonds. The ABX coefficients, included in the same regressions, are not jointly significant in any specification. This suggests that it was the interbank market that eroded spreads on non-subprime securitized assets, while changes in the ABX has no explanatory power whatsoever in predicting the spreads. Therefore, the contagion from subprime to non-subprime assets indeed appears to have transmitted through the interbank market.

2.6 Conclusion

Loan securitization is clearly one of the banking innovations that contributed to the 2008 global financial crisis. Fast ex ante bank screening combined with low ex post monitoring incentives particularly for the portfolios of subprime mortgage loans led to the drop in investor confidence that precipitated the crisis. Regulators did not have sufficient understanding of this innovation to intervene on time.

Since then, this market has transformed greatly. Both private and regulatory-based adjustments aimed at repairing the previous flaws, while maintaining the usefulness of this innovation as an efficient way to structure financing. These adjustments include an increase in the securitization of safer and more informationally transparent loans, requiring the originator to keep the ownership of larger fractions of the securitized portfolios or requiring banks to consolidate securitized off-balance sheet assets onto their balance sheet. Another important development, in particular in Europe, has been to allow banks to pledge these on-balance sheet portfolios of securitized loans as central bank collateral, in exchange for liquidity. This gave banks incentives to create new on-balance sheet assets. Understanding whether these recent measures have indeed been successful at correcting previous flows as well as studying the impact of this new phenomenon of on-balance sheet securitization in response to monetary policy are fascinating topics for future research. Given its important role in bank risk and liquidity management, securitization is here to stay.

CHAPTER 3

Interest Rate Risk

Financial intermediation may expose banks to interest rate risk by creating mismatches in the maturity structure and repricing terms of their assets and liabilities. Unlike credit risk which a bank can be more or less exposed to but requires credit derivatives to completely remove, it is possible for a bank to completely insulate itself from interest rate risk without trading interest rate derivatives. While banks may use interest rate derivatives to manage their interest rate risk exposure, they may also use on-balance sheet techniques, that is, managing the difference in maturity and repricing terms of their assets and liabilities. The difference in the maturity and repricing terms of their assets and liabilities is mostly determined by the maturity of their deposits (liabilities) and the variability of the interest rate charged on loans that they extend (assets).

Banks face frictions in the management of their on-balance sheet exposure to interest rate risk. These frictions stem from the stickiness of deposits which is partially determined by the level of competition in the banking industry (Drechsler et al. 2018). Further, they stem from the variability of the interest rate charged on the loans they extend, loan rate fixation (Hoffmann et al. 2018). There is substantial evidence that the loan rate fixation conventions vary across countries and time (Campbell 2013; Ehrmann and Ziegelmeyer 2017; Badarinza et al. 2018; Albertazzi et al. 2018). Hoffmann et al. (2018) shows that there is significant variation in the loan rate fixation conventions within the Eurozone, where some countries have up to 93% fixed-rate mortgages, while others have up to 96%

A. Bilan et al., *Banking and Financial Markets*, Palgrave Macmillan Studies in Banking and Financial Institutions,
https://doi.org/10.1007/978-3-030-26844-2_3

variable-rate mortgage. Further, there is evidence that these conventions are not the result of banks' decisions alone (Albertazzi et al. 2018; Basten et al. 2018). Hence, the literature finds that banks are not able to perfectly match the difference in maturity and repricing terms of their assets and liabilities.

If banks are not able to insulate themselves from interest rate risk using only on-balance sheet techniques, they may use interest rate derivatives to further reduce their exposure (hedge). Indeed, the literature finds that banks are exposed to interest rate risk using various measurements of on-balance sheet interest rate exposure (Purnanandam 2007; Gomez et al. 2016; Esposito et al. 2015; Hoffmann et al. 2018). Further, there is heterogeneity in banks' exposure to interest rate risk with some banks benefiting from an increase in interest rates, which creates a redistributive effect of monetary policy within the banking industry (Hoffmann et al. 2018). The literature further shows that banks do indeed use interest rate derivatives to manage their on-balance sheet exposure and that the extent to which they hedge depends on bank characteristics and derivative market conditions (Purnanandam 2007; Esposito et al. 2015; Hoffmann et al. 2018).

Finally, the literature finds that a bank's decision to manage and method of managing interest rate risk affects the transmission of monetary policy (Purnanandam 2007; Gomez et al. 2016; Hoffmann et al. 2018), the value of its equity (Flannery and James 1984b; English et al. 2018), its lending behaviour, and, hence, the investment and employment decisions of the firms to which they lend (Gomez et al. 2016).

The remainder of this chapter is organized as follows: we begin by reviewing the data sources and methodologies employed in the interest rate risk in banking literature. We continue by discussing the literature that seeks to uncover the following: (1) If and why banks are exposed to interest rate risk. (2) How and why banks manage interest rate risk. (3) What the consequences are of banks' decision to manage interest rate risk for the transmission of monetary policy and for the firms to which they lend.

3.1 Data

To conduct an analysis on bank's interest rate risk exposure, researchers need to estimate the degree to which banks are affected by changes in the interest rate. To do this, researchers need detailed information on the maturity of banks' assets and liabilities. A common measure for banks' on-balance sheet interest rate exposure is the income gap, that is, the difference between the bank's assets that mature (or reprice) within a year and its liabilities that mature (or reprice) within a year. Data to calculate this measure can typically be sourced from publicly available sources, such as quarterly accounting information from the FDIC Call Reports.

An alternative measure of interest rate risk exposure is the economic value-based measure. This measure is similar to the income gap-based measure as it is calculated using the repricing gap of assets and liabilities. The main difference is that the income-based measure focuses on assets and liabilities that will be repriced within one year, while the economic value approach considers all maturities (in most cases, 14 buckets). The economic value-based measure is thus more accurate as it takes into account a wider spectrum of banks' interest rate risk and is the preferred measure of regulators (Basel Committee on Banking Supervision 2016). However, to calculate the economic value-based measure, authors require detailed data on the maturity structure of banks' assets and liabilities. This level of granularity is only available in the confidential supervisory data sets of central banks, for example the Bank of Italy (Esposito et al. 2015) and the European Central Bank (Hoffmann et al. 2018).

Data on the derivative trading by banks is required to determine banks' total interest rate exposure and their off-balance sheet interest rate risk management practices. The publicly available data on banks interest rate derivative trading is scant. The quarterly accounting information from the FDIC Call Reports only contains "interest rate derivatives used for hedging purposes." From this data, researchers are only able to determine the net derivative position at a point in time, with no information on the maturity structure. Further, this data does not allow researchers to distinguish between different types of derivatives or the floating rate that the derivative linked to, for example, LIBOR or Eonia.

After the global financial crisis, the G20 pledged to increase transparency and resilience in global over-the-counter derivative markets through regulation. This has resulted in the availability of more granular data, for example, in Europe through the European Markets Infrastructure Regulation (EMIR).[1] This regulation requires that all derivative transactions with at least one counterparty residing in the European Union to be reported

[1] See Abad et al. (2016) for a detailed description of the data reported under EMIR.

to a trade repository. However, this data is confidential as only supervisory authorities are able to access the data from the trade repositories. The granularity of the EMIR data allows researchers to overcome the issues associated with the publicly available data as they are able to view each individual derivative transaction. Hence, researchers are able to determine which floating rate that the derivative is linked to, as well as construct more detailed information of the maturity structure of banks' off-balance sheet interest rate exposure.

3.2 Methodology

While the methods of managing interest rate risk and derivative trading is somewhat complex, the literature on the topic has mostly employed simple econometric techniques, ranging from correlation analysis to OLS regressions on cross-sectional data.

However, there are some topics in the literature that require more complex econometric techniques. Purnanandam (2007) analyses banks motives to trade interest rate derivative which he models as simultaneous to the decision to manage on-balance sheet interest rate risk. To account for the fact that banks may make their maturity GAP and derivatives decisions simultaneously, Purnanandam (2007) uses a system of equations and uses a two-stage least squares instrumental variable approach. In a first-stage regression, the authors model the level of on-/off-balance sheet hedging. He then uses the estimated on(off) balance hedging in the second-stage regression where he determines the motives to hedge off (on) balance sheet interest rate risk. By conducting the analysis using a 2SLS-IV approach, Purnanandam (2007) was able to account for potential simultaneity bias that arises out of the structure of the hedging decision process.

Another technique that is used in the literature, albeit infrequently due to data limitations, is the use of fixed effects. One fixed effect specification is the use of bank-time fixed effects to identify differences within bank-group observations or bank-firm observations. Albertazzi et al. (2018) use this specification to compare the loan rate variability observed by different banks in the same banking group across different countries. By including bank-time fixed effects, the authors are able to disentangle parent bank funding effects from country-level demand factors.

Another fixed effect specification is the use of firm-time fixed effects to control for loan demand factors at the borrower level. Gomez et al. (2016)

are able to use this fixed effect specification because they employ data from the syndicated loan market in which loans involve multiple banks and where banks lend to multiple firms, that is, bank-firm-level data. As a result, the authors are able to make statements about the effect of banks' funding gap on their lending to firms while controlling or the potential that banks and firms match based on interest rate risk exposure, loan demand, and other time-varying firm-specific effects.

3.3 Are Banks Exposed to Interest Rate Risk?

Financial intermediation may expose banks to interest rate risks by creating mismatches in the maturity structure and repricing terms of their assets and liabilities. Hence, determining the maturity structure of bank assets and liabilities is key in determining if banks are exposed to interest rate risk. There are two opposing views on banks' on-balance sheet exposure to interest rate risk, the "traditional view", and the "matching view". According to the traditional view, banks fund long-term loans with short-term deposits, exposing them to interest rate risk. The matching view purports that banks match the interest rate exposure of their assets with that of their liabilities. Further, under the matching view, there are two opposing theories. Hellwig (1994) develops a theory where banks' assets and liabilities are matched as they receive variable-rate deposits, which they use to extend variable-rate loans. Drechsler et al. (2018) argue that banks' market power in the deposit market causes banks to reduce the pass-through of changes in the interest rate to deposit rates. Thus, when banks exert market power, deposits behave as long-term liabilities. Hence, banks extending long-term loans would match the duration of their assets and liabilities under this view. Under the "matching view", if banks do bear interest rate risk, it would be caused by some friction that limits their ability to perfectly match the maturity structure of their assets and liabilities.

The empirical literature focuses on the maturity of banks deposits (liabilities) and the loans they extend (assets), where deposits are either considered short term, or long term, and the maturity of the loans depends on whether the interest rate is fixed or floating (fixed rate vs. adjustable rate). Indeed, Flannery and James (1984a) find that demand deposits are treated as long-term liabilities. To account for the potential for demand deposits to behave as long-term liabilities, the empirical literature often tests the assumption that deposits are short term but conduct robustness tests where they vary the maturity of deposits (Purnanandam 2007; Gomez et al. 2016; Hoffmann et al. 2018).

3.3.1 *Which Factors Determine the Choice of Adjustable or Fixed-Rate Debt?*

In terms of the frictions that limit banks' ability to determine the maturity structure of their assets, the literature focuses on the choice between adjustable and fixed-rate mortgages. The focus on mortgages is justified by the fact that they typically make up the largest portion of loans, for example Hoffmann et al. (2018) find that mortgages make up approximately 40% of total loans extended by the banks in their sample.

Do banks or borrowers (households) determine the choice or adjustable and fixed-rate mortgages? The empirical evidence is mixed. To begin answering this question, Basten et al. (2018) use a unique data set of households' requests for mortgage quotes, combined with the offer response from multiple banks. The authors find that both banks and households determine the choice to some extent. Households base their decision on the minimization of current mortgage payments over insurance against interest rate risk. Banks also play a role in the choice of loan rate fixation, where they balance their own exposure to interest rate risk against credit risk and household requests.

Campbell (2013) find that loan rate fixation conventions vary across countries, where mortgages tend to be fixed in some countries while being variable in others. The author find that this heterogeneity can be explained by past macroeconomic experiences, such as inflation volatility. As past macroeconomic experiences are exogenous to individual banks, these results suggest that banks do not determine the choice of loan rate fixation.

Hoffmann et al. (2018) show that the countries in the Eurozone can be split into two groups according to their loan rate fixation conventions. The first group, made up of Belgium, Germany, France, the Netherlands, and Slovakia, have a high share of fixed-rate mortgages (between 79% and 93%). The second group, made up of the remaining countries, have a high share of variable-rate mortgages (between 71% and 96%). The authors find the cross-country differences in loan rate fixation conventions to be persistent over time. This finding is in contrast with Badarinza et al. (2018), who find that the relative popularity of the two mortgage rate fixation types varies across time. Further, Ehrmann and Ziegelmeyer (2017) find that adjustable rate mortgages are more popular when the interest rate spread is high, economic growth is high, or the volatility in unemployment is low. This further suggests that these conventions can vary across time.

Using supervisory data from the Bank of Italy, Albertazzi et al. (2018) seek to uncover if banks determine the choice loan rate fixation. The authors compare the outcomes observed for the same banking group across different countries. This, combined with the observation that that funding conditions are normally determined at the parent level, allows the authors to distinguish between local demand conditions and banks choice of loan rate fixation. They find that local subsidiaries of Italian banks abroad tend to extend fixed-rate loans in countries with a fixed-rate convention, and variable-rate loans in countries with a variable-rate convention. These results suggest that banks do not determine the choice of loan rate fixation. The authors show that local demand conditions are more important in determining loan rate fixation conventions. Specifically, they find that the share of new loans with a fixed rate is larger when households' financial literacy is lower, the historical volatility of inflation is lower, the correlation between unemployment and the short-term interest rate is higher, and the use of local mortgages to back covered bonds and of mortgage-backed securities is more widespread. The latter finding is consistent with Fuster and Vickery (2015), who find that the share of fixed-rate mortgages is lower when mortgages are harder to securitize.

Hence, banks are potentially exposed to interest rate risk -where their exposure will be heterogeneous across countries, where loan rate fixation conventions vary-time, and different levels of competition in the banking market. Hoffmann et al. (2018) find that loan rate fixation conventions affect banks' interest rate exposures. In particular, the difference between loan rate fixation conventions across countries can account for up to 60% of one standard deviation (0.57) of bank's interest rate exposure. Further, the authors find that this finding is robust to controlling for differences in banks' business models. They find that while banks may not bear significant interest rate risk on the aggregate, there is significant cross-sectional variation. In their sample, approximately half the banks would benefit from an increase in interest rates, which contradicts the "traditional view" on banks' on-balance sheet exposure to interest rate risk. This benefit stems from the fact that these banks receive deposits that have a longer maturity, and extend variable-rate loans, and, hence, see an increase in their value when interest rates increase.

3.4 How and Why Do Banks Manage Interest Rate Risk?

If banks are indeed exposed to interest rate risk, the questions arise: How and why do banks manage interest rate risk? Unlike credit risk which a bank can be more or less exposed to but requires credit derivatives to completely remove, it is possible for a bank to completely insulate itself from interest rate risk without trading derivatives. While banks may use interest rate derivatives to manage their interest rate risk exposure, they may also use on-balance sheet techniques, that is, managing the difference in maturity and repricing terms of their assets and liabilities. A bank's decision to manage and how to manage interest rate risk affects the transmission of monetary policy, the value of its equity, its lending behaviour, and, hence, it may affect the investment decisions of the firms to which they lend. Before reviewing the literature that focuses on these effects, we begin with a discussion of the papers that seek to uncover the methods and motives for managing interest rate risk.

Purnanandam (2007) investigates the choice between on-balance sheet and off-balance sheet techniques as well as what motivates a bank to manage their interest rate risk in the first place. In the corporate finance literature, Petersen and Thiagarajan (2000) investigate the hedging practices of two goldmines and find that while they have significantly different derivative hedging practices (off-balance sheet hedging) their overall exposure to gold price fluctuations is similar. This is due to the ease with which they can adjust their operating costs in response to a change in the gold price (on-balance sheet hedging). Purnanandam (2007) puts this into a banking context where banks may have significantly different off-balance sheet hedging practices (derivative trading) but also different on-balance sheet hedging, potentially resulting in similar exposures to interest rate risk. Hence, when analysing the methods and motives for managing interest rate risk, it is important to consider both on- and off-balance sheet techniques. Therefore, the author investigates the decision to manage interest rate risk as well as the choice of on or off-balance sheet hedging to determine if these methods are complements or substitutes.

To analyse these questions, Purnanandam (2007) combines data from FDIC, Compustat, and the Federal Reserve. The author obtains historical bank failure data from the FDIC and quarterly accounting information from the FDIC Call Reports. He combines this data with executive compensation data from Compustat and macroeconomic data from the

Federal Reserve Bank of St Louis. The final data includes 1443 bank failures from 1980 to 2003 and bank interest rate exposure and derivative usage from the third quarter of 1997 to the third quarter of 2003.

Following Flannery and James (1984a,b), Purnanandam (2007) measures a bank's on-balance sheet exposure to interest rate risk as the difference between the bank's assets that mature (or reprice) within a year and its liabilities that mature (or reprice) within a year. The absolute value of this difference is then scaled by the total assets of the bank. The resulting variable, "GAP", captures the extent to which a bank manages interest rate risk using on-balance sheet techniques. Here, lower values correspond to more active on-balance sheet interest rate risk management. Purnanandam (2007) find that derivative user banks maintain higher maturity GAPs (17.58% of total asset) relative to non-user banks (13.56% of total asset).

Although widely used, this measure of interest rate risk exposure has two potential issues. Firstly, as deposits make up a large portion of banks' total liabilities (71% to 84%), determining the correct duration and interest rate risk of deposits is important. The duration and interest rate risk of deposits depends on the type, demand, or term deposits as well as the level of competition in the banking industry (Hannan and Berger 1991; Drechsler et al. 2018). The type of deposit affects the measurement of the duration of a bank's liabilities as demand deposits may be considered as a short-term or a long-term liability. The level of competition in the banking industry affects the interest rate risk of deposits, where banks exerting market power (low competition) limit the pass-through of market rates to deposit rates. Purnanandam (2007) accounts for this potential issue by varying the percentage of demand deposits that are included in short-term liabilities in his calculations.

Secondly, due to data limitations, Purnanandam (2007) measure of duration only accounts for assets and liabilities maturing in one year but fails to account for the composition of the duration of assets and liabilities beyond one year. This is a common issue in the literature as data limitations force authors to focus on short-term versus long-term assets and liabilities. This data limitation is resolved in more recent studies which employ more granular supervisory data (e.g., Esposito et al. (2015); Hoffmann et al. (2018)).

To measure a bank's off-balance sheet exposure to interest rate risk, or derivative hedging, Purnanandam (2007) uses the "interest rate derivatives used for hedging purposes" obtained from the FDIC Call reports. Approximately 4.5% of banks (385 out of 8000) in his sample use interest rate derivatives for hedging purposes, while interest rate derivatives make up approximately 92% of the total derivatives used for hedging purposes. This suggests that while only a small percentage of banks use interest rate derivatives for hedging purposes, interest rate derivatives are the most common when managing risk using derivatives. One potential issue with this measure of off-balance sheet interest rate risk is that it does not take the duration of the derivative contracts into account. Purnanandam (2007) account for this in robustness tests by using maturity-adjusted derivatives, that is, three buckets: interest rate derivatives with maturity of one year or less, maturity of one to five years, and maturity of more than five years. While this is an improvement, it still only allows for three levels of duration.

Another potential issue is that it assumes that all interest rate derivative trading for hedging purposes is linked to the same variable-rate as the bank's assets and liabilities. For example, a US bank may trade interest rate derivatives on LIBOR to completely hedge its interest rate risk to a loan given to a firm where the rate charged is linked to LIBOR. However, the remaining part of the bank's balance sheet is linked to the Federal Funds rate. Hence, the composition of interest rate derivatives is fixed. Again, this is a data limitation which resolved in more recent studies which employ derivative trade repository data (e.g., Hoffmann et al. (2018)).

Purnanandam (2007) begins by analysing the banks hedging motives along the lines of the findings from the corporate finance literature. In line with these findings, the author predicts that the interest rate risk management incentive of a bank should be increasing in its expected cost of financial distress (Smith and Stulz 1985) and its growth rate which proxies for its need for external financing (Froot et al. 1993).

There is a potential issue of simultaneity bias, a bank's risk management incentive is predicted to be increasing in its financial distress cost, while the likelihood of distress decreases as risk management increase. Hence, the author use a two-stage estimation approach, where in the first stage the bank's probability of failure is estimated using the following logit model, represented by Eq. (3.1):

$$Failure_{j,t} = \alpha + \beta * Z_{j,t} + \epsilon_{j,t} \tag{3.1}$$

where $Failure_{j,t}$ is an indicator that equals 1 if bank j failed in quarter t, and zero otherwise. $Z_{j,t}$ is a vector of variables determining the probability of failure of a bank. These include: bank size (log of total assets), as well as total deposits, non-deposit liabilities, non-performing assets, gross amount of loans and leases, and liquid assets. Further, this vector includes the growth rate of the bank, the average interest rate (three-month T-Bills), the volatility of the daily interest rates within the quarter, the term spread, and the credit spread. Here, a positive β represents the case where an increase in the explanatory variable increases the probability of failure of the bank.

Purnanandam (2007) finds bank failure to be increasing in total deposits, non-deposit liabilities, non-performing assets, and the average interest rate. Further, bank failure is found to be decreasing in bank size, liquidity, loans to total assets and growth in total assets. As the predicted probability of failure of a bank is used in later regressions, the goodness of fit of the model is important. The model has an area of the receiver operator characteristic (ROC) curve above 0.9 and a Kolmogorov-Smirnov test statistic with an associated p-value of 0.001, indicating that the model fits well in the cross-section.

Purnanandam (2007) uses the results from this first-stage regression as an explanatory variable in the second stage to analyse banks' hedging motives, as represented by Eq. (3.2):

$$Hedge_{j,t} = \alpha + \alpha_j + \beta * X_{j,t} + \gamma M_t + \delta Alt\_Hedge_{j,t} + \epsilon_{j,t} \tag{3.2}$$

where $Hedge_{j,t}$ is either the 12-month maturity GAP or an indicator that equals 1 if bank j used derivatives for hedging purposes in quarter t, and zero otherwise, or the log of the notional amount of derivatives used for hedging purposes scaled by total assets. α_j are bank fixed effects. M_t include macroeconomic variables: the average interest rate (three-month T-Bills), the volatility of the daily interest rate within the quarter, the term spread, and the credit spread. $X_{j,t}$ is a vector of variables which are expected to affect a bank's hedging motives, as previously discussed. These include: the estimated probability of failure from the first-stage regression, bank size, growth rate of assets, liquid assets, and the ratio of deposits to total assets.

To account for the fact that banks may make their maturity GAP and derivatives decisions simultaneously, Purnanandam (2007) uses a system of equations and uses a two-stage least squares instrumental variable approach. He estimates the probability of derivatives usage by a bank and the estimated maturity GAP in another regression, in a first-stage regression. The author estimates the probability of derivative usage by regressing the bank's interest rate derivative decision on an indicator variable that equals 1 if it uses other derivatives (foreign currency, commodity, or equity). This is motivated by the fact that banks which trade any derivative are more likely to trade other derivatives (Minton et al. 2009). The maturity GAP is estimated by using its lag which the author motives by arguing that frequent adjustments to the maturity GAP is costly. When $Hedge_{j,t}$ is the 12-month maturity "GAP", $Alt\_Hedge_{j,t}$ includes the estimated probability (from first-stage regression) of derivatives usage by bank j in quarter t and the lag of the 12-month maturity "GAP". When $Hedge_{j,t}$ is either of the two derivative measures, $X_{j,t}$ includes the estimated maturity GAP from the first-stage regression as well as an indicator variable that equals 1 if it uses other derivatives in quarter t.

In line with the theory, Purnanandam (2007) finds that banks with a higher probability of failure, a high growth rate, and less liquid assets are more likely to hedge their interest rate risk, by both maintaining a lower on-balance sheet GAP and using interest rate derivatives (Smith and Stulz 1985; Froot et al. 1993). Smaller banks are more likely to use on-balance sheet techniques to manage their interest rate risk, while large banks are more likely to use derivatives. Purnanandam (2007) finds that banks with a higher proportion of deposit financing are less likely to hedge using derivatives. This may be due to deposit insurance which creates a disincentive to manage risk, or deposit rates being insensitive to bank risk-taking for other reasons (e.g., bank market power).

In terms of the substitutability or complementarity between on- and off-balance sheet interest rate risk hedging, Purnanandam (2007) is unable to conclude in either direction as the results change depending on the specification used. To this end, Esposito et al. (2015) conduct an analysis on the exposure of Italian banking groups during the global financial crisis. The authors employ semi-annual data from Italian supervisory reports on 68 banks from 2008 to 2012. These data are at bank-time level where assets, liabilities, and off-balance sheet exposures are reported across 14 maturity buckets. The granularity of the data allowed for the use of an alternative and more precise estimate of banks' on- and off-balance sheet interest rate exposure. Using an alternative measure of interest rate exposure, they find that on- and off-balance sheet interest rate hedging are substitutes.

The authors measure interest exposure using the duration gap approach which is consistent with the principles of the Basel Committee on Banking Supervision (2004, 2006). The standardized method for measuring interest rate risk requires assets, liabilities, and off-balance sheet items to be allocated to 14 maturity buckets. For fixed-rate items, the allocation to the

14 maturity buckets is done according to the remaining time to maturity. For variable-rate items, the allocation is according to the items repricing.[2] The duration gap is calculated using Eq. (3.3):

$$GAP = \sum_{m=1}^{m=14} \frac{DUR_m}{(1+i)} \left(\frac{A_m^{ON} - L_m^{ON} + D_M^{OFF}}{Z} \right) \tag{3.3}$$

where the net position is calculated as on-balance sheet assets, A_m^{ON}, less on-balance sheet liabilities, L_m^{ON}, plus the net position of off-balance sheet instruments, D_M^{OFF}. The net position of every time band is then weighted by a factor based on a specified modified duration multiplied by a 200 basis point parallel shift in the yield curve (e.g., for the maturity bucket 1 year to 2 years, the modified duration is 1.38; thus, the weighting factor is $1.38 * 200bp = 2.76$). Further, the Basel Committee specifies that all positions in each time band have the same yield of 5%. The resulting value is then normalized by regulatory capital, Z.

A bank's interest rate risk, that is, the change in the value of a bank's capital, K, as a percentage of regulatory capital, Z, in response to a parallel shift in the yield curve by Δi, can be approximated by Eq. (3.4):

$$IRR \approx - \left[\sum_{m=1}^{m=14} \frac{DUR_m}{(1+i)} \left(\frac{A_m^{ON} - L_m^{ON}}{Z} \right) + \sum_{m=1}^{m=14} \frac{DUR_m}{(1+i)} \left(\frac{D_M^{OFF}}{Z} \right) \right] \Delta i \tag{3.4}$$

While banks are not subject to capital requirements for interest rate risk exposure, IRR, the regulatory provisions recommend an IRR value of 20% as an "alert threshold". Esposito et al. (2015) find that the Italian banking system's interest rate risk was limited and below this alert threshold, where 200 basis parallel downward shift of the yield curve would have decreased the economic value of the Italian banking industry by approximately 3.1% of regulatory capital.

[2] See Esposito et al. (2015) for details on these calculations and weighting factors for each maturity bucket.

Esposito et al. (2015) reformulate Eq. (3.4) to distinguish between on-balance sheet hedging and off-balance sheet hedging as in Eq. (3.5):

$$IRR \approx -\left[GAP^{ON} + GAP^{OFF}\right]\Delta i \tag{3.5}$$

Esposito et al. (2015) define banks with a positive on-balance sheet duration gap, $GAP^{ON} > 0$, as asset sensitive, while banks with a negative on-balance sheet duration gap as liability sensitive. While this measure of interest rate risk is an improvement on that used by Purnanandam (2007), it only takes into account interest rate risk stemming from repricing risk. Other sources of interest rate risk, yield curve risk (e.g., change in the shape or slope of the yield curve) and option risk (e.g., prepayment options embedded in residential mortgages), are not accounted for in this measure as it is a static method based on the composition of a bank's balance sheet at a particular time.

Following Purnanandam (2007), the authors model the choice between on- and off-balance sheet interest rate risk hedging as a simultaneous decision. The authors use a two-stage least squares instrumental variables (2SLS-IV) regression, where the first-stage regression is represented by Eq. (3.6):

$$\begin{aligned} GAP^{ON}_{j,t} &= \pi_0 + \alpha_j + \alpha_t + \pi_2 GAP^{ON}_{j,t-1} + \pi_3 SIZE_{j,t} + \pi_4 CAP_{j,t} \\ &\quad + \pi_5 ROE_{j,t} + \pi_6 NPL_{j,t} + \pi_7 LIQ_{j,t} + \pi_8 SLOPE_t + \eta j, t \end{aligned} \tag{3.6}$$

where $GAP^{ON}_{j,t}$ is the on-balance sheet duration gap of bank j in semester t. Bank-specific characteristics include $SIZE_{j,t}$(the logarithm of total assets), $CAP_{j,t}$ (the core tier 1 ratio), $ROE_{j,t}$ (the return on equity), $NPL_{j,t}$ (non-performing loans to total assets), and $LIQ_{j,t}$ (the ratio of the difference between loans and retail deposits to loans). α_j and α_t are bank fixed effects and semester-fixed effects, respectively. $SLOPE_t$ is the difference between the ten-year government bond yield and the three-month Euribor rate. When semester-fixed effects are included, $SLOPE_t$ is not, as it has no cross-sectional variation and, hence, would be absorbed by the semester-fixed effects. The inclusion of semester-fixed effects improves the estimation by removing unobservable time-specific effects.

The second-stage regression is represented by Eq. (3.7):

$$GAP_{j,t}^{OFF} = \beta_0 + \alpha_j + \alpha_t + \beta_2 \widehat{GAP}_{j,t}^{ON} + \beta_3 SIZE_{j,t} + \beta_4 CAP_{j,t} + \beta_5 ROE_{j,t} + \beta_6 NPL_{j,t} + \beta_7 LIQ_{j,t} + \beta_8 SLOPE_t + \epsilon_{j,t} \tag{3.7}$$

where $\widehat{GAP}_{j,t}^{ON}$ is the predicted value of $GAP_{j,t}^{ON}$, estimated in the first-stage regression. In analysing the relationship between on- and off-balance sheet hedging, the coefficient of interest is β_2. Here, a negative β_2 would imply a hedging strategy, that is, banks use their on-balance sheet exposure to hedge their off-balance sheet (derivative) exposure.

For the regressions where the on-balance sheet duration gap is the dependent variable, the first-stage regression is represented either by Eq. (3.8) or by Eq. (3.9):

$$GAP_{j,t}^{OFF} = \pi_0 + \alpha_j + \alpha_t + \pi_2 GAP_{j,t-1}^{OFF} + \Pi X' \eta j, t \tag{3.8}$$

$$GAP_{j,t}^{OFF} = \pi_0 + \alpha_t + \pi_2 Skill_j + \Pi X' \eta j, t \tag{3.9}$$

Here $Skill_j$ is included following the same justification as in Purnanandam (2007) but is calculated slightly differently due to data differences. $Skill_j$ is an indicator variable that is equal to 1 if a bank uses interest rates, commodities, or exchange rate derivatives for *trading purposes* over the *entire sample*. Hence, $Skill_j$ only has cross-sectional variation which precludes the use of bank fixed effects. The second-stage regression is the same as Eq. (3.7) but where the dependent variable becomes $GAP_{j,t}^{ON}$ and $\widehat{GAP}_{j,t}^{OFF}$ is included as an explanatory variable which is calculated either by Eq. (3.8) or by Eq. (3.9).

Esposito et al. (2015) find that Italian banking groups use on- and off-balance sheet interest rate exposures as substitutes (hedging strategy), as opposed to using them as complements (enhancing strategy). On average, Italian banks hedged approximately 20% of their on-balance sheet exposure using off-balance sheet exposures (derivatives) and 75% of their off-balance sheet exposure using on-balance sheet exposures (restructuring their balance sheet).

The authors find that small banks with more traditional business activity, about one-third of their sample, had a negative correlation between their interest rate risk and their credit risk. This suggests that these banks balance these two sources of risks. However, the remaining banks in their sample, asset-sensitive banks which were mostly larger banks, increased their off-balance sheet interest rate exposure when faced with a widening of the funding gap (liquidity risk). Further, they find banks' interest rate risk and liquidity risk to be negatively correlated. Additionally, the authors find a negative correlation between bank size and off-balance sheet duration gap. They argue that this is due to larger banks' use of interest rate derivatives to increase potential gains from an increase in the interest rate. This increased risk-taking, they argue, is due to larger banks having better access to capital markets, benefiting from greater diversification and moral hazard stemming from too-big-to-fail banks having an incentive to take on more risk.

Another innovation of the paper is the use of a non-parallel shift in the yield curve. As previously discussed, using only parallel shifts in the yield curve only allows for the measurement of repricing risk, while a non-parallel shift allows for the measurement yield curve risk in addition. The authors do this by testing two alternative scenarios where an increase in the interest rate results in the following: (1) an upward sloping yield curve, where short-term rates rise by 200bp and longer-term rates rise by 300bp. (2) a downward sloping yield curve, where short-term rates rise by 100bp and long-term rates by 200bp. As the authors have 14 maturity buckets, this is relatively straightforward to implement. Esposito et al. (2015) find their finding on the substitutability of on- and off-balance sheet interest rate risk management to be robust to the inclusion of yield curve risk.

While Esposito et al. (2015) make important contributions to the literature, three issues remain which relate to data. Firstly, the sample is comprised of a small number of Italian banks during the global financial crisis. This may be an issue as the findings may not relate to banks' risk management decisions but rather be the result of financial turmoil which affected Italian Banks heterogeneously (see for example, Bonaccorsi di Patti and Sette (2016)). Secondly, the data is only from one country which limits the external validity of the study, and is particularly important in the context of interest rate risk management given cross-country variation in interest rate fixation conventions (Campbell 2013). Finally, banks may trade interest rate swaps which are linked to interest rates other than the rate which they are exposed to (basis swap). This would present itself in the data as the bank hedging as the data does not differentiate between the different types of interest rate swaps, only their maturity.

Hoffmann et al. (2018) employs supervisory data sets that include on-balance sheet interest rate exposures of all banks directly supervised by the European Central Bank, which, as of December 31, 2015, includes 129 banks representing 82% of the total banking assets in the Euro-area. The maturity structure of the exposures is the same as in Esposito et al. (2015) but includes banks from 18 different Euro-area countries. Further, the authors restrict the data to include only Euro-denominated balance sheet items.

To obtain a measure of banks' off-balance sheet interest rate exposure, the authors merge this data with the EMIR transaction-level data on interest rate derivatives obtained from the DTCC-DDRL and Regis-TR, which cover almost all trades in interest rate derivatives by European financial institutions. The authors restrict the interest rate derivative data to include only interest rate swaps which are in reference to Eonia or Euribor, the two most common benchmarks for Euro-denominated interest rate swaps. As the EMIR transaction-level data contains the identities of both parties in a swap transaction, Hoffmann et al. (2018) are able to merge this data with the detailed on-balance sheet interest rate exposure data. The resultant data set covers 104 banks and is restricted to a single time period, December, 31, 2015. Finally, these data sets are merged with Orbis (formally Bankscope) to obtain bank interest income and expenses information, and other supervisory data sets from the ECB, which includes information on banks' business models and the composition of loans. The granularity and scope of data employed by Hoffmann et al. (2018) allow the authors to avoid the issues that arise from the data employed by Esposito et al. (2015).

For most of their analysis, Hoffmann et al. (2018) use three different measures of interest rate risk. The first is calculated based on the income gap, similar to that of Purnanandam (2007):

$$\Delta NIM = \left(CF_{t+1}^{A} - CF_{t+1}^{L}\right) \times \Delta r \tag{3.10}$$

where ΔNIM is the projected change in net interest margin in the short run (1 year) in response to a change in the interest rate of Δr.

The second measure of interest rate risk is based on economic value sensitivity, similar to that of Esposito et al. (2015):

$$\Delta PV = \sum_{m=1}^{m=14} \frac{CF_{t+m}^{A} - CF_{t+m}^{L}}{(1 + r_m + \Delta r)^m} - \sum_{m=1}^{m=14} \frac{CF_{t+m}^{A} - CF_{t+m}^{L}}{(1 + r_m)^m} \tag{3.11}$$

where ΔPV is the change in the present value of the bank's net worth in response to a change in the interest rate of Δr. The income gap-based measure, ΔNIM, and the economic value-based measure, ΔPV, are similar in the sense that they are both calculated using the repricing gap of assets and liabilities. The main difference is that the income-based measure focuses on assets and liabilities that will be repriced within 1 year, while the economic value approach considers all maturities (in this case, 14 buckets). Further, with regards to interest rate derivatives, two derivative contracts may have the same ΔPV but different ΔNIM, for example a two-year interest rate swap has a notional value of up to five times as large as a ten-year swap. The authors focus on the economic value sensitivity for most of their analysis as it is the most relevant in their context, and it is also the preferred measure of regulators (Basel Committee on Banking Supervision 2016).

The third measure is another income-based measure that is based on the measure used by Drechsler et al. (2018). The authors propose an income-based measure that measures the pass-through of short-term interest rates to interest income and expenses, as in Eq. (3.12):

$$\Delta NIM_t = \alpha + \sum_{m=1}^{m=14} \beta_m^{NIM} \times \Delta r_{t-m} + \epsilon_t \tag{3.12}$$

where the sum of the beta coefficients $\beta^{NIM} = \sum_{m=1}^{m=14} \beta_m^{NIM}$ is the average sensitivity of interest income to changes in interest rates over time. This income-based measure has an advantage over ΔNIM from Eq. (3.10) as it is calculated over many years and, hence, includes a larger part of the duration spectrum.

Hoffmann et al. (2018) find that the average off-balance sheet interest rate exposure, as measured by ΔPV^{OFF}, is equal to 0.09 basis points of total assets and exhibits significant cross-sectional variation. Further, the sign of the ΔPV^{OFF} is the opposite of the on-balance sheet interest rate exposure, ΔPV^{ON}, suggesting that banks use on- and off-balance sheet interest rate exposures as substitutes (hedging strategy). To test this more formally, the authors estimate a regression represented by Eq. (3.13):

$$\Delta PV_j^{OFF} = \beta_0 + \beta_1 \Delta PV_j^{ON} + \epsilon_j \tag{3.13}$$

where ΔPV_j^{OFF} is the change in the present value of the banks' net worth in response to a change in the interest rate of Δr based on the banks' off-balance sheet exposure, and ΔPV_j^{ON} is based on its on-balance sheet exposure. Hoffmann et al. (2018) find a negative and statistically significant relation, $\beta_1 = -0.71$, consistent with a hedging strategy. However, when running the same regression using income sensitivity, ΔNIM, the authors do not find a significant relation. From this, they conclude that banks use derivatives to hedge present value risk but not income risk.

In the next step, Hoffmann et al. (2018) analyse the effect of banks' off-balance sheet interest rate exposures on their total interest rate exposure. Here, the authors use the absolute value of bank's interest rate exposures before and after hedging, $|\Delta PV_j^{ON}|$ before hedging, and $|\Delta PV_j|$ after hedging. Taking the absolute value of these sensitivities is done to take an agnostic view of the final sign of the bank's interest rate exposure, that is, over-hedging (e.g., 150%) and incomplete hedging (e.g., 50%) are treated the same. The average exposure after hedging, $|\Delta PV_j|$, is 0.40, while the average exposure before hedging, $|\Delta PV_j|$, is 0.54. The difference −0.14 represents a reduction of interest rate risk exposure of approximately a quarter, and is statistically significant at the 5% level. Calculated differently, the authors compute the average percentage change in absolute exposures, $log(|\Delta PV_j|) - log(|\Delta PV_j^{ON}|)$ and find that on average hedging reduces interest rate exposures by 29%.

Finally, Hoffmann et al. (2018) test for cross-sectional variation in hedging by estimating a regression represented by Eq. (3.14):

$$\begin{aligned} log(|\Delta PV_j|) - log(|\Delta PV_j^{ON}| &= \beta_0 + \beta_1 |\Delta PV_j^{ON}| + \beta_2 Opp.\ Sign_j \\ &+ \beta_3 VRM_c + \beta_4 \% NPL_j + \beta_5 Size \epsilon_j \end{aligned} \tag{3.14}$$

Here, VRM_c is an indicator variable equal to 1 if the bank is located in a country with predominantly variable-rate mortgages. $\%NPL_j$ is the share of non-performing loans and $Size$ is the log of total assets. $Opp.\ Sign_j$ is an indicator variable that is equal to 1 for asset-sensitive banks, $\Delta PV_j^{ON} > 0$, in countries with predominantly fixed-rate mortgages, or liability-sensitive banks in countries with predominantly variable-rate mortgages. The authors use this variable to measure the ease at which a bank can find a local counterparty to their derivative transaction. If all banks have similar on-balance sheet exposures, the opportunities for risk-sharing are more limited. Hence, the expected sign of β_2 is negative, that is, banks hedge more when they have the opposite exposure compared to other local banks.

The coefficient for $|\Delta PV_j^{ON}|$, β_1, is negative and statistically significant at the 10% level. The authors conclude that this suggests that banks which are more exposed to interest rate risk hedge more. Further, the coefficient for $Opp.\ Sign_j$, β_2, is equal to -0.57 and statistically significant at the 5% level. Hence, banks whose on-balance sheet interest rate exposure has a different sign to the local prevailing exposure tend to hedge more. This is consistent with an increase in the ease of finding a counterparty (more trading opportunities) in a segmented market. In the context of the Eurozone, this result is particularly relevant given cross-country variation in mortgage market structure, particularly loan rate fixation conventions. This creates interbank risk-sharing opportunities through banks from different countries trading interest rate derivatives with one another.

The authors find no statistically significant difference in the hedging practice by banks domiciled in countries with differing loan rate fixation conventions, as measured by VRM_c.

Additionally, they find no evidence, that moral hazard, associated with the too-big-to-fail guarantees, as measured by $Size$, has an effect on banks' hedging activities. Further, theory suggests that financially constrained banks may choose to hedge less (Rampini and Viswanathan 2010), this is because both hedging counterparties and financiers require collateral, which requires net worth. Hence, financially constrained banks face a stronger trade-off between hedging and financing. The authors proxy for financial constraints using $\%NPL_j$ as a measure of risk and find no statistical significant evidence that financially constrained banks hedge less. This is in contrast with Rampini et al. (2019), who find that financial constraints impede both hedging and financing. A potential cause of the lack of evidence for the effects of moral hazard and financial constraints on hedging practices is the lack of within-bank variation, as the data only covers a single time period.

3.5 What Are the Consequences of Banks' Decision to Manage Interest Rate Risk?

3.5.1 *For the Transmission of Monetary Policy*

If banks' profits and economic value are exposed to interest rate risk and if they are not frictionlessly able to raise alternative financing, they may adjust their lending in response to monetary policy changes.

Purnanandam (2007) further investigates bank's interest rate hedging practices by analysing its effect on the transmission of monetary policy through the bank lending channel (Kashyap and Stein 2000).[3] To estimate the effect of bank's interest rate hedging practice, he estimates Eq. (3.15):

$$\Delta log(LOAN)_{j,t} = \alpha_0 + \sum_{k=1}^{k=4} \alpha_k \Delta log(LOAN)_{j,t-k} + \sum_{k=1}^{k=8} \beta_k \Delta FED_{t-k} + \sum_{k=0}^{k=3} \gamma_k \Delta log(NGDP)_{t-k} + \epsilon_{j,t} \tag{3.15}$$

where $log(LOAN)_{j,t}$ is the change in bank j's loan supply in quarter t. The equation includes four lags of the change in bank j's loan supply, $log(LOAN)_{j,t-k}$, as well as four lags of the growth rate of nominal GDP, $\Delta log(NGDP)_{t-k}$. Finally, the equation includes eight lags of the change in the Federal Funds rate, ΔFED_{t-k}, the measure of monetary policy.

Here, the sum of the β_k coefficients measures the response of banks' loan supply to changes in monetary policy. Purnanandam (2007) estimates Eq. (3.15) separately for a sample split by different size groups (as measured by total assets) and by derivative user and non-user banks. He finds that, across size groups, derivative user banks are able to insulate their loan supply from monetary policy changes, while non-user banks decrease their lending in response to a monetary policy tightening.

Further, the author tests for difference between the β_k coefficients for interest rate derivative user banks and non-user banks across different size groups. He finds the difference to be negative and statistically significant, implying derivative non-user banks decrease their lending significantly more than user banks. Finally, the author finds this result to hold when controlling for other findings in the bank lending channel literature: across size groups (Kashyap and Stein 2000) and when excluding banks that are affiliated to multi-bank holding companies (Campello 2002; Ashcraft 2006). These results indicate that banks' use of interest rate derivatives

[3] See Chap. 5: Global Banking, for a detailed description of the channels through which monetary policy is transmitted and the bank lending channel in particular.

reduces the potency of monetary policy and indicate a possible method through which larger banks are able to insulate their loan supply from monetary policy changes.

A common issue in the bank lending channel literature with regards to bank level analysis is the inability to disentangle loan demand from supply. Further, the results of Purnanandam (2007) may be the result of endogenous matching between banks and firms, for example a bank's high income gap may be an endogenous response to customers borrowing more when interest rates are high. Gomez et al. (2016) account for these potential sources of endogeneity by employing loan-level data. This loan-level data allows them to include borrower-time fixed effects which controls for time-varying loan demand (Khwaja and Mian 2008).

Gomez et al. (2016) use Dealscan data merged with quarterly accounting information from the FDIC Call Reports from 1986 to 2013. The authors calculate bank's interest rate income risk as in Purnanandam (2007). They then test banks' response to changes in the Federal funds rate, monetary policy, based on their income gap, while controlling for loan demand with borrower-time fixed effects. They find that in response to a 100bp increase in the Federal funds rate a bank with an income gap of 0.243 (75th percentile) increases its lending by approximately 0.4*bp* more than a bank with an income gap of 0.012 (25th percentile). The magnitude of this effect is economically significant as it is large in comparison to the unconditional quarterly loan growth, 1.8%. Further, the magnitude is similar to previously identified factors in the literature, such as bank size (Kashyap and Stein 2000).

Additionally, Gomez et al. (2016) find this effect to be larger for banks that do not use off-balance sheet hedging (interest rate derivatives) and for smaller banks. This finding is in line with Purnanandam (2007) as small banks are more financially constrained and off-balance sheet hedging reduces the potency of monetary policy. Further, the authors find that the income gap of bank holding companies affects the response of their subsidiaries to monetary policy, through internal capital markets.

Furthermore, the authors test the sorting hypothesis, where high/low income gap banks may lend to specific firms. They do this using two methods. Firstly, they compare the sensitivity of bank lending to monetary policy including and excluding borrower-time fixed effects which controls for this sorting. They find the results to be similar in magnitude and statistical significance, suggesting that banks and firms match randomly.

In a more formal test of the sorting hypothesis, Gomez et al. (2016) use the granularity of their data by comparing banks lending to the same firm. Here, they regress the income gap of a firm's largest lender on that of its second largest lender. Alternatively, they compare the income gap of a firm's future largest lender on that of its current largest lender. If the sorting hypothesis were to hold, the authors would find a positive relation in either regression, that is if high income gap banks lend to specific firms, there should be a correlation between the income gaps of a firm's banks. The authors find no statistical evidence for the sorting hypothesis in either of the two regressions.

Banking theory suggests that monetary policy may have redistributive effects between the banking sector and non-financial sectors (Diamond and Rajan 2012; Brunnermeier and Sannikov 2016). This is done through a "stealth recapitalization" where a decrease in the monetary policy rate increases banks' net worth, when they face liquidity constraints, at the expense of non-financial sectors. A key assumption of this theory is that banks' equity value is decreasing in the monetary policy rate, that is, a decrease in the monetary policy rate raises banks' equity value (Brunnermeier and Koby 2018). This assumption is confirmed by Flannery and James (1984b), who find a negative correlation between banks' equity returns and interest rate changes. It is further causally confirmed by English et al. (2018), who show that banks' stock prices decline in response to an unanticipated increase in monetary policy rates or a steeping of the yield curve.

However, Hoffmann et al. (2018) find that this assumption does not hold for all banks in the Eurozone, as net worth is increasing in interest rates for about half the banks in their sample. This has two implications: firstly, the magnitude of these "stealth recapitalization" may be lower than expected based on the findings of Flannery and James (1984b) and English et al. (2018). Secondly, the differential response of banks' net worth within the banking sector implies a redistributive effect within the banking sector. Hoffmann et al. (2018) find that in their sample a 25-basis point increase in interest rates would have resulted in asset-sensitive banks, $\Delta PV > 0$, gaining €6.6$billion$. Liability-sensitive banks, $\Delta PV < 0$, would have lost €11.2 $billion$. This implies a redistributive effect, or net transfer between the banking sector and non-financial sectors, of €4.6$billion$ and a transfer within the banking industry of €6.6 $billion$. Hence, the redistributive effects of changes in the interest rate within the banking sector are 40% larger than the standard redistributive effects.

3.5.2 *For Their Borrowers*

When banks are not exposed to on-balance sheet interest rate risk due to reasons such as loan rate fixation convention, they may still be indirectly affected as households and firms may bear interest rate risk. If this is the case, monetary policy would be transmitted through borrowers' balance sheets, which affects consumption and investment. Hoffmann et al. (2018) finds that in countries with mainly variable-rate mortgages, households suffer from higher interest rates, while households in other countries are relatively unexposed to interest rate risk. Households in countries with mainly variable-rate mortgages are exposed as their balance sheet consists of fixed-rate assets (sticky deposits) and variable-rate liabilities (variable-rate loans). Hence, these households are liability sensitive. This finding is important when considering the external validity of single country analyses as the findings may be due to the loan rate fixation conventions of the country. Further, for multi-country currency areas, that is, the Eurozone, it implies that monetary policy is subject to heterogeneity due to the heterogeneity in loan rate fixation within the area.

Due to switching costs and information asymmetry, bank-firm relationships tend to be "sticky", and firms cannot frictionlessly substitute to a new bank when their relationship bank reduces its lending. Hence, firms which borrow from banks with a high income gap may have better access to financing than firms which borrow from a low income gap bank, when interest rates increase. Gomez et al. (2016) test if firms which borrow from banks which are more or less exposed to interest rate risk are able to invest and grow more. They do so by regressing firms level variables (firm debt growth, employment growth, and total asset growth) on the income gap of the lead arrange in the syndicate of the firms' debt.

The authors find that firms' total debt increases by 2.9% in response to a 100bp increase in the federal funds rate, similar in magnitude to the effect on individual loans. This suggests that firms do not substitute between lenders, for example they do not switch to a more accommodative lender when another contracts its loan supply. Further, they find a differential response of firms which lend from banks with an income gap of 0.3 (top quartile) and from banks with an income gap of 0.15 (bottom quartile). In response to a 100bp increase in interest rates, firms which lend from banks with an income gap of 0.3 increase their employment by 0.3 p.p. more and asset growth (investment) by 0.2 p.p. more than firms which lend from banks with an income gap of 0.15. Hence, the level and the distribution of banks' exposure to interest rate risk, and their off-balance sheet hedging, has important real consequences for the economy.

3.6 Conclusion

While financial intermediation may expose banks to interest rate risk, they may not be exposed to a large extent on aggregate. However, there is substantial heterogeneity in interest rate risk across banks (Purnanandam 2007). This heterogeneity is caused by the heterogeneous frictions which banks face in managing their on-balance sheet interest rate exposure (Hoffmann et al. 2018). These fictions vary across countries with differing loan rate fixation conventions (Campbell 2013; Albertazzi et al. 2018).

Banks use off-balance sheet techniques (derivative trading) to hedge their net on-balance sheet exposure (Esposito et al. 2015). Consistent with the segmented market theory, the ease with which banks are able to hedge their interest rate risk using derivatives depends on their interest rate exposure relative to other banks in the country in which they are domiciled (Hoffmann et al. 2018).

Further, banks' exposure to interest rate risk has consequences for the transmission of monetary policy (Gomez et al. 2016). Additionally, banks' exposure to interest rates affects the response to interest rate changes of the firms to which they lend (Gomez et al. 2016). Finally, banks' use of interest rate derivatives reduces the potency of monetary policy transmission (Purnanandam 2007; Esposito et al. 2015).

The core issue in the literature is that the measurement of interest rate risk requires granular data. Post-crisis regulation has made more granular data available to researchers on both on- and off-balance sheet interest rate exposures. This has allowed for more precise estimates of banks' interest rate risk (Esposito et al. 2015; Hoffmann et al. 2018). Further research into how and why banks' interest rate risk varies over time and across boarders, as well as how banks interest rate risk management affects their other sources of risk, is warranted. Table 3.1 offers a compact overview of the papers reviewed in this chapter.

Table 3.1 Interest rate risk

Paper	*Research question*	*Data*	*Methodology*	*Main findings*
Albertazzi et al. (WP, 2018)	Which **factors** determine the choice of **adjustable or fixed rate** debt?	Individual Monetary and Financial Institution Interest Rates (IMIR) data set held by the Bank of Italy.?	**Exogenous Variation:** Funding conditions are determined at the parent level and exogenous to country-level macroeconomic conditions.	Local subsidiaries of Italian banks abroad tend to extend fixed-rate loans in countries with a fixed-rate convention, and variable-rate loans in countries with a variable-rate convention.
			Correlations and within-group variation: comparing a bank's share of fixed-rate loans within the same banking group across different countries as explained by local demand factors.	The share of new loans with a fixed rate is larger when households' financial literacy is lower, the historical volatility of inflation is lower, the correlation between unemployment and the short-term interest rate is higher, and the use of local mortgages to back covered bonds and of mortgage-backed securities is more widespread.

Basten et al. (WP, 2018)	Data from a Swiss website, Comparis, on households' requests for mortgage quotes and the offer response from multiple banks combined with the supervisory data set of the Swiss Financial Market Supervisory Authority (FINMA) containing bank characteristics.	**Correlations and within-group variation:** the terms and conditions of a bank's offer explained by bank characteristics. **Fixed effects:** include borrower-fixed effects to account for differences in demand across borrowers.	Both banks and households determine the choice of loan rate fixation to some extent. Households base their decision on the minimization of current mortgage payments over insurance against interest rate risk. Banks balance their own exposure to interest rate risk against credit risk and household requests.
Ehrmann and Ziegelmeyer (JMCB, 2017)	Data from the Eurosystem Household Finance and Consumption Survey combined with Residential Property Price Index Statistics of the ECB Statistical Data Warehouse and the ECB MFI interest rate statistics.	**Two-Stage Heckman Selection Model:** where in the first stage a probit model is estimated for the decision for households to take out a mortgage. The second-stage probit model estimates the probability of the household obtaining an adjustable rate mortgage as explained by household and mortgage characteristics as well as macroeconomic conditions.	Adjustable rate mortgages are taken out more frequently when the interest rate spread is high, economic growth is high, or the volatility in unemployment is low.

(continued)

Table 3.1 (continued)

Paper	*Research question*	*Data*	*Methodology*	*Main findings*
Hoffmann et al. (RFS, Forth-coming)	How and why do banks **manage interest rate risk?**	On-balance sheet interest rate exposures from the European Central Bank supervisory data sets, merged with EMIR transaction-level data on interest rate derivatives and Orbis.	**Correlations and cross-sectional variation:** where a banks use of interest rate derivatives is explained by its on-balance sheet interest rate exposures, bank characteristics, and country characteristics.	Banks which are more exposed to interest rate risk hedge more. Banks whose on-balance sheet interest rate exposure has a different sign to the local prevailing exposure tend to hedge more. On average, hedging reduces interest rate exposures by 29%. Banks use derivatives to hedge present value risk but not income risk.
Esposito et al. (JBF, 2015)		Italian supervisory reports on the on- and off-balance sheet interest rate exposures of Italian banking groups, separated into 14 maturity buckets.	Similar to Purnanandam (JME, 2007)	Italian banking groups use on- and off-balance sheet interest rate exposures as substitutes (hedging strategy), as opposed to using them as complements (enhancing strategy). Italian banks hedged approximately 20% of their on-balance sheet exposure using off-balance sheet exposures (derivatives), and 75% of their off-balance sheet exposure using on-balance sheet exposures (restructuring their balance sheet).

Purnanandam (JME, 2007)	How does banks' exposure to **interest rate risk** affect the transmission of **monetary policy transmission?**	Bank failure data from the FDIC and quarterly accounting information from the FDIC Call Reports, with executive compensation data from Compustat and macroeconomic data from the Federal Reserve Bank of St. Louis.	**Two-stage least squares instrumental variable approach**: In a first-stage regression, the level of on(off)-balance sheet hedging is modelled. In the second stage, the estimated on(off)-balance hedging is instrumented for its observed value in a regression that explains the off(on)-balance sheet interest rate risk management motives with this instrument and other bank characteristics.	Banks with a higher probability of failure, higher growth rate, and less liquid assets are more likely to hedge their interest rate risk, by both maintaining a lower on-balance sheet GAP and using interest rate derivatives. Smaller banks are more likely to use on-balance sheet techniques to manage their interest rate risk, while large banks are more likely to use derivatives. Banks with a higher proportion of deposit financing are less likely to hedge using derivatives.
			Correlation and two-step approach: The sample is split along two dimensions (size and if the bank uses derivatives); a separate regression is run for each split, and where the change in credit is explained as the change in the monetary policy rate. Differences in the beta estimates of the separate regressions implies difference in response to monetary policy along that dimension.	Banks of all sizes, which don't use derivatives, reduce their lending volume in response to a contractionary monetary policy.

(continued)

Table 3.1 (continued)

Paper	*Research question*	*Data*	*Methodology*	*Main findings*
Gomez et al. (WP, 2016)	How does banks' exposure to **interest rate risk** affect their **borrowers**?	Dealscan data merged with quarterly accounting information from the FDIC Call Reports.	**Correlations and within-group variation:** banks' response to changes in monetary policy, as explained by their income gap. **Fixed effects:** include borrower-fixed effects to account for differences in demand across borrowers.	In response to an increase in the interest rates, banks with more positive income gaps, increase their lending by more.
			Correlations and cross-sectional variation: where the firms' investment or employment decision is explained by the funding gap of the bank from which it lends the most.	In response to an increase in the interest rates, firms which lend from banks with more positive income gaps increase their lending, employment, and investment by more.

CHAPTER 4

Credit Risk

CDS are traded in an over-the-counter (OTC) market, where a limited number of dealers (typically, large investment banks) create markets for buyers and sellers of credit risk, such as banks, insurance companies, and mutual funds. CDS allow for the transfer of credit risk between participants in the CDS market; this allows for both risk-sharing and risk-taking. This is to say that banks may trade in the CDS market to hedge existing credit exposures or to speculate on credit risk.

A number of contributions seek to uncover why banks trade CDS in the first place. Banks' propensity to use CDS as a hedging instrument is increasing in their capital constraints as CDS allows for the offsetting of credit exposure under capital regulations (Minton et al. 2009; Beyhaghi et al. 2016). Additionally, if banks use other risk transfer instruments, they are more likely to use CDS to hedge their credit risk (Minton et al. 2009).

This suggests that if a firm obtains a larger proportion of its credit from banks that are more active hedgers, for example foreign exchange hedging, or are more capital constrained, it is more likely to have CDS traded on its debt (Saretto and Tookes 2012; Subrahmanyam et al. 2014). Further, the decision to trade CDS on a firm is based on the riskiness of the firm, the characteristics of the banks' relationship with the firm, and the banks' reputation in other credit markets (Beyhaghi et al. 2016; Streitz 2016; Gündüz et al. 2016).

Another strand of the CDS literature focuses on the effects of CDS trading on other credit markets (e.g., the bond market) and a banks choice

A. Bilan et al., *Banking and Financial Markets*, Palgrave Macmillan Studies in Banking and Financial Institutions,
https://doi.org/10.1007/978-3-030-26844-2_4

to use CDS over other credit risk transfer instruments. As a primary role of banks is to monitor their borrowers, banks' use of CDS to hedge their credit risk may reduce their incentive to monitor their borrowers, with possible negative effects on firm performance. If other creditors expect the current lenders of these firms to reduce their monitoring activities, they might be less willing to provide credit to these firms. The literature has shown that riskier borrowers' debt is more likely to be sold than hedged using CDS (Beyhaghi et al. 2016). Further, there is evidence for a credit enhancement channel where a bank uses CDS to facilitate loan sales by selling CDS on the firm to their counterparty in the loan sale (Hasan and Wu 2017).

In general, new securities and markets can affect related markets by altering their characteristics such as liquidity, efficiency, and quality, as the new markets act as substitutes or complements to the related markets. The initiation of CDS trading on a firms' debt (CDS initiation) has mostly detrimental effects for the secondary market for a referenced firm's bonds. The bond market becomes less efficient, and there are no improvements in terms of an increase in liquidity or a reduction in pricing errors (Das et al. 2014). Additionally, on CDS initiation, the firm sees its loan spreads in the syndicated market increase by 13% (Amiram et al. 2017).

A consequence of banks' participation in both CDS and credit markets is that their use of CDS impacts the way in which they interact with their borrowers. As CDS allows for the banks to hedge existing exposures, their use of CDS to hedge may allow them to increase their credit supply to CDS-referenced firms. Further, under certain conditions, CDS improves the bargaining power of banks in debt restructuring negotiations, which ex ante improves their willingness to lend to these firms. This in turn improves CDS-referenced firms access and cost of debt (Ashcraft and Santos 2009; Saretto and Tookes 2012).

However, creditors who purchase CDS contracts may have an increased incentive to push the CDS-referenced entity into bankruptcy in order to collect the payout from the CDS contract. While creditors hold control rights under the debt contract, CDS allow for formal ownership of debt claims to be decoupled from the economic exposure to credit deterioration. This gives rise to "empty creditors" who have less incentives to participate in firm restructuring but retain their voting rights. While the evidence is mixed, there is growing support for the view that this results in banks inefficiently pushing firms into default (Subrahmanyam et al. 2014; Colonnello et al. 2016; Degryse et al. 2019).

Firms may change their financing and investment policies in response to having CDS traded on their debt. The literature on firms' response to becoming a CDS-referenced firm shows that firms respond by increasing their cash buffers to avoid having to negotiate with empty creditors (Subrahmanyam et al. 2017). Further, there is evidence that firms increase the riskiness of their R&D project, which results in them becoming more innovative, registering more patents, and receiving a larger number of citations on their patents (Chang et al. 2017).

This chapter is organized as follows: We begin by providing an expanded definition of CDS contracts and the key events that affected these contracts. We then review the data and methodologies employed in the literature. Following this, we then discuss the literature that focuses on why and how banks lay off credit risk, followed by how CDS trading affects the other credit markets. Next, we discuss the findings and methodologies from the literature on the effects of CDS trading on the referenced firm and how these referenced firms respond to having CDS traded on their debt. Finally, we discuss the findings on the spillover effects of CDS trading.

4.1 Credit Default Swap Contracts

A credit default swap (CDS) contract is similar to an insurance contract where one party pays another party for protection from a particular event.[1] In the case of CDS, a protection buyer (buyer of the CDS) makes periodic payments to the protection seller (seller of the CDS) and the protection seller pays the buyer a protection value if a "credit event" occurs.

The CDS contract specifies the parties (protection buyer and seller) as well as the reference entity on which credit risk protection is being purchased (Fig. 4.1). Further, it specifies the maturity, which ranges from one to ten years, with the most liquid being five-year maturity. Further, CDS contracts define what the parties agree to be a credit event (restructuring or bankruptcy), which triggers a payment from the protection seller to the protection buyer. For this protection, the CDS buyer pays a periodic premium to the protection seller, called the CDS spread.

[1] CDS differ from standard insurance contracts as a protection buyer does not need to hold the underlying asset, and it may purchase protection that exceeds the value of its position in the underlying. This can be thought of as buying insurance on your neighbour's house, or insuring your own home for more than its worth.

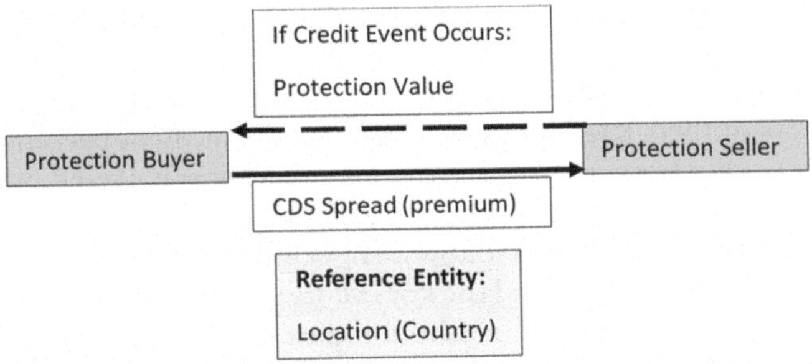

Fig. 4.1 CDS Contract Payment Diagram
Note: This figure illustrates the payment structure of a CDS contract. A protection buyer (buyer of the CDS) makes periodic payments (CDS spread) to the protection seller (seller of the CDS). The protection seller pays the buyer a protection value if a "credit event" occurs. The definition of a "credit event" depends on the standardized contract used, which is determined based on the domicile country of the underlying reference entity

Once the event occurs, a settlement takes place where the value of the compensation that the protection buyer receives from the seller is determined. Finally, the contract specifies the way in which this payment from the protection seller to buyer is to be settled. This can be done through a cash settlement where the protection buyer receives the difference between the protection value and the current value of the underlying debt, or by physical settlement, where the protection buyer delivers a certain bond of the reference entity to the seller and receives the full insured amount in cash, in return (ISDA 2003).[2]

Clearly, there are many points that could potentially be negotiated in these bilateral contracts. This could harm the liquidity of the CDS market, as parties would have to negotiate these before entering into agreements. To address this, the International Swap and Derivative Association released the 2003 ISDA Credit Definitions, which aimed to standardize many of the contract terms and thus improve liquidity in the CDS market (ISDA 2003). These contracts were standardized by reference entity type and location of the reference entity. For the single name corporate CDS

[2] The residual value of the underlying debt is typically determined by polling the dealers in the market.

(CDS where the reference entity is a single firm), there are two main standardized contracts, the Standard European Corporate CDS Contract and the Standard North American CDS Contract (ISDA 2009a,b). The type of contract is determined by the location of the reference entity (i.e., a CDS contract on a European firm trades with a Standard European Corporate CDS contract).

The main difference between European CDS contracts and North American CDS contracts is their definition of a credit event, called the restructuring clause. Under the 2003 ISDA Credit Definitions, there are four types of restructuring clauses: Old Restructuring (CR), Modified Restructuring (MR), Modified-Modified Restructuring (MMR), and No Restructuring (XR). European corporate CDS mostly trade with an MMR clause, under which restructuring is recognized as a credit event. With an MMR clause, the deliverable obligation is limited to debt with a maturity no more than 60 months for restructured obligations and 30 months for all other obligations. Prior to 2009, most North American corporate CDS contracts traded with an MR clause, which limits the deliverable obligation to debt with a maturity no more than 30 months. However, in 2009, with the CDS Big Bang protocol, the restructuring clause was standardized and changed to XR for North American CDS corporates (Markit 2009a).

In 2009, the ISDA further standardized both European CDS corporate and North American CDS corporate contracts. The CDS Big Bang was implemented in April 2009, while the CDS Small Bang was implemented in June 2009. The CDS Big Bang Protocol further standardized the contracts of North American CDS corporate contracts, while the CDS Small Bang Protocol did the same to European CDS corporate contracts. Both standard contracts had terms changed to improve the liquidity of the respective CDS markets, these changes included standardization of the settlement auctions, amongst other changes (Markit 2009a,b). The main difference between the changes is that the North American contract was standardized to trade only with an XR restructuring clause, while the European contract's restructuring clause remained MMR.

4.2 Data

To explore the interaction between CDS and credit markets, researchers require both CDS and credit data, typically at the bank-firm level, along with data on bank and firm characteristics. In most applications in the

CDS literature, the more granular the data on CDS is, the less authors have to rely on assumptions and deal with the measurement error of their proxies for CDS trading. Further, the lack of granular data may impede the depth to which researchers are able to investigate a particular topic. For example, measuring CDS trading at bank level limits the ability to test for borrower characteristics that determine the choice of the credit risk transfer instrument.

As CDS are traded in an over-the-counter market, there is a lack of transparency, even post trade, and, hence, a lack of granular data on CDS trading. It is possible to identify which firms have CDS traded on them, through CDS pricing databases, or which banks trade CDS, through information contained in their balance sheets. However, without trade data researchers were unable to determine which banks were trading CDS on a particular firm, or what their exposures were. Historically, this meant that researchers had to create proxies for CDS trading which were often prone to measurement error. Typically, researchers have relied on the CDS pricing data sets to identify which firms have CDS traded on them, and when CDS begins to trade on these firms' debt (CDS initiation).[3]

Through post-crisis regulation, granular transaction data have become available from trade repositories such as the Trade Information Warehouse (TIW) of the Depository Trust and Clearing Corporation (DTCC). The European Parliament along with the European Securities and Markets Authority (ESMA) has implemented the European Markets Infrastructure Regulation (EMIR). Article 9 of EMIR requires the reporting of OTC and exchange traded derivative transactions to one of the trade repositories.[4] The DTCC-TIW data sets are the most comprehensive data sets on granular CDS positions available, containing between 90% and 95% of global CDS activity (Mayordomo et al. 2014). The DTCC position-level data set contains individual bank's CDS positions on a reference entity with a particular counterparty, at a weekly frequency. While not public, supervisory authorities, such as central banks, are eligible to obtain data on trades which involve a party or a reference entity under their jurisdic-

[3] These are: Bloomberg CMA CDS data, Markit CDS data, CreditTrade, and GFI. See Mayordomo et al. (2014) for a detailed comparison of these databases.

[4] These include DTCC Derivatives Repository Ltd., Krajowy Depozyt Papierów Wartosciowych S.A, Regis-TR S.A., UnaVista Ltd., CME Trade Repository Ltd., ICE Trade Vault Europe Ltd., Bloomberg Trade Repository Limited, and NEX Abide Trade Repository AB.

tion/supervision. For example, the Deutsche Bundesbank has access to CDS transactions that involve German banks as party or counterparty and transactions on German reference entities. This data allows researchers to exactly identify which banks are trading CDS on a particular firm and what their net position is. This level of granularity is not available from the public database of the DTCC, which only shows CDS positions aggregated at firm level, and only for the top 1000 reference entities by gross notional.

To investigate the impact of CDS trading, researchers may additionally require bank-firm-level credit exposures. These have been obtained from either country-specific credit registries or the LPC DealScan database. The Dealscan database contains information on syndicated loans. These loans typically are granted jointly by several financial intermediaries towards the same firm. These loans tend to be large and, hence, the database mainly includes large firms. This creates a bias towards large firms, which in many applications may be an issue. However, this bias is not so important in the CDS literature as CDS firms tend to be large firms.

4.3 Methodology

To identify the effect of CDS trading on a referenced entity the literature most often employs a methodology that uses the initiation of CDS trading as treatment. An indicator variable, $CDS\ Trading$ is created which equals 1 if a firm has CDS traded on its debt in the quarter. This is included in a specification which contains either firm fixed effects or another indicator variable, $CDS\ Traded$, which equals 1 if a firm ever has CDS traded on its debt, as well as time fixed effects. By including firm fixed effects, or $CDS\ Traded$, and time fixed effects, the $CDS\ Trading$ dummy captures the treatment effect of CDS being initiated on the firm. By including $CDS\ Traded$, authors are able to account for the potential endogeneity that arises out of the potential that CDS firms are different to non-CDS firms in a way that affects their variable of interest, in a non-time-varying manner.

To further account for the differences between CDS firms and non-CDS firms, many authors conduct robustness tests by matching the treatment and control group using varied matching techniques. Matching is a non-parametric method for preprocessing data in order to reduce the imbalance between CDS (treatment) and non-CDS (control) groups. Most common is the use of propensity score with 1-to-1 matching. This 1-to-1 match, that is, 1 control firm matched to 1 treatment firm, reduces the imbalance between the treatment and control group but comes at a cost of fewer observations, which reduces the precision of the estimated coefficients. The literature employs other matching techniques including propensity score with a 1-to-2 matching or a calliper , overlap weighting and coarsened exact matching (Li et al. 2018; Iacus et al. 2012). The different techniques trade off the balance of matched treatment and control group with the reduction in observations and hence precision of the estimated coefficients.

Additionally, the literature has employed an instrumental variable methodology to account for the potential endogeneity of the timing of CDS initiation. Here, the instrument is $Lender\ FX\ Usage$, which measures the extent to which a firm's lenders use the foreign exchange derivatives to hedge. The key to this instrumental variable approach is the finding from Minton et al. (2009) that banks which use credit derivatives for hedging purposes are also more likely to hedge using other derivatives. This implies that $Lender\ FX\ Usage$ meets the relevance condition. Further, it is argued that $Lender\ FX\ Usage$ is unlikely to be directly related to firm-level characteristics which are being tested and, hence, the exclusion restriction is met.

As CDS is initiated on firms in different time periods, the use of CDS initiation is an event in a staggered difference-in-differences methodology. An alternative approach is the use of a single-event difference-in-differences methodology in which the event is either a major event in the CDS market (Danis 2016; Gündüz et al. 2016) or changes to the bankruptcy law of the country in which the CDS firms are domiciled (Degryse et al. 2019). The use of these events allows researchers to avoid issue of the endogeneity of CDS initiation. However, the issue of differences between CDS firms and non-CDS firms remains, and, hence, authors tend to employ matching techniques to account for this imbalance.

The major events in the CDS market, namely the implementation of the CDS Big Bang or Small Bang protocol, do not always take place in random time periods potentially limiting their applicability. The CDS Big Bang and Small Bang protocols were implemented in 2009, a turbulent time period where many changes occurred in financial markets. Therefore, the use of these events may be an issue given the potential for confounding events. The use of bankruptcy law changes limits the study to a single country which limits external validity of these studies.

4.4 Why and How Do Banks Trade Credit Risk Transfer Instruments

Banks may mitigate their exposure to the credit risk of their borrowers using credit risk transfer instruments.[5] The literature on why and how banks trade credit risk transfer instruments focuses on the two most frequently used instruments: loan sales and CDS. This strand of the literature has broadly focused on three questions. First, do banks use credit derivatives to lay off credit risk? Second, what factors affect banks' propensity to lay off credit risk? Third, what determines their choice of credit risk transfer instrument (loans sales vs. CDS)?

Minton et al. (2009) investigate the degree to which banks use credit derivatives to hedge loans. The authors gather data on credit derivative usage from US bank holding companies' 10-K filings and merge it with the US bank holding companies' data. They find that only 23 out of their sample of 395 banks use credit derivatives. Further, most of the banks' credit derivative exposures are due to banks activities as dealers rather than for their own hedging purposes.

Minton et al. (2009) also document that banks that are net buyers of credit derivatives are also more likely to use other derivatives (e.g., commodity, equity, foreign exchange, and interest rate derivatives). The subsequent literature that investigates the effects of CDS trading has used this finding to justify the use of an instrumental variable that potentially resolves a key identification challenge in the literature (Saretto and Tookes 2012; Subrahmanyam et al. 2014). That is, they instrument banks' credit derivative trading with their foreign exchange hedging. This fulfils the relevance condition given the correlation documented by Minton et al. (2009). The exclusion restriction is fulfilled as banks' foreign exchange hedging is unlikely to be determined by any borrower characteristics.[6]

[5] Banks may trade credit risk transfer instruments for other reasons. As one of the primary functions of banks is the monitoring and collection of information on their borrowers, banks gain insider information about their borrowers. Banks may trade credit risk transfer instruments to exploit their informational advantage. Indeed, Acharya and Johnson (2007) find significant evidence for insider trading in the credit derivatives.

[6] For example, in Subrahmanyam et al. (2014) a bank's foreign exchange hedging behaviour is correlated with its CDS hedging behaviour but does not determine the borrowers credit rating directly.

Minton et al. (2009) further investigate why banks use credit derivatives. As their data is at bank level, they analyse the characteristics of banks that use credit derivative to hedge credit risk stemming from their loans to firms versus those that do not hedge using derivatives. The authors find that banks which are net buyers of credit derivatives are larger, and have a larger fraction of commercial and industrial loans and foreign loans and a lower fraction of loans secured by real estate. Further, the authors find that the likelihood that a bank uses credit derivatives to hedge is negatively related to its net interest margin, equity capital, and tier I risk capital. Finally, Minton et al. (2009) find that banks which sell or securitize loans are more likely to use credit derivatives to hedge loans. Hence, the authors conclude that credit derivatives, loan sales, and securitization are complements rather than substitutes.

Beyhaghi et al. (2016) follow on with this line of research by trying to uncover why and how banks use credit risk transfer instruments. The authors investigate these questions individually using separate logit models and jointly using a nested logit model. The separate logit models represent the problem as a series of discrete choices, that is, the choice to lay off credit risk or not, and, secondly, if laying off credit risk, then which financial instrument to use. The nested logit model considers these decisions as a joint decision, that is, retain the credit risk or lay off credit risk using CDS or lay off credit risk using loan sales, or lay off the credit risk using both CDS and loan sales.

To answer these questions, Beyhaghi et al. (2016) combine multiple data sets. They obtain loan facility data from the DealScan database. They merge this with borrower information from Compustat and CRSP using the link data provided by Wharton Research Data Services (Chava and Roberts 2008). The authors add bank characteristics from the Uniform Bank Performance Reports obtained from the Federal Financial Institutions Examination Council. They merge Markit CDS data to the data set to obtain CDS spread information on borrowers. Finally, they merge data on loan sales from the Loan Syndication and Trading Association (LSTA) database. The analysis is conducted at loan level with a sample of quarterly data from January 2003 to December 2007.

The LSTA database include neither the identities of the loan sellers or buyers nor whether the loan was actually traded. Nevertheless, it provides information on whether the loan is quoted in the market suggesting a market willing to sell the loan. Thus, the authors create an indicator variable *Loan Sale*, which is equal to 1 if the loan facility has an LSTA record.

To construct the proxy for a bank's trading of CDS on a particular borrower, Beyhaghi et al. (2016) employ CDS spread data obtained from Markit. The authors measure the cumulative abnormal change in CDS spreads around the loan initiation date, that is, the date on which the loan was given to the borrower. The authors use an estimation window which begins 5 days before loan initiation and ends 30 days after. They then construct an indicator variable $CDS\ Hedging$, which is equal to 1 if the abnormal return was greater than 0. The authors argue that a positive abnormal increase in the CDS spread is an indication that there was an increase in demand for the CDS. They further argue that an increase in the demand for the CDS around the loan initiation date indicates that the bank giving the loan traded CDS on the borrower.

This measure suffers from two main issues. First, an increase in spread may not necessarily imply an increase in demand for credit protection; it may be related to the underlying risk of the reference firm that is not accounted for in the equity returns. Second, if one accepts that the abnormal increase in spread is a result of an increase in demand, this is not necessarily the demand of the creditors of the firm; it may be investment banks or hedge funds.

In a first stage, Beyhaghi et al. (2016) test the bank and borrower characteristics that affect a bank's propensity to use any credit risk transfer instrument. Banks' use of credit risk transfer instruments should be related to their capital and liquidity constraints (Pennacchi 1988; Allen and Carletti 2006). Loan sales have a direct effect on these constraints as the process of selling a loan replaces the risky, illiquid asset (the loan) with a safe, liquid asset (cash).

The effect of CDS trading on a bank's liquidity and capital constraints is less direct. The Basil capital regulations allow for the offsetting of credit exposures with the purchase of CDS, which reduces regulatory capital requirements.[7] Beyhaghi et al. (2016) argue that a bank's purchase of CDS alleviates its liquidity constraints as the decrease in credit risk allows it to borrow more easily and obtain better interest rates on the interbank market. Thus, the more binding a bank's capital and liquidity constraints, the more likely it is to use credit risk transfer instruments.

[7] In the Basel regulation, CDS is considered to be a hedging instrument. The risk weight on a retained unhedged loan is 100% under Basel III. Under Basel III, the credit risk weight on OTC CDS contracts is 20% while only 2% if centrally cleared. Basel I and Basel II did not make a distinction between OTC and centrally cleared CDS.

Indeed, Beyhaghi et al. (2016) find that the propensity of banks to use credit risk transfer instruments is increasing in their capital and liquidity constraints. Additionally, the authors find that while transactional lenders are more likely to use credit risk transfer instruments, lead syndicate lenders are less likely to use credit risk transfer instruments. Further, while the riskiness of the borrower does not appear to affect a bank's propensity to use credit risk transfer instruments, banks are more likely to use these instruments for larger borrowers whose debt have a longer maturity.

In a second stage, Beyhaghi et al. (2016) investigate bank's choice of credit risk transfer instruments. This decision is modelled by Duffee and Zhou (2001) and Parlour and Winton (2013). The models differ along many dimensions but both predict that banks are more likely to sell ex ante low-quality loans than hedge using CDS. A bank's decision to sell a loan or hedge it using CDS has implications for its incentive to monitor the borrower and the maintenance of its control rights. While CDS only removes the economic exposure to a borrower, a loan sale removes the bank's control rights over the firm too. Hence, selling a loan reduces the incentive to monitor a borrower more than hedging using CDS does.

In line with the theory, Beyhaghi et al. (2016) find that loans to ex ante low-quality (high-risk), or longer maturity loans, are more likely to be sold. Further, loans to borrowers with higher return on assets are more likely to be hedged with CDS. A lenders capital or liquidity constraints do not appear to determine the choice of credit risk transfer instrument.

As the decision to hedge credit risk is a nested one (i.e., the bank makes the decision to hedge using a particular hedging instrument), the authors use a nested logit model. This is an econometric approach that allows for a discrete choice model with more than two choices. Here, the choices are: (1) retain the credit risk, *Ret*; (2) lay off credit risk using CDS, CDS; (3) lay off credit risk using loan sales, *Sale*; (4) lay off the credit risk using a both CDS and loan sales, *Both*. The utility of these choices is represented as follows:

$$U_{Ret,i} = V_{Ret,i} + \epsilon_{Ret,i} \tag{4.1}$$

$$U_{CDS,i} = V_{CDS,i} + V_{CRT,i} + \epsilon_{CDS,i} + \epsilon_{CRT,i} \tag{4.2}$$

$$U_{Sale,i} = V_{Sale,i} + V_{CRT,i} + \epsilon_{Sale,i} + \epsilon_{CRT,i} \tag{4.3}$$

$$U_{Both,i} = V_{Both,i} + V_{CRT,i} + \epsilon_{Both,i} + \epsilon_{CRT,i} \tag{4.4}$$

where $U_{i,j}$ is the random utility function of choice j for loan i. $\epsilon_{i,j}$ represents the random error component and $V_{i,j}$ represents the deterministic portion estimated by:

$$V_{i,j} = \beta Z_{i,j} \tag{4.5}$$

where $Z_{i,j}$ is a vector containing characteristics of the loan, i, and credit risk transfer choice, j.

The multinomial logit model imposes a restriction that the random errors are independent and identical across choices. From Eqs. (4.2), (4.3), and (4.4), we can note that the credit risk transfer instruments share a common error term and, hence, the total error terms will not be independent and identical across choices. The nested logit model allows the error terms of nests to be correlated, as is the case here. The parameters of the model are then calculated using maximum likelihood. If a certain characteristic is more prevalent to a given choice, it is considered to positively affect the choice. A key assumption of the nest logit model is that all alternatives have to be identified and, hence, modelled. Beyhaghi et al. (2016) state that this is indeed the case in their setting. However, it may be noted that they do not account for the ability of banks to have negative CDS position (i.e., sell CDS). This rules out the credit enhancement option in which a bank sells the loan and offers CDS protection to the buyer of the loan for part of the loan sale amount.

Hasan and Wu (2017) examine three channels in the choice of credit risk transfer instruments. One, the substitute channel, where the choice is either CDS hedging or loan sales. Two, the complementary channel, where CDS hedging and loan sales are used together. Three, the credit enhancement channel, where a loan sale is combined with a negative CDS position. The authors find that the complementary channel dominates the substitution channel. Further, they find a negative relation between a bank's net CDS position and its loan sales, if the bank is a net seller of CDS protection (i.e., the credit enhancement channel).

The optimal data set to analyse the choice of credit risk transfer instrument would be CDS and loan sale trade data at the bank-borrower level, combined with credit exposures at the same level. With this data, a researcher would be able to identify exactly which banks are trading CDS or selling loans on a particular borrower around a loan initiation date. Hasan and Wu (2017) get closer to the optimal data set by employing the Shared National Credit (SNC) data combined with the US bank holding companies' data, Markit CDS data, Compustat, and CRSP. The SNC data track each syndicate member's loan share after origination. This allows the authors to calculate the loan sales of a bank on a particular borrower.

The authors construct a proxy for CDS trading at bank level using the bank holding companies' data. They define a bank as a CDS net buyer if the reported CDS bought minus CDS sold is positive. Similarly, a CDS net seller is a bank with a higher value of CDS sold than bought.

Measuring CDS trading at the bank level limits the ability to test for borrower characteristics that determine the choice of the credit risk transfer instrument. Further, it may mask a bank's heterogeneous choices of credit risk transfer instrument. For example, if a bank sells CDS on nine of its borrowers but purchases a large position on its tenth borrower that is greater in magnitude than the sum of the nine other positions, it would be classified as a CDS net buyer but its behaviour would be that of a CDS net seller. Finally, as reported by Minton et al. (2009), the majority of banks' credit derivative exposures are due to dealer activities rather than hedging purposes. Hence, a bank's net CDS position is more likely to reflect the net position from its market-making activities than its decision to purchase or sell CDS on its borrowers.

While Gündüz et al. (2016) does not investigate the decision to use credit risk transfer instruments or the trade-off between loan sales and CDS, they are among the first to employ CDS trade data. The authors obtain CDS position data at party-counterparty level from the DTCC and combine this with creditor positions from the German Credit Registry. They find that banks purchase more CDS protection on riskier firms and firms to which they have higher existing credit exposures.

4.5 What Are the Consequences of CDS Trading for Other Credit Markets?

Having discussed the determinants of a bank's decision to lay off credit risk and its choice of risk transfer instrument, we turn our focus to the consequences of these decisions. As CDS allows creditors to both lay off and take on credit exposure, the trading of CDS may affect other credit markets, for example the syndicated loan market and the secondary market for a CDS-referenced firm's bonds.

4.5.1 Syndicated Loans

Streitz (2016) provides empirical evidence for the effect of CDS trading on loan syndication. The author merges CDS spread data obtained from Bloomberg's CMA database, the LPC DealScan database, and borrower financial information from Compustat. He begins by determining the change in the likelihood of a bank to syndicate a loan and the fraction of loans sold in response to CDS beginning to trade on the borrower (CDS initiation). As an initial step, Streitz (2016) measures the effect of CDS trading on loan syndication using the model represented by Eq. (4.6):

$$Syndication_{ijt} = \alpha_{ij} + \alpha_t + \beta * CDS\,Trading_{it} + \gamma * X_{it-1} + \delta * Y_{ijt} + \epsilon_{ijt} \tag{4.6}$$

where $Syndication_{ijt}$ represents either of the two variables of interest: $SoleLender$ or $LeadShare$. $Sole\ Lender$ is an indicator that equals 1 if the loan is a single lender loan or zero if it is a syndicated loan whereby bank j is the lead lender at time t. $Lead\ Share$ equals the fraction of the loan retained by bank j, the lead arranger, in time t. $CDS\,Trading_{it}$ equals 1 if firm i had CDS traded on its debt at the loan origination date.

As CDS firms may be different from non-CDS firms in a way that affects a banks propensity to sell a loan, the author included a set of borrower controls X_{it-1} and a set of loan characteristics Y_{ijt}. Finally, Streitz (2016) includes time fixed effects, α_t, and borrower-lead arranger fixed effects, α_{ij}, to account for unobservable time-invariant borrower and bank characteristics.

Here, a positive β represents the case where CDS initiation decreases the propensity of lead arrangers to syndicate a loan and increases the share of the loan that lead arranges retain. Indeed, Streitz (2016) finds this to be the case with banks being 2.9% less likely to syndicate a loan once CDS is traded on a borrower and retain 5.48% more of the loan.

Further, consistent with notion that smaller firms are more opaque and therefore suffer more intense moral hazard and adverse selection problems, the author finds that the lead arranger retains a larger share if the borrower is small, or if the loan is small with a shorter maturity. This is in line with previous findings in the syndicated loan literature that lead arrangers can sell a larger fraction of a loan where moral hazard and adverse selection problems are less severe (Sufi 2007).

There are two competing reasons for the finding that banks are less likely to syndicate a loan and retain more of the loan once CDS is traded on the borrower. First, banks may be less likely to syndicate a loan if they are able to trade CDS as it is a more flexible, and less permanent method to offload credit risk. Second, an important role of a lead arranger is to continue to monitor the borrower. Lead arrangers may choose to offload their remaining credit risk using CDS at a later stage to avoid having to monitor the borrower. Hence, a second potential reason for the finding is that it may be that potential investors in the loan syndicate are less willing to participate if the lead arranger cannot credibly commit to monitor the borrower (Parlour and Winton 2013).

In line with the first argument, flexibility of CDS, Streitz (2016) finds that the more liquid the CDS market, as measured by the borrowers' CDS bid-ask spread to loan size, the stronger is the effect of CDS trading on the syndicated loan market. Similarly, the author finds the effect to be stronger if the lead arranger is more able to trade CDS. He measures this using two variables: first, if the bank reports a positive CDS position at any point in the sample period and, second, if it reported a high CDS holding in the quarter prior to issuing the loan.

This moral hazard problem should be more severe for banks with weaker reputations and borrowers which require more intense monitoring (Parlour and Winton 2013). The author uses two measures of borrower opacity to proxy for the importance of monitoring for a borrower: analyst coverage and the tangibility of the borrower's assets. Firms with higher asset tangibility and analyst coverage are assumed to be less informationally opaque. Following Sufi (2007), Streitz (2016) measures the reputation of the bank as its market share in the syndicated loan market in the prior year. As alternative proxies for reputation (Streitz 2016) constructs two indicator variables that are equal to 1 if the bank is one of the three (or ten) largest banks, and 0 otherwise.

The author finds no evidence that the importance of monitoring a borrower affects the impact of CDS on the retention of loans. Finally, contrary to the moral hazard argument, Streitz (2016) finds that lenders with better reputations retain a larger fraction of the loan once CDS begins to trade on the borrower. This finding is consistent with the observation that larger, more reputable banks are more likely to trade CDS.

Further, to measure if CDS trading affects the monitoring incentives of banks, the author analyses the effect of CDS trading on covenant violations, which he argues is a loan outcome that is correlated with monitoring services. Streitz (2016) finds that there is reduction in the likelihood of covenant violations once CDS is traded on the borrowers' debt. As discussed later in this chapter, CDS trading may affect the propensity of firms to violate covenants or banks to push firms to violate these covenants (Bolton and Oehmke 2011) and for covenants to be attached to the loan in the first place (Arping 2014). Hence, it is unclear if the reduction in the likelihood of covenant violations is a result of a reduction in monitoring or due to these confounding effects.

Streitz (2016) notes that unobserved differences between CDS and non-CDS firms influence the decision to syndicate a loan and to initiate trading CDS. That is, the selection of firms into CDS traded firms and the timing of the inception of CDS trading on a firm may be endogenous. Following Ashcraft and Santos (2009), Saretto and Tookes (2012), and Subrahmanyam et al. (2014), the author employs an instrumental variable approach (Heckman correction procedure) by constructing a model to predict CDS trading on a particular firm and then using this prediction as an instrumental variable in later regressions.

Common to many papers in the CDS literature, the authors follow Saretto and Tookes (2012) by constructing an instrumental variable, $Lender\ FX\ Usage$, which is calculated as the average amount of foreign exchange derivatives held by all lead arrangers that have lent to the firm in the previous five years as a fraction of the lenders' total assets. $Lender\ FX\ Usage$ measures the extent to which a firm's lenders use the foreign exchange derivatives to hedge. The key to this instrumental variable approach is the finding from Minton et al. (2009) that banks which use credit derivatives for hedging purposes are also more likely to hedge using other derivatives. This implies that $Lender\ FX\ Usage$ meets the relevance condition. Further, $Lender\ FX\ Usage$ is unlikely to be directly related to loan syndication (i.e., the exclusion restriction is met).

Streitz (2016) use $Lender\ FX\ Usage$ to predict the probability of CDS trading in a first stage which is used as an instrument for CDS trading in the second stage. The results from the first stage confirm the relevance condition as $Lender\ FX\ Usage$ is statistically significant with a 1 percentage point increase in $Lender\ FX\ Usage$ resulting in a 3.23 percentage point increase in the probability of CDS trading. However, the results from the second-stage regression shows that while the instrument is highly significant, it has the opposite sign to the original result.

Amiram et al. (2017) has a large overlap with Streitz (2016) as both papers measure the effect of CDS initiation on the share of loans retained by the lead arranger in a syndicate. While Streitz (2016) also measures the change in the propensity for banks to syndicate a loan, Amiram et al. (2017) measure the change in loan spread. Amiram et al. (2017) find that upon CDS initiation lead arrangers retain 4.2% more of the loan. This is similar in magnitude as the finding of 5.48% from Streitz (2016). Further, they find that the loan spread increases by 13%, implying that the average firm that faces a loan spread of 197 basis points prior to CDS trading sees its loan spread increase to approximately 228 basis points after CDS trading. The authors conduct the same robustness test as Streitz (2016) following Saretto and Tookes (2012) and find that their results are robust to the potential source of endogeneity.

The similarity in results between Amiram et al. (2017) and Streitz (2016) for loan retention is a good indicator for the external validity of both studies given the extent to which the samples differ. Amiram et al. (2017) obtain their CDS trading data from Markit, while Streitz (2016) obtains CDS trading data from Bloomberg. Further, Amiram et al. (2017) sample contains 836 CDS traded firms with 7046 loans issued from 1993 to 2014, while Streitz (2016) sample contains 327 CDS traded firms with 14,379 facilities from 2000 to 2010.

Amiram et al. (2017) further test how the intensity of the effect of CDS trading varies with bank, firm, and CDS market characteristics. Using the same theoretical justification as Streitz (2016), but different measures, Amiram et al. (2017) test if borrower opacity, the reputation of the lead arranger, or the liquidity in the CDS market affect the intensity of the effect of CDS trading.[8] Amiram et al. (2017) find that the effect is less intense for less opaque borrowers, lead arrangers with a strong reputation, and borrowers with relatively illiquid CDS markets. The authors use these findings to argue that CDS initiation reduces the potency of a lead arranger's stake in the loan as an incentive device, which alleviates adverse selection and moral hazard problems within a syndicate.

In constructing their measure of borrower opacity, Amiram et al. (2017) calculate a borrower's debt-contracting value (DCV) of accounting information (Ball et al. 2008). The DCV measure is the Somers' D association

[8] Following Ashcraft and Santos (2009), Amiram et al. (2017) proxy for the liquidity of CDS contracts with the number of dealers providing CDS quotes for a borrower, while Streitz (2016) used borrowers' CDS bid-ask spread to loan size as a measure of liquidity. As in Streitz (2016), Amiram et al. (2017) follow Sufi (2007) and measure the reputation of the lead arranger as its market share of in the syndicated loan market in the prior year.

statistics obtained from industry-specific probit regressions that predict credit ratings using the following equation:

$$P(Rating_{q,i} \leq N) = \Phi(\sum_{n=1}^{N} \mu_n + \sum_{k=1}^{4} \alpha_k EBITDA_{q-k,i} + \sum_{k=1}^{4} \beta_k COV_{q-k,i} + \sum_{k=1}^{4} \delta_k LEVERAGE_{q-k,i} + \sum_{k=1}^{4} \gamma_k NW_{q-k,i}) \tag{4.7}$$

where $Rating_{q,i}$ is equal to 1 if a firm's credit rating is AAA, 2 if AA+, et cetera. $EBITDA_{q-k,i}$ is the EBITDA in quarter $q-k$ divided by total assets at the beginning of the quarter. $COV_{q-k,i}$ is the interest coverage of firm i in quarter $q-k$. $LEVERAGE_{q-k,i}$ is the long-term debt in quarter $q-k$ divided by total assets. $NW_{q-k,i}$ is common equity in quarter $q-k$ divided by total assets. DCV is measured as Somers' D, a goodness-of-fit statistic. DCV measures the ability of a firm's public information (hard information) to reflect its credit quality. DCV ranges from 0, low transparency, to 1, high transparency.

As an additional measure to account for the potential endogeneity of CDS trading, Amiram et al. (2017) conduct a robustness test by matching the treatment and control group using propensity score matching. Matching is a nonparametric method for preprocessing data with the aim of reducing imbalance between control and treatment groups in order to control for the potentially confounding influence of pretreatment control variables.

Following Ashcraft and Santos (2009), Amiram et al. (2017) use propensity score matching with the nearest neighbour method of matching. That is, they construct a matched sample by keeping CDS firms from 2001 Q1 till the first quarter CDS begins to trade on their debt. They combine this with a sample of firms that never have CDS traded on in the sample. They then estimate a probit model where the dependent variable is equal to 1 for firms which become traded in a given quarter. The explanatory variables are the lag of all borrower specific characteristics.[9]

[9] The borrower characteristics are: ROA, Profit, Tangible Assets, Leverage, Log(total asset), Credit Rating, and DCV (a measure of opacity).

The estimated coefficients are used to construct a control group which is assigned counterfactual trading dates using firms with the highest predicted probability of being traded in a given quarter, conditional on the firm having bond issues in 12 quarters before and 8 quarters after the start date. Each CDS firm is matched to the closest, in terms of propensity score, non-CDS trading firm. This is done without replacement to avoid the case where in an extreme case all CDS firms are matched to the same non-CDS firm.

This 1-to-1 match (i.e., 1 control firm matched to 1 treatment firm) reduces the imbalance between the treatment and control group but comes at a cost of fewer observations, which reduces the precision of the estimated coefficients. Amiram et al. (2017) show that the results are robust to using a propensity score matched sample.

4.5.2 *Corporate Bonds*

In general, new securities and markets can affect related markets by altering their characteristics such as liquidity, efficiency, and quality. Das et al. (2014) empirically investigate if CDS initiation is beneficial for the market for corporate bonds in terms of these characteristics. The authors find that CDS initiation has mostly detrimental effects on the secondary market for a referenced firm's bonds. They find that bond markets become less efficient and that there is neither an improvement in liquidity nor in market quality (i.e., a reduction in pricing errors).

Oehmke and Zawadowski (2015) model the effects of CDS trading on bond markets and find that the introduction of CDS has opposing effects on the market for CDS-referenced firms' bonds. On the one hand, given that CDS have lower trading costs than bonds, it cannibalizes existing demand for the bond as investors are able to sell CDS in place of purchasing the bond. On the other hand, it may improve the demand for bonds as CDS allows long-term investors to absorb more of the bond supply and hedge this risk on the CDS market. In a follow-up paper, Oehmke and Zawadowski (2017) employ DTCC transaction data and test these predictions.

Oehmke and Zawadowski (2017) find that CDS is indeed a substitute for trading bonds. The authors find that when trading for hedging purposes both bond and CDS markets are used, while when trading for speculative reasons trading concentrates in the CDS market. Further, they find CDS trading volumes and positions are larger for firms which have multiple bond issuances with varying contractual terms. As both markets trade the credit risk of the referenced firm, there is potential for cross-market arbitrage via the basis trade. Oehmke and Zawadowski (2017) find that this potential arbitrage trade compresses the negative basis and reduces the price impact in the bond market.

4.6 How Does CDS Trading Affect the Referenced Firm?

CDS trading on a firm affects bank's behaviour and the markets for the firm's debt. Further, while creditors hold control rights under the debt contract, CDS change the relationship between creditors and borrowers as the formal ownership of debt claims can be decoupled from the economic exposure to credit deterioration (Hu and Black 2008a,b). Creditors who purchase no-restructuring CDS contracts may have an increased incentive to push the CDS-referenced entity into bankruptcy in order to collect the payout from the CDS contract. This gives rise to "empty creditors" who have less incentives to participate in firm restructuring (Bolton and Oehmke 2011). Hence, CDS potentially has an impact on the referenced entity by altering the behaviour of its creditors. The theory of the economic effects of CDS trading on the referenced entity mostly relies on asymmetric information between the lender and the borrower. Specifically, moral hazard (e.g., Arping (2014)) and cash flow manipulation (e.g., Bolton and Oehmke (2011), Colonnello et al. (2016)).

Bolton and Oehmke (2011) develop a model in which creditors are able to purchase CDS, which improves their bargaining power in restructuring negotiations. Through this, CDS act as a commitment device as creditors are more easily able to force bankruptcy in the case of default. This reduces a firm's incentive to strategically default (cash flow manipulation), which, ex ante, increases its financing capacity. The improved financing capacity leads to an increase in firms' investment, leverage, value, and a decrease in their cost of debt. However, Bolton and Oehmke (2011) show that creditors will "over insure" (i.e., purchase more CDS on a firm than is socially optimal) in equilibrium, which results in an increase in the probability of default for these firms. The latter reflects the impact of empty creditors on CDS firms. The increase in the probability of default, due to over-insurance, may lead to a decrease in the financing capacity of firms. This leads to an ambiguous effect of CDS trading on firms financing capacity. Similarly, the increase in leverage may lead to an increase in the probability of default for these firms. Thus, in the case of over-insurance, the costs and benefits of CDS are unclear, even theoretically.

Danis and Gamba (2018) take a different approach and model the effects of CDS trading with a calibrated dynamic structural model. The authors construct a partial equilibrium dynamic model with equity and debt financing, as well as CDS trading. They capture the effects of CDS trading on firms by measuring the changes to the firms' fundamentals when CDS markets are introduced. In this way, the authors are able to predict changes to firm value, investment, and leverage while taking into account the increased default probability. The authors find that the introduction of CDS trading leads to an increase in firm liquidation, which, through bankruptcy costs, reduces firm value. The authors predict that the introduction of CDS trading leads to an increase in firm leverage, investment, and the probability of default. These effects should be most pronounced for small, financially constrained firms with low productivity. Lastly, the model predicts that the degree of hedging by CDS to be positively related to firm leverage, intangibility of assets, and to be negatively related to Tobin's Q.

As Fig. 4.2 illustrates, there are two conditions for the positive and negative effects of CDS on an underlying firm to be felt. Firstly, restructuring has to be permitted under the law of the country in which the CDS-referenced firm is domiciled. As CDS has a positive effect on the underlying firm though changing the bargaining power of the lender in restructuring negotiations . If no restructuring is possible, then the positive effects are not felt, but the incentive to push a firm into default remains.

The second condition is that the CDS contract should not recognize restructuring as a credit event. If restructuring is recognized as a credit event, then the CDS pays out regardless of the outcome of restructuring negotiations. Hence, CDS loses its role as a commitment device. Further, if it is paid out on restructuring, the lender need not push the referenced entity into default to collect its payment.

The empirical investigations into the effects of CDS and empty creditors on financially distressed firms have produced mixed findings. Subrahmanyam et al. (2014) show in a large sample of distressed and healthy firms that the introduction of CDS increases the probability of bankruptcy. However, Caglio et al. (2018) find that CDS hedging by a firm's creditors may in fact decrease the probability of default of these firms. Using a small sample of distressed companies, Bedendo et al. (2016) find that CDS do

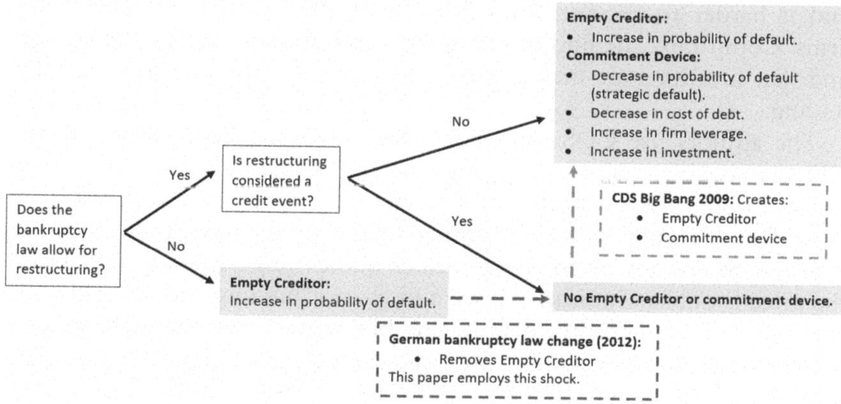

Fig. 4.2 CDS credit events and bankruptcy law
Note: This figure illustrates the two conditions for the positive and negative effects of CDS on an underlying firm to be felt. The first is the ability to restructure a company under the domicile country's law. The second condition only plays a role if the first condition is met. The second condition is that the CDS contract type should not pay out when the underlying debt is restructured. If restructuring is not permitted under law, then the CDS contract type is irrelevant and the firms have no incentive to strategically default (as they will be liquidated). However, the incentive for empty creditors to push a firm into bankruptcy remains. If restructuring is permitted and defined as a credit event, in this context, CDS has no effect on the underlying firm. Finally, if restructuring is permitted and not defined as a credit event, then CDS acts as a commitment device as well as increases the probability of default through the effect of empty creditors

not have a significant effect on the likelihood of bankruptcy. Danis (2016) contributes to this debate by providing further evidence that empty creditors have a negative effect on out-of-court debt restructuring. Colonnello et al. (2016) find that the relative bargaining power of shareholders and creditors affects the intensity of the real effects of empty creditors.

Subrahmanyam et al. (2014) find that the inception of CDS trading on a reference entity increases the likelihood of bankruptcy and ratings downgrade. Specifically, the authors find that the probability of bankruptcy increases from 0.14% to 0.47% upon the inception of CDS trading. Further, they find that distressed firms are more likely to file for bankruptcy if they have CDS traded on their debt. This implies that CDS traded firms find it harder to recover from financial distress than non-CDS traded firms. Confirming the findings of Saretto and Tookes (2012), the authors find that firm leverage increases significantly upon the inception of CDS trading.

The authors use CDS transaction records from CreditTrade and the GFI Group which includes the date when CDS trading began, the type of contract trade, price, volume, and settlement terms. The advantage of using these data sets is that with transaction data the quotes and specifications are binding, whereas with voluntary dealer quotes (e.g., Markit CDS Data) the price is only an indicative price and are not binding. Additionally, the authors obtain bankruptcy data by combining data from multiple sources on North American firms filing for bankruptcy in US courts. They combine data from the BankruptcyData Database (www.BankruptcyData.com), the Altman-NYU Salomon Center Bankruptcy List, the Mergent Fixed Income Securities Database, Moody's Annual Reports on Bankruptcy and Recovery, and the UCLA-LoPucki Bankruptcy Research Database. Their final data set covers the period 1997 to 2009 and includes 1628 bankruptcy filings and 901 North American firms with CDS traded on their debt.

The authors are among the first to distinguish between the types of CDS contracts. The predictions from the theory of Bolton and Oehmke (2011) rely on the CDS contract only paying out in bankruptcy, that is, not on restructuring. Thus, the empty creditor effect should be more intense and the proportion of no restructuring contracts is higher than other types of CDS contracts. Indeed, Subrahmanyam et al. (2014) find this to be the case.

Further, the authors find that the number of creditors a firm has increases after CDS begins to trade on its debt. This could exacerbate the effect of empty creditors as the larger the number of creditors, the larger is the competition to "empty themselves first", that is, become empty creditors before other creditors of the firm (Bolton and Oehmke 2011). Additionally, an increase in the number of creditors could either increase or decrease a firm's probability of bankruptcy outside of increasing the effect of empty creditors. An increase in the number of creditors increases the chances of a creditor coordination failure when a firm is financially distressed. However, it also improves firms' financing options as they are more easily able to substitute between creditors. Hence, it is unclear how the number of creditors should affect a firm in financial distress. However, CDS firms have an additional impact of creditors competition to "empty themselves first".

Subrahmanyam et al. (2014) use both the instrumental variable approach and the matching approach as robustness tests to mitigate potential endogeneity issues around the timing of CDS inception and the selection of firms into becoming CDS firms. Following Saretto and Tookes (2012), the authors use *Lender FX Usage* as an instrument for CDS trading by the bank. Additionally, they include the Tier One capital ratio of lenders. The authors argue that this meets the relevance condition as banks are more likely to trade CDS if they experience capital constraints. Further, they argue that the instrument meets the exclusion restriction as individual borrower credit risk is unlikely to be affect by individual banks capital constraints when aggregated across lenders. That is, the selection issue is mitigated due to aggregation across all lenders. The authors find that their results are indeed robust to potential endogeneity issues around the timing of CDS inception and the selection of firms into becoming CDS firms.

In conducting the robustness test with a matched sample, Subrahmanyam et al. (2014) use three different matching rules to further test for robustness to their choice of matching restriction. The authors restricted the matching sample to a 1-to-1 match, as in Amiram et al. (2017). They further show that the results are robust to a "tighter" match of using a 1-to-1 match and then dropping those pairs that are more than 1% different in propensity score (calliper). Finally, the authors show that the matched results are robust to a "looser" match of using a 1-to-2 match. Here, they match the two closest control firms to each treatment firm. By tightening and loosening the matching protocol, the authors show that the results are robust to matching using propensity score matching and that they consider the bias/precision trade-off of matching.

Given the lack of CDS transaction data, the authors are forced to make the assumption that the trading of CDS on the firm is done by the creditors of the firm and not third parties. Hence, the authors need to assume the existence of empty creditors in the absence of CDS transaction data at the bank-firm level. Further, the use of the introduction of CDS trading on a firm's debt as an exogenous shock may not hold. While this is the case for the majority of the papers that use this event, it is especially so in this case as the variable of interest is the probability of bankruptcy. As CDS is a type of insurance against default, the initiation of CDS may occur around times that the probability of bankruptcy of a firm is increasing, or prior to an increase as the creditors anticipate an increase. Therefore, while the authors conduct multiple robustness tests to show that they are indeed providing causal evidence, the required assumptions given the data limitations and the potential for reverse causality of probability of bankruptcy on CDS trading are still areas of concern.

Colonnello et al. (2016) model the impact of shareholder bargaining power on the propensity for banks to trade CDS on a firm and thus become empty creditors. Their model predicts that creditors are more likely to trade CDS on firms with strong shareholders in order to improve their bargaining power in debt restructuring negotiations. Creditors' bargaining power is improved by improving their outside option (i.e., CDS payment in bankruptcy). While Bolton and Oehmke (2011) predict that firms with weaker creditors are more likely to benefit from the commitment device effect and hence experience the positive effects of CDS trading on their debt, Colonnello et al. (2016) predict that firms with stronger shareholders are more likely to experience the effects of empty creditors. Therefore, the net effect on firms with strong shareholders is uncertain.

Using a similar methodology as Subrahmanyam et al. (2014), Colonnello et al. (2016) test the predictions of their model. They employ the Markit CDS data to determine the date CDS begins to trade on a firm, which they merge with the LPC DealScan data set, Compustat, CRSP, and Thomson Reuters Institutional Holdings. The authors use the institutional investor classification from the Institutional Investor Classification Data website, of Brian Bushee, coupled with the Thomson Reuters Institutional Holdings database to distinguish between active and passive investors. The authors distinguish between active and passive institutional ownership as they argue that the higher the presences of active institutional owners, the higher is the shareholder bargaining power. They find that a 1% increase in institutional ownership is associated with a 0.32% increase in CDS purchasing. Their results suggest that creditors of firms with more powerful shareholders purchase CDS to improve their bargaining power in debt restructuring. They further find that a firm's distance-to-default decreases only when conditioning on the top quartile of firms with the highest shareholder bargaining power.

The authors follow Bartram et al. (2018) in their matching protocol. They employ an overlap weighting approach that results in the covariates of the CDS and non-CDS firms having similar distributions (Li et al. 2018). In this matching protocol, each firm is assigned a weight that is proportional to the probability of the firm being assigned to the opposite group (i.e., a CDS firm (treated) being assigned to the non-CDS (control) firm group, and the other way around). This is formally described in the following equation:

$$w_{i,t}(x_t) = \begin{cases} p_{i,t}(x_t) & for\ Z_{i,t} = 0 \\ 1 - p_{i,t}(x_t) & for\ Z_{i,t} = 1 \end{cases} \tag{4.8}$$

where $Z_{i,t} = 1$ for treated observations (observations where CDS begins to trade on the firm's debt); $p_{i,t}(x_t)$ is the propensity score for treatment, and $1 - p_{i,t}(x_t)$ is the propensity score for control; $p_{i,t}(x_t)$ is defined as $Pr(Z_{i,t}|X_{i,t} = x_t)$ and $X_{i,t}$ are covariates included in the logit model. Hence, a firm-quarter with CDS trading as treated observations is weighted by its propensity to be assigned to the control group, and the control observations are weighted by their propensity of to be firm-quarters with CDS trading observations. The main advantage of using this method is that it results in a matched data set that has the most overlap in the covariates between treatment groups (Li et al. 2018). This method also reduces the need to trade off balance with precision (number of observations) as observations are not discarded but assigned a lower weight. Using this method of matching, Colonnello et al. (2016) show that their results are robust to matching their treatment and control groups.

The initiation of CDS trading presents endogeneity issues, even after the techniques authors have employed to limit their impact. Using an event in the CDS market, the CDS Big Bang Protocol, Danis (2016) test for the effect of CDS on the restructuring of distressed firms. Danis (2016) shows that empty creditors have a negative effect on out-of-court debt restructuring.[10] The CDS Big Bang Protocol changed the standard CDS contract for North American firms to no restructuring contracts, amongst other changes. As the effect of empty creditors relies on CDS contracts trading with a no restructuring clause, this event should have increased the effect of empty creditors. Danis (2016) finds supportive evidence for this hypothesis as the average participation rate is 29 percentage points lower for firms with CDS traded on their debt and that the average participation rate further decreases for CDS firms after the implementation of the CDS Big Bang Protocol.[11] Hence, the author finds evidence in support of the

[10] Colonnello et al. (2016) use this event as a robustness test and find that their results are robust to using this event.

[11] Danis (2016) defines the participation rate as the face value of bonds tendered divided by the total face value of bonds outstanding. The author states that the participation rate is

effects of empty creditors and that they have a negative impact on the restructuring of distressed firms.

However, the issue remains that CDS behaves both as a commitment device and allows for the creation of empty creditors. Hence, the authors cannot disentangle the effect of CDS as a commitment device increasing the leverage of the firm, from the effect of empty creditors. Further, while Danis (2016) is among the first to show the existence of empty creditors, given data limitations he still relies on the proxy for the existence of empty creditors, the fact that CDS trades on a firm at all.

Degryse et al. (2019) test for the existence of empty creditors by employing an exogenous change to the bankruptcy code in Germany, effectively removing their impact on CDS firms. The authors employ a unique data set on bank-firm CDS net notional and credit exposures. They combine CDS position data at party-counterparty level from the Depository Trust & Clearing Corporation (DTCC), and combine this with creditor positions from the German Credit Registry (MiMik).[12] They then merge this with a database containing detailed firm information (USTAN), and another containing CDS spreads (Markit). Lastly, they combine the resulting data set with macroeconomic data obtained from DataStream.

Given the granularity of the data, the authors avoid making the assumption that CDS trading on a firm implies that the creditors are trading CDS, and hence these firms are exposed to empty creditors. Further, they do not employ the initiation of CDS trading as their event, but rather a change to the bankruptcy code in Germany. Hence, their analyses avoid some of the potential sources of endogeneity, which the previous literature had to contend with (e.g., Subrahmanyam et al. (2014), Colonnello et al. (2016)).

Degryse et al. (2019) find that the probability of default for firms with CDS traded on them decreases by 1.3 to 2 percentage points when the effect of empty creditors is removed. This effect increases in the book leverage of a firm, in its efficiency, in the concentration of its debt, and in the average CDS hedge position of its creditors. Specifically, a one standard deviation increase in the average CDS hedge position of a firm's creditors

an indicator of the success of restructuring as it is positively associated with debt reduction for the firm.

[12] Caglio et al. (2018) employ a similar data set from the DTCC. While the data in Degryse et al. (2019) is from German banks and firms, the data in Caglio et al. (2018) is from US banks and firms.

increases the intensity of the effect of empty creditors by 90 basis points. Further, the authors find that larger firms, more profitable firms with more tangible assets, and firms with higher average collateral ratios of their debt are less affected by empty creditors. Finally, while financially vulnerable firms are severely affected by empty creditors, safe firms are not affected.

Degryse et al. (2019) test an assumption of the Bolton and Oehmke (2011) model that the incentive for empty creditors to push CDS firms into default is "priced in" to the CDS spreads. They do so by comparing CDS spreads of treated German entities with those of other European companies unaffected by the change in German insolvency law. They find that when the incentive for empty creditors to push firms into default is removed, CDS spreads on average drop by 120 basis points. This suggests that the effect of empty creditors is indeed priced into the CDS spreads of affected firms.

The empirical literature is not limited to the negative effects of CDS through empty creditors and has investigated a wide range of effects of CDS. Hirtle (2009) shows that greater use of CDS leads to an increase in bank credit supply and an improvement in credit terms, such as maturity and required spreads, for large loans that are likely to be issued by companies that are "named credits" in the CDS market. These findings are in line with the predictions of Bolton and Oehmke (2011) that CDS behaves as a commitment device and hence decreases strategic default, increases the financing capacity of CDS firms, decreases cost of debt, increases investment, and firm value. These benefits are dampened by the effects of empty creditors. Further, there is some support for the theory that CDS increases the duration of CDS firms' debt (Arping 2014).

Saretto and Tookes (2012) find that firms with CDS traded on them can sustain higher leverage and borrow at longer debt maturities. The line of argument that the authors take does not rely on the theory of Bolton and Oehmke (2011) or Arping (2014). Instead, they argue that the ability of suppliers of credit to hedge their credit exposure should make them more willing to lend to a firm and lend at longer durations. The authors show that the initiation of CDS trading on a firm's debt increases the firm's leverage ratio by 0.009 to 0.055, which is between 6% and 22% of the average leverage ratio in their sample. Further, the authors find that the duration of debt increases by 0.68 to 1.79 years, which is between 8% and 32% of mean debt maturity in their sample. This finding is in support of the predictions from Arping (2014); however, the specific channel, that of roll over risk, has not been shown empirically.

Ashcraft and Santos (2009) show that the improvement of credit terms hinges on the riskiness of the firm. Where safe and transparent firms see an improvement in their borrowing terms when CDS begins to trade on them, riskier as well as more opaque firms see an increase in their cost of debt financing. This finding could be explained by the findings of Degryse et al. (2019), where ex ante safer firms are not affected by the empty creditor problem and, hence, experience a reduced dampening effect of empty creditors which results in a net benefit from CDS trading on their debt.

As in the other strands of the CDS literature, the increasing availability of bank-firm-level CDS transaction data, combined with bank-firm-level credit exposures, allows authors to rely less on econometric techniques to reduce endogeneity concerns. Gündüz et al. (2016) employ bank-firm-level CDS transaction data obtained from the DTCC with bank-firm-level credit exposures from the German credit registry. The authors find that when liquidity in the CDS market improves, an increase in a bank's CDS position leads to a relatively higher credit exposure to safer firms. The authors use the implementation of the CDS Small Bang as an exogenous shock to the liquidity of the CDS market for European reference entities.

Bartram et al. (2018) conduct the first cross-country analysis on the propensity to trade CDS and the effects of CDS trading by employing a sample of more than 56,000 firms from 50 countries during the period 2001-2015. The authors find that CDS is more likely to be traded on firms domiciled in countries with stronger orientation towards bank financing, lower levels of ownership concentration, and weaker creditor rights. The authors show that the initiation of CDS trading on firms' debt affects real decisions within these firms, such as leverage, investment, and the riskiness of their investments. Further, they find these effects to be larger in countries where CDS help to mitigate weak property rights and where there is less uncertainty about the enforcement of obligations due under the CDS contract.

4.7 How Do Referenced Firms Respond to Being CDS-Referenced Firms?

If firms are able to observe whether or not CDS is traded on their debt, and if they are aware of the potential consequences, it stands to reason that they may change their behaviour in response to having CDS traded on their debt. Subrahmanyam et al. (2017) investigate firms' response to having CDS traded on their debt and, in their sample, being exposed to empty creditors. The authors use the same method and data as in their previous paper, but change the variable of interest from probability of bankruptcy to cash holdings (Subrahmanyam et al. 2014). Common to the literature, the authors employ the following IV model to account for the endogeneity of CDS trading:

$$\begin{aligned}
&Cash_{i,t} = \beta X_{i,t} + \gamma CDS\ Trading_{i,t} + \delta Y_{i,t} + \epsilon_{i,t} \\
&CDSTrading^{\star} = \lambda Z_{i,t} + \omega \\
&CDSTrading = 1, \quad if\ CDSTrading^{\star} > 0 \\
&CDSTrading = 0, \quad otherwise
\end{aligned} \tag{4.9}$$

Where $Cash_{i,t}$ is the cash ratio of firm i in quarter t, $X_{i,t}$ is a vector of control variables determining cash holdings and $Y_{i,t}$ is a vector of other control variables. As in Subrahmanyam et al. (2014), $Z_{i,t}$ includes the average amount of foreign exchange derivatives held by all lead arrangers that have lent to the firm in the previous five years as a fraction of the lenders' total assets ($Lender\ FX\ Usage$), as well as the lenders' Tier One capital ratio. Following Ashcraft and Santos (2009), $Y_{i,t}$ either includes firm fixed effect or an indicator variable, $CDS\ Traded_i$, which is equal to 1 if a firm ever has CDS traded on it in the sample period. This is included to control for any time-invariant differences between CDS firms and non-CDS firms.

Here, the coefficient of interest is γ with a positive γ indicating an increase in cash holdings after the initiation of CDS trading on the firm. Subrahmanyam et al. (2017) find that firms increase their cash holdings by 2.6 percentage points after CDS begins to trade on their debt. They further find that this effect is increasing in the degree of financial distress of the CDS firm, the intensity of CDS trading on its debt. Finally, they find that this effect is only significant for firms without bank debt, which may suggest that an offsetting effect for CDS firms with bank financing. Indeed, it may be that firms increase their risk-taking behaviour by reducing their cash holdings in response to a decrease in monitoring by banks. These findings suggest that CDS firms take both the treat of empty creditors and their marginal value of liquidity into account when determining their cash holdings.

Chang et al. (2017) investigate the effect of CDS trading on a firm's debt on its technological innovation output. For their main results, the authors follow Subrahmanyam et al. (2014), in terms of both data sources and methodology. The authors argue that CDS affects innovation by increasing a CDS firm's risk-taking behaviour, which they argue is key for innovation. They find that CDS trading on a firm's debt increases its technological innovation output as measured by patents and patent citations. They find that after CDS begins to trade on a firm's debt, the firm registers 14.8% more patents and receives 20.2% more citations on its patents compared to non-CDS firms.

4.8 How Does CDS Trading Affect Firms with Economic Links to Referenced Firms (Spillovers)?

As the literature has shown, CDS trading on a firm impacts it in many ways, including their bankruptcy risk, capital structure, and borrowing costs. However, CDS only trades on a handful of firms which brings into the question the importance of understanding the effects of CDS trading on the referenced entities. CDS firms tend to be large, and hence changes to these firms can have significant economic effects on economically linked firms.

Li and Tang (2016) investigate the impact of CDS trading on the suppliers of CDS-referenced firms. The authors argue that suppliers tend to be smaller than CDS firms and should be concerned with their exposure to CDS firms. If a supplier is dependent on a CDS-referenced customer, and the CDS-referenced customer is exposed to empty creditors, the supplier faces higher revenue risk. Hence, a supplier of a CDS-referenced firm may have an incentive to maintain lower leverage. However, CDS spreads provide information about the customers of these suppliers. The authors argue that creditors of the supplier may use the CDS of CDS-referenced customers to manage their credit exposure to the supplier. The ability of the supplier's creditors to hedge may make them more willing to lend to the firm. Hence, a supplier of a CDS-referenced firm may be able to maintain higher leverage.

Indeed, Li and Tang (2016) find that a firm's leverage is lower when it obtains a larger portion of its revenue from CDS-referenced customers. Specifically, they find that a one standard deviation increase in the proportion of sales to CDS-referenced customers (0.138) is associated with a 0.5 to 0.8 percentage point decrease in the firm's leverage ratio. Further, Li and Tang (2016) find that these firms achieve lower leverage ratios by issuing equity, which they do at a lower cost. This finding lends itself to the notion that CDS trading on customers improves the information environment of suppliers. Therefore, while CDS is only traded on a small number of large firms, the effects of CDS trading generates externalities (spillovers) to connect firms in an economically meaningful way.

4.9 Conclusion

The credit derivative literature has shown that the decision to trade CDS is complex. Banks are more likely to use CDS to hedge their credit risk if they use other risk transfer instruments, such as foreign exchange derivatives (Minton et al. 2009). Additionally, banks' propensity to use CDS as a hedging instrument is increasing in their capital and liquidity constraints (Minton et al. 2009; Beyhaghi et al. 2016). Further, the decision to trade CDS on a firm is based on the riskiness of the firm, the characteristics of the bank's relationship with the firm, and the bank's reputation in other credit markets (Beyhaghi et al. 2016; Streitz 2016; Gündüz et al. 2016). Moreover, it has found that firms which obtain a larger proportion of their credit from banks that are more active hedgers are more likely to have CDS trading their debt (Saretto and Tookes 2012; Subrahmanyam et al. 2014). The literature has shown that riskier borrowers' debt is more likely to be sold than hedged using CDS (Beyhaghi et al. 2016). Further, there is evidence for a credit enhancement channel where a bank uses CDS to facilitate loan sales by selling CDS on the firm to their counterparty in the loan sale (Hasan and Wu 2017).

Another strand of the CDS literature focuses on the effects of CDS trading on other credit markets (e.g., the syndicated loan market and the bond market). The initiation of CDS trading on a firm's debt (CDS initiation) has mostly detrimental effects for the secondary market for a referenced firm's bonds. The bond market becomes less efficient, and there are no improvements in terms of an increase in liquidity or a reduction in pricing errors (Das et al. 2014). Additionally, on CDS initiation, the firm sees its loan spreads in the syndicated market increase by 13% (Amiram et al. 2017).

A consequence of banks' participation in both CDS and credit markets is that their use of CDS impacts the way in which they interact with their borrowers. The credit derivative literature has shown that CDS ex ante improves creditors' willingness to lend to CDS firms which improves these firms access and cost of debt (Ashcraft and Santos 2009; Saretto and Tookes 2012). While the evidence is mixed, there is growing support for the view that CDS trading results in banks inefficiently pushing firms into default (Subrahmanyam et al. 2014; Colonnello et al. 2016; Degryse et al. 2019).

The literature on firms' response to becoming a CDS-referenced firm shows that firms respond by increasing their cash buffers to avoid having to negotiate with empty creditors (Subrahmanyam et al. 2017). Further, there is evidence that firms increase the riskiness of their R&D project, which results in them becoming more innovative, registering more patents and receiving a larger number of citations on their patents (Chang et al. 2017).

There are two key challenges in the literature which authors have mitigated through the use of econometric techniques. The first challenge stems from the potential issue that CDS trading on a firm is endogenous to the effect being studied. This could either be in the form of the timing of CDS trading, where CDS initiation is used as an event in a difference-in-differences set-up, or in the form of omitted variable bias where CDS firms are different to non-CDS firms in a manner that impacts the effect being studied. These issues have mostly been mitigated through the use of firm fixed effects to control for the difference between CDS and non-CDS firms, and time fixed effect to control for time-specific effects. Another method that is frequently used to control the differences between CDS firms and non-CDS firms is the use of matching techniques, which aim to match CDS and non-CDS firms according to some characteristics, for example firm size.

The second challenge in the literature stems from the lack of granular transaction-level data, where authors have had to use proxies for banks' CDS trading behaviour. Post-crisis regulations have made granular transaction data available to researchers, and, hence, this challenge should be alleviated. The literature on the effects of CDS trading on the referenced firm has begun to use this data, which has benefited identification. The literature on the reason to trade CDS and the spillovers to economically linked firms and other credit markets may be further developed using the granular transaction-level data sets. Table 4.1 offers a compact overview of the papers reviewed in this chapter.

Table 4.1 Credit risk

Paper	*Research question*	*Data*	*Methodology*	*Main findings*
Minton et al. (JFSR, 2009)	Do Banks Lay off Credit Risk?	US bank holding companies' 10-K filings merged with the US bank holding companies data from the Federal Reserve Bank of Chicago Bank Holding Companies Database.	**Correlations and cross-sectional variation**: comparing the characteristics of banks that are net buyers of credit derivatives to other banks.	23 out of their sample of 395 banks use credit derivatives. Banks' credit derivative exposures are mainly due to their dealer, rather than hedging activities. Banks which use other derivatives are also more likely to use credit derivates Banks which are net buyers of credit derivatives are larger, have a larger fraction of commercial and industrial loans, foreign loans, and a lower fraction of loans secured by real estate. The likelihood that a bank uses credit derivatives to hedge is negatively related to its net interest margin, equity capital, and tier I risk capital Banks which sell or securitize loans are more likely to use credit derivatives to hedge loans

(*continued*)

Table 4.1 (continued)

Paper	*Research question*	*Data*	*Methodology*	*Main findings*
Gündüz et al. (WP, 2016)	Why do Banks lay off credit risk?	DTCC CDS position-level data combined with CDS spreads from Bloomberg and bank-firm credit exposures from the German Credit Registry.	**Difference-in-differences**: exploiting the intensity of a bank's credit exposure to a firm, as well as the riskiness of the firm, before the implementation of the CDS Small Bang protocol.	When liquidity in the CDS market improves, banks purchase more CDS protection on riskier firms and firms to which they have higher existing credit exposures
Beyhaghi et al. (JCF, 2016)	How do banks lay off credit risk	The Uniform Bank Performance Reports obtained from the Federal Financial Institutions Examination Council, combined with Markit CDS data, loan sale data from the Loan Syndication and Trading Association database, loan facility data from the DealScan database, and borrower information from Compustat and CRSP.	**Correlations and cross-sectional variation**: across banks with differing capital and liquidity constraints, and business models. Variation across firms with differing ex ante risk, size, and debt maturity. **Nested Logit**: to account for the nested decision process of laying off credit risk.	The propensity of banks to use credit risk transfer instruments is increasing in their capital and liquidity constraints Relationship lenders and lead syndicate lenders are less likely to use credit risk transfer instruments. Banks are more likely to use these instruments for larger borrowers whose debt have a longer maturity.
				Loans to ex ante low-quality (high-risk), or longer maturity loans, are more likely to be sold. Loans to borrowers with higher return on assets are more likely to be hedged with CDS.

Hasan and Wu (WP, 2017)		The Shared National Credit data combined with the US bank holding companies' data, Markit CDS data, Compustat, and CRSP	**Correlations and within-group variation**: the change in a bank's retained loan share explained by its net notional CDS protection relative to its total assets.	CDS hedging and loan sales are complements rather than substitutes. If the bank is a net seller of CDS protection, loan sales are combined with a negative CDS position.
Streitz (RoF, 2016)	What are the consequences of CDS trading for other credit markets?	CDS spread data obtained from Bloomberg's CMA database, loan information from LPC DealScan database, and borrower financial information from Compustat.	Similar to Saretto and Tookes (RFS, 2012)	Banks are 2.9% less likely to syndicate a loan once CDS is traded on a borrower. Banks retain 5.48% more of a loan once CDS is traded on a borrower. The effect is less intense for smaller borrowers with shorter debt maturity, lead arrangers with a poor reputation, and borrowers with relatively illiquid CDS markets. Reduction in the likelihood of covenant violations once CDS is traded on the borrowers' debt.
Amiram et al. (JFE, 2017)		CDS trading data from Markit combined with the LPC DealScan database and Compustat.	Similar to Saretto and Tookes (RFS, 2012)	Banks retain 4.2% more of a loan once CDS is traded on a borrower and the loan spread increases by 13%. The effect is less intense for less opaque borrowers, lead arrangers with a strong reputation, and borrowers with relatively illiquid CDS markets.

(continued)

Table 4.1 (continued)

Paper	*Research question*	*Data*	*Methodology*	*Main findings*
Das et al. (JFE, 2014)		Corporate bond trading data from TRACE combined with Bloomberg CDS data. Bond issue-specific data from the Fixed Income Securities Database and equity data from CRSP.	**Time series variation**: where the contemporaneous and lagged values of a firm's stock and CDS returns are used to explain the contemporaneous bond return.	
			Difference-in-Differences: exploiting the initiation of CDS trading on a firm's bonds to measure the change in the quality of the market for a firm's bonds.	CDS initiation has mostly detrimental effects on the secondary market for a referenced firm's bonds. Bond markets become less efficient, and there is neither an improvement in liquidity nor in market quality
Oehmke and Zawad-owski (RFS, 2017)		DTCC public position-level data combined with Markit CDS spread data, as well as Compustat, Mergent FISD,TRACE Enhanced, CRSP, and IBES.	**Correlations and cross-sectional variation**: where the CDS or Bond trading volume is explained by different trading motives which vary at firm level. The coefficients from the regressions using the CDS and Bond market are then compared to each other for differences. **Tobit estimation**: to account for the fact that they only observe the top 1000 CDS firms.	CDS is indeed a substitute for trading bonds. When trading for hedging purposes, both bond and CDS markets are used, while when trading for speculative reasons, trading concentrates in the CDS market.

Subrahmanyam et al. (RFS, 2014)	How does CDS trading affect the referenced firm?	CDS transaction records from CreditTrade and the GFI Group combined with bankruptcy data from multiple sources. The instrumental variable was constructed using the Dealscan syndicated loan database and Federal Reserve's Call Report data.	Similar to Saretto and Tookes (RFS, 2012) **Instrumental variable**: instrumenting CDS trading on a particular borrower with its lenders' Foreign Exchange usage and their Tier One capital ratio.	The probability of bankruptcy increases from 0.14% to 0.47% upon the inception of CDS trading. Distressed firms are more likely to file for bankruptcy if they have CDS traded on their debt. Firm leverage increases significantly upon the inception of CDS trading. The number of creditors a firm has increases after CDS begins to trade on its debt.
Colonnello et al. (Forthcoming JFE, 2016)		Markit CDS data combined with the LPC DealScan data set, Compustat, CRSP, and Thomson Reuters Institutional Holdings and the Institutional Investor Classification Data of Brian Bushee.	Similar to Ashcraft and Santos (2009) (JME, 2009) **Overlap Weighting Method of Matching**: where CDS traded firms (treated) are weighted by their propensity to be assigned to the control group and non-CDS traded firms (control) weighted by their propensity to be assigned to the treatment group. **Difference-in-differences**: exploiting the increase in the empty creditor effect for CDS firms through the change to the restructuring clause of CDS contracts in the CDS Big Bang protocol.	A 1% increase in institutional ownership is associated with a 0.32% increase in CDS purchasing. A firm's distance-to-default decreases only when conditioning on the top quartile of firms with the highest shareholder bargaining power.

(*continued*)

Table 4.1 (continued)

Paper	*Research question*	*Data*	*Methodology*	*Main findings*
Bedendo et al. (JMCB, 2016)		Markit CDS data combined with Moody's Default and Recovery Database, Factiva, and the Dealscan syndicated loan database.	**Correlations and cross-sectional variation**: where the likelihood of a firm experiencing a default is explained by the firm having CDS traded on its debt at the time of default.	CDS do not have a significant effect on the likelihood of bankruptcy.
Danis (Management Science, 2016)		Markit CDS data combined with Moody's Default and Recovery Database, Bloomberg, Factiva, and Compustat.	**Difference-in-differences**: exploiting the increase in the empty creditor effect for CDS firms through the change to the restructuring clause of CDS contracts in the CDS Big Bang protocol.	Empty creditors have a negative effect on out-of-court debt restructuring. The average participation rate is 29 percentage points lower for firms with CDS traded on their debt, and further decreases for CDS firms after the implementation of the CDS Big Bang Protocol.
Degryse et al. (WP, 2019)		Bank-firm-level CDS transaction data obtained from the DTCC, combined with bank-firm-level credit exposures from the German credit registry, firm information from USTAN, CDS spreads information from Markit, macroeconomic data obtained from DataStream.	**Difference-in-differences**: exploiting the removal of the empty creditor effect for CDS firms through the change to the German Bankruptcy law in 2012. **Coarsened Exact Matching**: Improving the covariate balance between the CDS traded firm sample (treated) and a non-CDS traded firm sample (control) based on firm characteristics.	The probability of default for firms with CDS traded on them decreases by 1.3 to 2 percentage points when the effect of empty creditors is removed. This effect increases in the book leverage of a firm, its efficiency, in the concentration of its debt, and in the average CDS hedge position of its creditors. Larger firms, more profitable firms with more tangible assets, and firms with higher average collateral ratios of their debt are less affected by empty creditors.

			Financially vulnerable firms are severely affected by empty creditors, and safe firms are not affected.
Hirtle (JFI, 2009)	Bank level CDS trading data from the Federal Reserve's Call Report data combined with loan-level data from the Federal Reserve's Survey of Terms of Business Lending.	**Correlations and cross-sectional variation**: where the a bank's credit supply is explained by its use of CDS for credit protection purposes.	Greater use of CDS leads to an increase in bank credit supply and an improvement in credit terms, such as maturity and required spreads, for large loans that are likely to be issued by companies that are "named credits" in the CDS market.
Ashcraft and Santos (JME, 2009)	Information on implied equity market volatilities from Optionmetrics and information on analyst coverage from IBES combined with Markit CDS data, Compustat, and CRSP.	**Difference-in-differences**: exploiting the initiation of CDS trading on a firm's debt. **Propensity score matching**: CDS traded firms (treated) to non-CDS traded firms (control) based on the firms' propensity to have been treated.	Safe and transparent firms see an improvement in their borrowing terms when CDS begins to trade on them. Riskier as well as more opaque firms see an increase in their cost of debt financing.
Saretto and Tookes (RFS, 2012)	CDS quotes from Bloomberg, combined with firm information from Compustat and capital structure information from Capital IQ. The instrumental variable was constructed using the Dealscan syndicated loan database and Federal Reserve's Call Report data.	Similar to Ashcraft and Santos (JME, 2009) **Instrumental variable**: instrumenting CDS trading on a particular borrower with its lenders' Foreign Exchange usage.	Initiation of CDS trading on a firm's debt increases the firm's leverage ratio by 0.009 to 0.055. The duration of debt increases by 0.68 to 1.79 years.

(*continued*)

Table 4.1 (continued)

Paper	*Research question*	*Data*	*Methodology*	*Main findings*
Gündüz et al. (WP, 2016)		DTCC CDS position-level data combined with CDS spreads from Bloomberg and bank-firm credit exposures from the German Credit Registry.	**Difference-in-differences**: exploiting the change in a bank's CDS trading on a firm around the implementation of the CDS Small Bang protocol, as well as the riskiness of the firm before the implementation.	When liquidity in the CDS market improves, an increase in a bank's CDS position leads to a relatively higher credit exposure to safer firms.
Bartram et al. (WP, 2019)	How does the propensity to trade CDS vary across countries?	Markit CDS data combined with Worldscope, country-level financial market, legal and institutional characteristics obtained from previous studies (e.g., Djankov et al. (JFE, 1998), amongst other data sets.	**Difference-in-differences**: exploiting the initiation of CDS trading on a firm's debt. **Overlap Weighting Method of Matching**: where CDS traded firms (treated) are weighted by their propensity to be assigned to the control group and non-CDS traded firms (control) weighted by their propensity to be assigned to the treatment group. **Correlations and cross-sectional variation**: where the introduction of CDS trading is explained by firm and country characteristics.	On introduction of CDS trading on a firm, firms increase leverage by 6.8%; and where leverage increases, the level of capital investment of CDS firms also increase. These firms reduce the riskiness of their investments as seen in a reduction in R&D spending by close to 8%. These effects are larger in countries where CDS help to mitigate weak property rights and where there is less uncertainty about the enforcement of obligations due under the CDS contract. CDS is more likely to be traded on firms domiciled in countries with stronger orientation towards bank financing, lower levels of ownership concentration, and weaker creditor rights.

Subrahmanyam et al. (JFE, 2017)	How do firms respond to being CDS-referenced firms?	CDS transaction records from CreditTrade and the GFI Group combined with corporate cash holdings and other firm characteristics from the Compustat database. The instrumental variable was constructed using the Dealscan syndicated loan database and Federal Reserve's Call Report data.	Similar to Subrahmanyam et al. (RFS, 2014)	Firms increase their cash holdings by 2.6 percentage points after CDS begins to trade on their debt. This effect is increasing in the degree of financial distress of the CDS firm, the intensity of CDS trading on its debt.
Chang et al. (Forthcoming JFE, 2017)		CDS data from Markit, CreditTrade, and the GFI Group. Patent information obtained from the US Patent and Trademark Office and patent citations from the Harvard Business School Patent Network Dataverse. The instrumental variable was constructed using the Dealscan syndicated loan database and Federal Reserve's Call Report data.	Similar to Saretto and Tookes (RFS, 2012)	After CDS begins to trade on a firm's debt, the firm registers 14.8% more patents and receives 20.2% more citations on its patents compared to non-CDS firms.

(*continued*)

Table 4.1 (continued)

Paper	*Research question*	*Data*	*Methodology*	*Main findings*
Li and Tang (JFE, 2016)	How does CDS trading affect firms with economic links to referenced firms (spillovers)?	DealScan and the Fixed Income Securities Database (FISD). Compustat Segment files	**Correlations and within-group variation**: the change in non-CDS-referenced firms' leverage explained by the proportion of their sales to CDS-referenced customers. Similar to Subrahmanyam et al. (RFS, 2014) but at supplier level. **Difference-in-differences**: exploiting the initiation of CDS trading on a firm's customers debt. **Instrumental variable**: instrumenting CDS trading on a particular firm's customer with the customer's lenders' Foreign Exchange usage and the industry concentration the customer's lenders' debt.	A one standard deviation increase in the proportion of sales to CDS-referenced customers (0.138) is associated with a 0.5 to 0.8 percentage point decrease in the firm's leverage ratio. These firms achieve lower leverage ratios by issuing equity, which they do at a lower cost.

CHAPTER 5

Collateral and Lending

Credit markets are vulnerable to information imperfections, such as adverse selection or moral hazard, which may lead to financing constraints (Barro 1976; Stiglitz and Weiss 1981; Hart and Moore 1994). Two main economic theories explain how pledging collateral might alleviate these constraints. First, collateral can mitigate *ex ante* information asymmetries between borrowers and lenders because it acts as a signalling device (Bester 1985, 1987; Chan and Thakor 1987). According to this interpretation, lenders will offer menus of contract terms, with different collateral requirements. Less risky borrowers will choose to pledge higher collateral in order to signal their higher quality and obtain more favourable loan terms. A second economic explanation contends that collateral reduces *ex-post* frictions such as moral hazard and costly state verification (Boot et al. 1991; Holmstrom and Tirole 1997; Townsend 1979). The reason is that collateral disciplines the firm managers, by giving outside investors the option to liquidate the firm's assets. To reduce such ex post frictions banks are likely to require the riskiest borrowers to pledge collateral.

Irrespective of whether the ex ante or the ex post theories are empirically more prevalent, a growing academic literature agrees that collateral plays

A. Bilan et al., *Banking and Financial Markets*, Palgrave Macmillan Studies in Banking and Financial Institutions,
https://doi.org/10.1007/978-3-030-26844-2_5

an important role in easing financial constraints.[1] This is the so-called "collateral channel". Moreover, since collateral is widely used across a variety of lending markets, it can directly affect macro stability. Because the value of the assets pledged typically fluctuates with the business cycle, holding collateral can accentuate the balance sheet volatility of lenders, making the booms and the busts more pronounced (Bernanke and Gertler 1990; Kiyotaki and Moore 1997). Such collateral-driven booms might also lead to longer periods of low growth. For example, Asriyan et al. (2018) argue that whenever collateral prices are high lenders have less incentives to screen investment projects, which in aggregate decreases the stock of information available in the economy.

In this chapter, we review the empirical evidence establishing the importance of collateral availability for firm creation and growth. Since collateral is often thought to be mainly real estate (Calomiris et al. 2017; Davydenko and Franks 2008), we start with contributions that study how fluctuations in real estate prices affect economic growth, because they change the value of the collateral stock individuals and firms hold. We then review recent evidence on the role that movable and patent collateral play in easing lending frictions. Finally, we comment on the importance of legal frameworks enforcing creditor rights, which should complement the use of pleadgeable assets. Table 5.1 offers a compact overview of the papers reviewed.

5.1 Data

To measure whether collateral eases financing constraints at firm and individual levels, two sets of data are needed: a data set measuring changes in collateral values or proxies for these changes, and a second data set collecting economic outcomes. Depending on the type of collateral studied, the former data can be sourced from general economic indicators when the

[1] Berger et al. (2011) measure which among the ex ante and the ex post theories of collateral is stronger empirically, by exploiting gaps in the disclosure requirements of the Bolivian Credit Registry. The registry offers the holder access to a wider set of information than the information disclosed to prospective lenders. Based on this, the authors build indicators of observed and unobserved borrower risk and then test the incidence of collateral in the different subgroups of borrowers. Their findings provide support both for the ex post theories, which are prevalent among long-term borrowers, and the ex ante theories, empirically prevalent among short-term borrowers.

Table 5.1 Collateral and lending

Paper	*Research question*	*Data*	*Methodology*	*Main findings*
Hurst and Lusardi (JPE, 2004)	*Are financing constraints an obstacle for business creation?*	US Panel Study of Income Dynamics (PSID) on households, merged with firm information from the National Survey of Small Business Finances(NSSBF)	**Instrumental variable:** instrumenting household wealth with proxies: inheritances and housing capital gains	Credit constraints not empirically important in deterring business creation in the US: – positive correlation between household wealth and the propensity to start a business strong only for the top 5% of the wealth distribution – households in regions with strong housing appreciation no more likely to start a business than households in other regions
Schmalz et al. (JF, 2017)		French administrative micro-level surveys: French Labor Force Survey to identify business creations and homeownership; and a large-scale survey of SMEs, run by the French Statistical Office, for firm financial information	**Difference-in-differences:** homeowners versus home renters, across 25 French regions with heterogeneous variation in real estate prices	An increase of 16 percentage points in house prices leads to an 11% increase in the probability of becoming an entrepreneur

(continued)

Table 5.1 (continued)

Paper	*Research question*	*Data*	*Methodology*	*Main findings*
Cloyne et al. (AER, forthcoming)	*What is the effect of housing collateral on household borrowing?*	Administrative panel on the universe of mortgage contracts in the UK, collected by the UK's Financial Conduct Authority (FCA) and available at the FCA and the Bank of England	**Exogeneous variation and within borrower identification:** from predetermined refinancing dates on mortgage contracts interacted with the business cycle	House price appreciation increases individual borrowing, but the effect is smaller than in Schmalz et al. 2017: elasticity of borrowing with respect to house prices between 0.2 and 0.3
Chaney et al. (2012) (AER, 2012)	*Are financing constraints an obstacle for firm investment?*	Compustat financial data on listed firms; real estate prices at state and MSA level, provided by the US Department of Housing and Urban Development, as well as by Global Real Analytics	**Difference-in-differences:** across firms that own real estate and firms that do not across regions with different real estate price appreciation **Instrumental variable:** local variation in real estate prices instrumented with long-term interest rates*local house supply elasticity	Average US corporation invests approximately US$0.06 out of each US$1 of additional collateral

Catherine et al.	*What is the economic importance of financing constraints?*	Same as Chaney et al. (2012) (AER, 2012)	**Simulated Method of Moments:** comparison between an economy with financing constraints and an economy without financing constraints	Aggregate welfare loss from financing constraints of 9.4% and output loss of 11% wrt counterfactual
Asriyan et al. (WP, 2018)	*Do credit booms driven by real estate collateral lead to information depletion and slower recovery?*	Similar to Chaney et al. (AER, 2012)	Similar to Chaney et al. (AER, 2012) **Correlation** between collateral values and investment measured in the cross-section of firms with more versus less public information available Three proxies for information: the bid-ask spread on the firm's stock, the number of financial analysts that follow the firm, and the ratio of intangible assets to tangible fixed assets of the sector in which the firm operates	A one standard deviation increase in real estate collateral increases the investment rate of high information by 0.8 percentage points more than the investment rate of low-spread firms After a credit boom, US states which had previously invested more into firms with less available information experiment a lower growth in new investment than states had previously invested more into firms with more information available

(*continued*)

Table 5.1 (continued)

Paper	*Research question*	*Data*	*Methodology*	*Main findings*
Campello and Larrain (RFS, 2015)	*Are firms that employ relatively more movable assets credit constrained?*	Amadeus database with financial information on European firms, covering the majority of privately held firms in Romania	**Difference-in-differences**, exploiting the introduction of a new legal provision in Romania in 2000 ("Law 99"), which allowed firms to pledge movable collateral for the first time. Firms divided into treatment and control groups according to whether they belong to sectors intensive in movable assets	Reform increased the leverage of firms in movable-intensive sectors by 3.7 percentage points more than in firms in non-movable-intensive sectors
Cerqueiro et al. (JF, 2016)		Proprietary data: loan portfolio of one large Swedish bank	**Difference-in-differences**, exploiting a law change in Sweden which excluded floating liens as collateral. Compare borrowers that had previously pledged floating liens as collateral to a matched sample of borrowers who did not	The bank increases the interest rate on outstanding treated versus control loans by 20 basis points

Hochberg et al. (JFE, 2018)	*Are technological start-ups credit constrained?*	Loans to start-ups identified patents pledged as collateral and reported to the US Patent and Trademark Office (USPTO) Start-up characteristics extracted from a database of US venture capital-backed firms from the Dow Jones VentureSource (DJVS)	**Correlation** between the probability of obtaining a loan backed by patent collateral and trading intensity in the secondary market for related patents	A 1 percentage point increase in patent trading associated with an increase in predicted debt rate of 1.10 percentage points
Calomiris et al. (JFE, 2017)	*Do legal enforcements of creditor rights ease collateral constraints?*	Proprietary data: loan portfolio of a global bank active in several emerging market countries	**Difference-in-differences:** proxy for credit supply using actual loan-to-value ratios for loans secured with movable versus real estate collateral, and across countries with different legal treatment of movable collateral	Loan-to-value ratios of loans collateralized with movable assets on average 27.6 percentage points higher relative to loans collateralized with immovable assets, in strong-law countries relative to weak-law countries

(continued)

Table 5.1 (continued)

Paper	*Research question*	*Data*	*Methodology*	*Main findings*
Degryse et al. (WP, 2016)		Proprietary data: loan portfolio of a global bank active in several emerging market countries	**Difference-in-differences:** using lender-estimated loan recovery rates on movable relatively to immovable collateral, across countries with different legal treatment of movable collateral	Liquidation values for movable assets are on average 30.7 percentage points higher relative to real estate assets, in countries with strong creditor protection relative to countries with weak credit protection
Mann (JFE, 2018)	*Do stronger creditor rights for patents increase investment among technological firms?*	Records from the United States Patent and Trademark Office (USPTO) on the use of patents as collateral, matched to Compustat	**Difference-in-differences**, exploiting four court decisions, from 2002, 2003, 2007, and 2009, that strengthened creditor rights for patenting firms incorporated in Delaware. Compare financing and investment for Delaware-relative to non-Delaware-incorporated firms	Total debt rises by 4% of assets in the quarter when a patent portfolio is pledged. Pass-through of US$0.17 of annual R&D spending for each marginal US$1 of total debt

collateral is tradable-such as house price indicators for real estate collateral or secondary market trading on patents. For non-tradeable collateral, typically the literature has relied on law changes: differential legal systems for movable versus non-movable collateral, or laws changing the grasp of creditor rights on one specific type of asset pledged as collateral.

To study economic outcomes at individual or firm level, a variety of data sources have become available. Studies identifying transitions to entrepreneurship and individual borrowing typically rely on panel surveys conducted by market supervisors. Examples of such surveys are the National Survey of Small Business Finances (NSSBF), which used to be conducted by the Board of Governors of the Federal Reserve System, the French Labor Force Survey, and regulatory data on the universe of mortgages in the UK, which is collected by the Financial Conduct Authority. Firm-level outcomes are estimated based on available financial indicators from common sources such as Compustat or Amadeus. Other studies have used proprietary data, such as loan portfolios of large banks. Recently, researchers have started to address questions in fields where the data is still scarce, such as patent collateral. So far, the main source of information on patents pledged as collateral has come from the United States Patent and Trademark Office (USPTO).

5.2 Methodology

This literature emerged with the goal to establish whether financing constraints are economically relevant. The main empirical challenge was to disentangle whether financing outcomes-such as the observed number of new firms or the investment level of existing firms-are the result of efficient market equilibria. Or, on the contrary, if they result from constrained equilibria in which the supply of finance is insufficient to address existing demand. To do this, the first studies looked at correlations between proxies for individual wealth and the probability of starting new businesses (Evans and Jovanovic 1989). The economic reasoning backing this approach is that poorer households should have similar rates of business creation as the richer ones if they had unconstrained access to finance. But such results could be biased by individual ability, which is likely to be correlated with wealth.

Subsequent studies have searched for better instruments for wealth, both at individual and at firm level. Relying on changes in local asset prices, Hurst and Lusardi (2004) first measured whether regions that experienced house price increases were more likely to see a higher number of new businesses. The studies that followed tried to rid the analyses of confounders at a regional level, by using improved research designs: comparing houseowners and house renters within region (Schmalz et al. 2017), using exogenous variation from predetermined mortgage refinancing dates (Cloyne et al. 2017), or instrumenting house prices with the elasticity of the supply of housing (Chaney et al. 2012; Asriyan et al. 2018).

Most of these contributions studied real estate collateral, but a parallel stream of literature emerged to investigate financing constraints which are not alleviated by real estate assets. A more mature literature considers the role of movable collateral. These papers exploit law changes that affect movable assets and study the reaction of firms holding relatively movable collateral with respect to firms holding non-movable collateral. A novel literature addresses the role of patents in alleviating financial constraints (Hochberg et al. 2018). This work uses scarce patent data creatively, albeit with weaker identification.

Finally, a complementary body of the literature takes a public policy evaluation approach to study the effect of legal frameworks on alleviating collateral constraints. These papers typically study laws related to creditor rights on different types of collateral. The identification exploits either law changes (Mann 2018), or legal regimes with differential strength of enforcement (Calomiris et al. 2017; Degryse et al. 2016). The research design is based on difference-in-differences methodologies across firms with heterogeneous exposures to the law change.

5.3 Types of Collateral

This section reviews recent literature on the relationship between collateral and financial constraints for three types of collateral: real estate assets, movable assets, and patents.

5.3.1 *Real Estate Collateral and Firm Creation*

The economic literature has long been concerned with how access to finance affects business creation. Earlier contributions document a positive correlation between existing individual wealth and entrepreneurship, suggesting that financing constraints might be one of the reasons why less wealthy individuals are also less likely to start new businesses (Evans and Jovanovic 1989; Evans and Leighton 1989). Acknowledging concerns of simultaneity in these results-as individuals could be both likely to accumulate wealth and become entrepreneurs due to unobserved characteristics such as ability-subsequent studies have used inheritances as an instrument for individual wealth (Holtz-Eakin et al. 1994; Blanchflower and Oswald 1998). Consistent with the hypothesis of financing frictions, they found that the propensity to start a business responds strongly to inheritances received in the recent past.

Hurst and Lusardi (2004) challenge most of these findings. They continue studying the previously documented positive correlation between individual wealth and entrepreneurship, but look across the distribution of wealth. Their work documents that this relationship is strong only at the top of the wealth distribution, for individuals in the top 95th percentile of wealth (with $300,000 or more in wealth). In fact, the authors argue, the estimated probability of starting a business for someone with $20,000 in wealth is nearly identical to the estimated probability of starting a business for someone with $200,000 in wealth. Using data from the US Panel Study of Income Dynamics on household wealth and business ownership, matched with information from the National Survey of Small Business Finances, they then reassess the importance of financing constraints by using two instruments for individual liquidity: inheritances and capital gains on real estate.

The first estimations confirm existing results: past inheritances have a positive effect on the propensity to start a business. But so do future inheritances. This leads the authors to conclude that inheritances proxy for more than just liquidity, which is why they are not a suitable instrument to study financial constraints. In a second step, they use capital gains on housing as an instrument. Housing capital gains are arguably less correlated with other unobservable individual factors that could also determine entrepreneurial propensities. Hurst and Lusardi (2004) hypothesize that, if liquidity shortages were significant, households in areas with larger housing capital should be more likely to start a business, controlling for regional economic conditions. The instrumental variable estimates show that while the coefficient on wealth-instrumented with regional house price appreciations-is negative, it is not statistically different from zero. Therefore, the study concludes that financing constraints are not a significant factor deterring the creation of new businesses in the US in the 1990s.

More recently, Schmalz et al. (2017) conducted a similar exercise but found a different result: that collateral frictions do reduce the creation of firms, as well as the size of resulting firms and their growth prospects. They exploited shocks to individual collateral originating in cross-regional variation in house prices in France, and found that firm creation by homeowners, as a treated group, is more responsive than firm creation by renters and homeowners with outstanding mortgages, as control group.

Unlike Hurst and Lusardi (2004), Schmalz et al. (2017) address this question using a within-region difference-in-differences methodology. They use changes in house price dynamics observed across 25 regions in France to compare at a micro level, within region, the entrepreneurial outcomes of homeowners versus home renters. This detail of analysis enables them to difference out local economic shocks that could simultaneously influence house prices and the creation of local businesses.[2] For example, if increases in house prices coincided with salary increases in the industries where start-ups are most common, then there could be less people opting for entrepreneurship in those regions. This scenario would be consistent both with the existence of financing constraints and with the estimates obtained by Hurst and Lusardi (2004).

Schmalz et al. (2017) investigate entrepreneurial outcomes from two perspectives: at the extensive margin, by studying entry decisions, and at the intensive margin, concerning the growth and survival of businesses that have previously entered the market. Both analyses employ French administrative micro-level data. For the decision to start new firms, they rely on the French Labor Force Survey from 1992 to 2002, which allows them to identify transitions from employment to entrepreneurship, as well as to gather information on individual homeownership and geography. For the analysis at the intensive margin, the authors use a large-scale survey run by the French Statistical Office to construct a sample of entrepreneurs who created firms in 1998. The survey provides detailed information about the entrepreneurs, as well as their location and homeownership prior to creating their firms. The firms are then matched with accounting information, covering the following years. Both analyses also use information on local house prices for 25 regions in France.

[2] The underlying assumption behind this approach is that such regional shocks, when they occur, are likely to affect in the same way homeowners and renters, *but for* the housing collateral channel.

A first econometric specification tests whether increases in the availability of housing collateral raise the probability to start new firms:

$$E_{i,j,t+1} = \alpha + \beta Owner_{i,t} * \Delta p_j^{t-6 \to t-1} + \theta Owner_{i,t} + \gamma Z_{i,t} + \\ + \tau Z_{i,t} * \Delta p_j^{t-6 \to t-1} + \gamma_l + \gamma_{jt} + \epsilon_{i,j,t} \quad (5.1)$$

where $E_{i,j,t+1}$ is a dummy variable equal to 1 if individual i, living in region j and surveyed in year t, becomes self-employed at date $t+1$. $\Delta p_j^{t-6 \to t-1}$ captures the cumulative increase in house prices in region i, for the five years prior to the survey. $Owner_{i,t}$ identifies the treatment group made of individuals who own their houses. To alleviate concerns that homeowners might be fundamentally different from renters, $Z_{i,t}$ includes controls for observables, such as education dummies, gender, foreign dummies, past wage, industry, age, and father's job. Interacting these controls with the variation in house prices should substantially alter the estimates if the response of self-employment to local house prices is determined by individual heterogeneity, and not strictly by the mechanics of the collateral channel.[3] Finally, γ_l and γ_{jt} are department and region*time fixed effects.

A positive β would indicate that entrepreneurial activity reacts to changes in the collateral available to individuals. The estimate is identified from two sources of variation. In the cross-section, regions experiencing larger house price growth should exhibit a relatively larger share of new entrepreneurs among house owners relative to house renters. And, across time, within a given region, the difference in entrepreneurial activity between homeowners and renters should increase, as house prices increase.

A second model measures whether businesses created when collateral availability increases are larger and more likely to survive. The specification employed is as follows:

$$Y_{i,j}^{1999} = \alpha + \phi Owner_i * \Delta p_j^{1992-1997} + \theta Owner_i + \gamma Z_i + \\ + \tau Z_i * \Delta p_j^{1992-1997} + \gamma_l + \gamma_{indXregion} + \epsilon_{i,j} \quad (5.2)$$

[3] For example, older individuals could be more likely to both own a house and open a business in industries that are more exposed to local economic upswings. In this case, failing to control for age and its interaction with house prices would bias the estimate of beta upwards.

$Y_{i,j}$ measures outcomes in 1999 (the first year after firm creation), among which the logarithm of assets, total sales, number of employees, total debt, and total wage bill. The $Owner_i$ is here equal to 1 when the business is created by a houseowner and 0 when the entrepreneur is a renter. The same model is then employed to measure outcomes in the medium term, by replacing the outcomes with their values in subsequent years. Hazard rates for firm survival can also be estimated, by constructing dummies equal to 1 when firm exits occur. Here, a positive ϕ would indicate that, in regions with high house price growth, homeowners create larger firms than renters, compared to regions with low house price growth.

The results of the estimations show that homeowners located in regions where house prices appreciate more are significantly more likely to create businesses than renters in the same regions. The effects are economically large: an increase of 16 percentage points in house prices leads to an 11% increase in the probability of becoming an entrepreneur. And, conditional on entry, firms created by homeowners have 13% larger assets. Treated firms-with higher owner collateral-also use more debt and create more value added than controls.

Therefore, contrary to Hurst and Lusardi (2004), who find that households from regions with strong house price appreciation are not more likely to start a business than households in other regions, Schmalz et al. (2017) present empirical evidence consistent with the collateral channel. By looking within region, at the relative outcomes of homeowners versus renters, they arrive at an effect that is better identified than in previous work.

While the analysis in Schmalz et al. (2017) could still be vulnerable to endogeneity-if, for example, shocks to local income expectations affected differentially homeowners and renters—, Cloyne et al. (2017) study the impact of house prices on individual borrowers by relying on an instrumental variable approach. They look at borrowing behaviour around the exogenously determined timing of home loan refinancing, using administrative panel data on the universe of mortgage contracts in the UK from 2005 to 2015.

In the UK, most mortgage loans have a predetermined, idiosyncratic reset date, typically within two to five years from the signing of the initial contract. And most borrowers do choose to refinance their mortgages at the reset date, as interest rates typically increase significantly after the initial fixed period. However, depending on when they signed their first loan contract, some borrowers are able to refinance their mortgage terms during stable economic times, while others have to do so during the Great Recession. Combining the predetermined individual contract reset dates with the macro context at the time of the reset, Cloyne et al. (2017) create quasi-experimental variation in house value. Because the same individual is observed multiple times as they reach more than one refinancing dates, the identification relies on within-individual variation.

The estimates show that house price appreciations indeed induce homeowners to increase borrowing, suggesting that they were previously constrained. Moreover, the new borrowing is financed mainly by home equity extraction. This provides additional and more robust evidence for the existence of a real estate collateral channel, at least at the individual level.

5.3.2 Real Estate Collateral and Credit

Chaney et al. (2012) study the collateral channel *at the firm level.* They investigate whether firm investment is sensitive to changes in the value of their assets. For this, they use local variations in the prices of real estate. As many firms pledge real estate assets when asking for a loan, these price variations are, effectively, shocks to the collateral the firms have available. The study focuses in US listed firms, and it uses Compustat accounting data covering 9211 firms, over the period 1993-2007. For each firm-year observation, the authors obtain the real estate assets of each firm, the location of the firm headquarter, and a range of financial indicators. The data is then combined with real estate prices at state and MSA levels, both for residential real estate, provided by the US Department of Housing and Urban Development, and with commercial real estate data from Global Real Analytics.

The identification relies on two sources of variation. First, Chaney et al. (2012) compare, within a local area, the sensitivity of investment to real estate prices across firms with or without real estate. Second, they compare investment by landholding firms across areas with different variations in real estate prices. The main econometric specification is as follows:

$$INV_{it} = \alpha_i + \delta_t + \beta * RE\ Value_{it} + \gamma P_t^l + controls_{it} + \epsilon_{it} \tag{5.3}$$

where INV is the ratio of investment to lagged tangible assets, and $RE\ Value$ is the ratio of the market value of real estate assets in year t to lagged tangible assets. P_t^l controls for the overall impact of real estate prices in location l, in year t, irrespective of whether a firm owns real estate or not. Controls include the ratio of cash flows to lagged tangible assets, and the market to book value of assets. The coefficient β estimates a composite measure of firm heterogeneity in both the strength of financing frictions and the available real estate assets that the firm can pledge. For the average firm in the sample, β measures what fraction of the increase in the value of its real estate collateral is allocated to financing investment.

While this specification is vulnerable to two main sources of endogeneity, the authors take additional steps to address them. A first possible concern is that real estate prices may be correlated with the investment opportunities of landholding firms. This could occur as a result of reverse causality-if large firms which increase investment have a non-negligible impact on the local demand for real estate-or due to omitted variables-if the real estate price measures are in fact good proxies for local demand shocks and if landowning firms are more sensitive to such shocks. To address this first source of endogeneity, Chaney et al. (2012) instrument local real estate prices with the interaction between long-term interest rates and local housing supply elasticity. A second source of endogeneity stems from the fact that a firm's decision of whether to own or lease real estate may be correlated with its investment opportunities. To measure whether this bias exists, the authors control for observable determinants that are likely to be correlated with the ownership decision (age, assets, return on assets, as well as industry and state dummies), and for their interaction with the main explanatory variable. The estimates remain unchanged in the main equation, suggesting that the coefficient on the real estate price variable identifies indeed collateral frictions, and not unobserved firm investment opportunities. The complete instrumental variable model employed is as follows:

$$INV_{it} = \alpha_i + \delta_t + \beta * RE\ \hat{Value}_{it} + \gamma \hat{P}_t^{\,l} + \sum_k \kappa_k * X_k^i * \hat{P}_t^{\,l} + controls_{it} + \epsilon_{it} \tag{5.4}$$

where $RE\ \hat{Value}_{it}$ and $\hat{P}_t^l$ use price estimates from the first stage regression:

$$P_t^l = \alpha_l + \delta_t + \gamma * Elasticity^l * InterestRates_t + u_t^l \tag{5.5}$$

The estimates of both models show consistently that over the 1993-2007 sample period, the representative US corporation invested approximately \$ 0.06 out of each \$ 1 of additional collateral. This provides support for the existence of the "collateral channel" at firm level: firms with more valuable collateral secure more funding, and invest more.

Catherine et al. (2018) follow up on this finding as they set out to quantify in a the effect of these collateral constraints on overall economic output. Starting from a simplified version of the empirical specification in Chaney et al. (2012), Catherine et al. (2018) first confirm the elasticity of firm investment to real estate collateral. This estimated elasticity is then used to estimate a structural model of firm dynamics where investment is conditioned by collateral constraints. Finally, this model is included in a general equilibrium model which allows the authors to quantify the total output loss associate with the constraints. This is relative to a theoretical benchmark: an economy without financing constraints.

The estimates show that the output loss from financing constraints can be as large as 11%. Moreover, most of this effect cannot be explained by resource misallocation across firms, but rather by aggregated under-investment in the economy. In fact, when firms are constrained, the stock of capital in the economy is smaller. This implies that the representative consumer undersaves and supplies too little labour relative to the unconstrained economy.

In addition to this direct effect that collateral constraints can have on the economy, Asriyan et al. (2018) introduce a different type of misallocation possibly caused by inflated values of real estate collateral. Collateral and direct borrower screening are to a certain extent substitute tools that lenders can use to deal with asymmetric information in the pool of borrowers. When credit booms increase the value of the overall collateral pledged, lenders might prefer to use relatively more collateral as a screening device. In return, they might allocate less resources into screening. In aggregate, this could lead to a suboptimal level of information production. As booms are typically followed by busts, the recovery period from a credit booms might be particularly hard as the economic agents need to rebuild the stock of information. This is a possible theoretical explanation as to why credit booms are usually followed by periods of low economic growth.

To test this hypothesis, Asriyan et al. (2018) use US-firm-level data from Compustat and an empirical approach based on regional real estate price variations such as in Chaney et al. (2012). In a first step, the authors confirm that a rise in collateral values coincides with an increase in investment and output. The second step-and the most challenging one-is a test of whether an increase in collateral values leads to information depletion through a decline in screened investment. But measuring the informational content of investment is challenging. Asriyan et al. (2018) employ three common measures of information from the corporate finance literature: the bid-ask spread on the firm's stock, the number of financial analysts that follow the firm, and the ratio of intangible assets to tangible fixed assets of the sector in which the firm operates. Then they show that the reaction of investment to collateral is stronger for firms with less information available. A final test assesses the implications for the subsequent recovery. Investment during the bust years (2007-2012) appears negatively correlated with the investment undertaken during the boom (2001–2006) into firms with less available information.

5.3.3 *Movable Collateral and Credit*

Another way to ease financing constraints, especially for firms that do not own sufficient real estate, is to enlarge the collateral contracting space by allowing borrowers to pledge more types of collateral. However, in countries with weaker institutions, pledging movable assets will not really resolve asymmetric information problems. Institutional improvement may then "solve" this by regulating the use of movable assets-machinery and equipment-as collateral. In financially constrained sectors, such changes in eligible collateral should directly translate into increases in the number of loans backed by such collateral, thereby increasing access to credit and investment for firms that rely more intensively on machinery and equipment in their production process. This is what Campello and Larrain (2015) show, using as a research design the introduction of a new legal provision in Romania in 2000 ("Law 99"). This law allowed Romanian firms to pledge movable collateral for the first time.

They collect data from Amadeus, the most comprehensive data repository gathering financial statement information on European firms, which is compiled by Bureau van Dijk. While Amadeus includes very comprehensive information on Romanian firms, the coverage in Eastern Europe is typically more reduced. However, the authors are able to extend parts of their analysis to a sample of ten Eastern European countries, which implemented similar laws regarding movable collateral, but at different points in time.

For their empirical strategy, Campello and Larrain (2015) first divide firms into treatment and control groups according to whether they belong to sectors intensive in movable assets (i.e., sectors with a ratio of movable assets/total assets in the top quartile). Then, they estimate the following difference-in-differences specification to capture the effect of the law on the change in leverage of firms reliant on movable assets:

$$\Delta Leverage_{ist} = \alpha_i + \alpha_t + \beta * Post_t * HighMovableAssets_s + \gamma X_{ist} + \epsilon_{ist} \tag{5.6}$$

where $Post_t$ is a dummy that equals zero before the reform year and one afterwards, $HighMovableAssets_s$ is a dummy that equals one if the firm belongs to the treated group (sectors in the top quartile of the "movable assets/total assets" ratio), and zero if the firm belongs to the control group (sectors in the bottom quartile of the "movable assets/total assets" ratio). X_{ist} denotes a vector of firm-level controls that includes size, age, profitability, and overall tangibility, while α_i and α_t are firm fixed effects and year fixed effects.

The estimation points to a positive and significant β, suggesting that the reform indeed increased the leverage of firms in movable-intensive sectors by 3.7 percentage points more than in firms in non-intensive sectors. The effect is confirmed in cross-country specifications, across the sample of ten Eastern European countries, enhancing the external validity of the estimate. Moreover, replacing the dependent variable with other financial indicators shows that relaxing the collateral menu can have important real effects. After the law, treated firms increased investment employment, productivity, and sales relative to controls.

Beyond the effects at firm level, such laws affecting the interplay between movable and non-movable collateral in loan contracts could have large reallocation effects, if they tilt industry composition towards sectors intensive in movable assets. To measure whether this was indeed the case in Romania, Latvia, and Poland, Campello and Larrain (2015) calculate the share of aggregated fixed assets allocated to sectors intensive in movable assets out of total assets. Plotting this share across time, they observe important increases immediately following the introduction of collateral reforms, for the three countries. This is evidence suggesting that collateral reforms indeed led to a fast and pronounced sectoral change in the industrial structure and asset utilization mix of the three countries, with implications for the profile of the industrial workforce.

While analysing also a change in the legal framework that affected the value of movable collateral in Sweden, Cerqueiro et al. (2016) rely on detailed lending data to document how banks adjust loan contracts and their own monitoring behaviour in response. They study a specific type of movable collateral, floating liens. A floating lien is a security interest in prespecified classes of "movable" property, such as inventories or accounts receivable, in which the individual assets are not specifically identified. Before 2004, in Sweden, floating liens were special priority claims that enabled creditors to seize a firm's property outside bankruptcy and without court intervention. However, since January 1, 2004, that special priority has been abolished, reducing the pool of eligible assets as collateral. Cerqueiro et al. (2016) use this change in law to generate quasi-experimental variation in collateral value and study the effects on the remaining terms of the loan contract. As interest rates, loan amounts, and collateral values are typically co-determined, this set-up allows the authors to separately identify the role of collateral. To do so, they employ bank loan-level data, covering 2002 to 2005, with information on loan volumes, interest rates, collateral values, borrower characteristics assigned by the bank, and the frequency of monitoring.

By comparing the reaction to this legal shock of borrowers that pledged floating liens outstanding around the change in the law with a group of similar control loans granted to borrowers in the same industry that did not pledge floating liens during our sample period, Cerqueiro et al. (2016) document four empirical results. First, following the change in the law, the bank reduces the estimated value of the outstanding collateral by 13%. Second, the bank increases the interest rate on outstanding treated loans by 20 basis points. Third, following the legal change, the bank reviews less frequently the condition of both the borrower and the assets they pledged as collateral. This finding empirically confirms theoretical models claiming that collateral and monitoring are complementary.[4] And, fourth, following the abolishment of the special priority rights, the tightening credit conditions and the reduction in bank monitoring, 12 percentage points more borrowers experience payment delinquency problems.

[4] For example, Rajan and Winton (1995) argue that, in the presence of other claimants, monitoring is valuable because it allows the lender to demand (additional) collateral if the firm is at increased risk of distress.

5.3.4 *Patent Collateral and Credit*

While the previous evidence suggests that firms in sectors reliant on real estate or movable assets can at least partially ease financing constraints by pledging these assets as collateral, ensuring sufficient funding can be a bigger challenge for start-ups. Among these, technological start-ups might have the highest need for debt but they might simultaneously experience more difficulties in securing the funds. This is because they are mostly reliant on risky, unproven technologies. Such intangible assets are typically hard to value ex ante and sell in case of distress. Assessing the importance of financing constraints for technological start-ups has been difficult so far, because loans to these types of firms are typically underreported.

Hochberg et al. (2018) take the first step in addressing this question in a new approach: they identify loans to start-ups from a list of patents pledged as collateral and reported to the US Patent and Trademark Office (USPTO). In the US, lenders have strong incentives to record the security interest on a patent. This ensures that the lender is the first in line to be paid if assets are liquidated, and reveals their status to outside parties. Hochberg et al. (2018) then match these reports with a database of US venture capital-backed firms from the Dow Jones VentureSource (DJVS). To focus on technological start-ups, they restrict the sample to start-ups owning patents and active in three innovation-intensive sectors (software, semiconductor devices, and medical devices). The period studied extends from 1987 to 2008.

In empirical tests, the authors measure the correlation between the probability of obtaining a loan backed by patent collateral and trading intensity in the secondary market for similar patents. The results suggest that patents are indeed useful as collateral in the market for venture capital. Patents expand entrepreneurial financing opportunities, so long as they can be sold in a relatively liquid secondary market. Overall, a 1 percentage point increase in patent trading is associated with an increase in the predicted debt rate of 1.10 percentage points. This correlation increases when start-ups have patents that are more redeployable to alternative uses and, hence, less firm-specific. Again, this is consistent with the mechanics of the collateral channel: lenders are more inclined to provide loans against patent collateral when the value of the collateral is maintained in case its owner enters distress.

In fact, as Mann (2018) shows, pledging patents is an important source of funding, particularly of innovations, even for listed US corporations. In

2013, 38% of the US firms that held patents used them as collateral. These firms accounted for 20% of the R&D expenses recorded in Compustat. Therefore, policy initiatives aimed at increasing the pledgeability patents, such as granting and recording patents, might be particularly powerful in alleviating financing frictions for innovation. Developing secondary market infrastructure for trading patents could substantially reduce such frictions for technological start-ups, if their patents can be easily purchased and redeployed by larger corporations.

5.4 Collateral and Law

So far, this chapter reviewed the existing evidence supporting empirically the collateral channel, according to which borrowers can ease financing constraints when they pledge assets that lenders can claim in default. The fact that collateral in whichever shape it comes-real estate, movable assets, or patents-alleviates financing constraints suggests that lending markets do not function perfectly. A complementary stream of literature (Calomiris et al. 2017; Degryse et al. 2016; Mann 2018) shows that the strength of the collateral channel varies with the legal framework. Therefore, regulators looking to improve lending flows can simultaneously act on the opportunity value of collateral and on the legal frameworks allowing lenders to extract value from it.

Calomiris et al. (2017) and Degryse et al. (2016) illustrate the importance of legal frameworks by studying how lending terms on loans secured with movable collateral vary in a cross-section of countries with different creditor rights. Calomiris et al. (2017) explore how this differential strength in creditor rights affects the supply of loans for loans secured with movable versus immovable collateral. Their data comprises the loan portfolio of a global bank active over 2002-2004 in 16 emerging market countries. The key here is that each loan contains the liquidation value of the asset pledged as collateral. This allows the authors to construct loan to value ratios across loans secured with the two types of collateral and across countries with different legal sophistication. The ratios are the main proxy used for loan supply.

Cross-country differences in the quality of movable collateral laws are summarized in an index based on information from World Bank's Doing Business report. The index is a summary measure of the binary scores allocated by the World Bank to eight different components that enforce a favourable legal regime for movable collateral. The components refer to the scope of the assets that can be pledged, whether formal registries exist for the monitoring of these transactions and the ease with which lenders can take possession of the collateral in default. The index ranges from 0 to 7, with seven being the most favourable legal framework.

Using again a methodology, Calomiris et al. (2017) first document that the loan-to-value ratios for loans collateralized with movable assets are stronger in strong-law countries, that is, in countries with a higher value of the index. This difference is likely to be explained by the legal treatment of movable collateral, because-the authors find-loan-to-value ratios for loans collateralized by immovable assets are similar across the countries in the sample. The magnitudes documented are large: the loan-to-value ratios of loans collateralized with movable assets are on average 27.6 percentage points higher relative to loans collateralized with immovable assets, in strong-law countries relative to weak-law countries. To ensure that these results are not driven by unobservable variables at country level, the analysis then focuses on one country, Slovakia. Slovakia passed a legal reform that significantly facilitated the use of movable collateral in 2003. Analysing leading terms within this one country, but also comparing them with the evolution of its neighbour, Czech Republic, where there was no legal reform, upholds the results.

Second, Calomiris et al. (2017) study the real consequences of collateral legal frameworks, by looking at whether cross-country law differences affect the sectoral allocation of resources among manufacturing firms. They estimate the following equation:

$$Share_{sc} = \alpha_s + \beta * Law_c * REI_s + \gamma X_c REI_s + \epsilon_{sc} \tag{5.7}$$

where $Share_{sc}$ is the ratio of sectoral output-across 22 industries or sectors, in 10 emerging countries-Law_c is a 0/1 dummy separating countries in weak-versus-strong law enforcement, and REI_s is a 0/1 dummy separating sectors in weak-versus-strong real estate intensity. The model is further saturated with sector fixed effects and country characteristics which might have an impact on sectoral allocation.[5]

[5] These additional country characteristics are time to enforce a contract, time to resolve insolvency, prevalence of rule of law, and strength of property rights.

The estimates imply that weak-law countries allocate 15.4% more production to immovable-intensive sectors than strong-law countries. These differences are plausibly driven by the combination of financing frictions and collateral laws that discriminate by asset type. In consequence, improvements in legal frameworks might reduce distortions in the allocation of resources in weak-law countries.

In contemporaneous work, Degryse et al. (2016) underline the precise channel through which better creditor protection affects bank lending and real outcomes. While they also rely on the international portfolio of a large bank, Degryse et al. (2016) include in their analysis loan-level liquidation values estimated by the lender for different types of collateral, as well as interest rates on the loans. This allows the authors to observe that the same lender will estimate lower recovery rates on movable relatively to immovable collateral, in countries with a relatively weaker law enforcement. In return, the lender will charge higher interest rates on these loans. As a result, economies where the prevailing law guarantees better enforcement of creditor rights might experience more vigorous credit growth and higher output.

To empirically measure how different legal frameworks affect the liquidation value of collateralized assets, Degryse et al. (2016) rely on detailed loan-level data from the SME lending branch of a large international bank. The data uniquely includes the type of asset pledged behind every loan, as well as its expected liquidation value and market value. The authors devise an indicator of creditor rights, which describes the local efficiency of debt enforcement, and is heterogeneous across countries. This indicator is based on three pillars: the strength of the written laws, or "rules in the book"; the efficiency of enforcement in practice; and whether the country set up any formal information-sharing mechanisms on borrower credit history. Each country in the sample is rated according to how well it performs along these dimensions, and then allocated to one of two groups: low-credit rights country or high-creditor-rights country.

While the legal framework is naturally heterogeneous across countries, there is also substantial heterogeneity on how it impacts different types of assets. Discrepancies between the market value and the liquidation value of different assets occur, for example, when the design of contracts is imperfect, their enforcement is too lengthy, and the lender struggles to find buyers to monetize the assets. The discrepancies tend to be larger for movable collateral (such as machinery, equipment, inventory, and accounts receivable) and smaller for non-movable collateral (real estate or financial assets). Since movable collateral tends to be more business-specific, it is generally sold in less liquid markets.

The empirical analysis exploits this double layer of heterogeneity, as it proceeds in three mains steps. First, the authors document a positive relationship between the average liquidation value of collateral and the strength of country-level enforcement of credit rights. They find that, on average, liquidation values are 17.6% higher in high-creditor-rights countries. Second, they employ the following econometric specification to measure, at a loan level, and within country, whether there are any discrepancies in the recovery rates of loans collateralized with the two types of assets, movable or non-movable:

$$RecoveryRate_{k,i,c,t} = \alpha_c + \alpha_t + \alpha_j + \beta_1 * Movable_k + \gamma_1 Firm_{i,t} + \epsilon_{k,i,c,t} \tag{5.8}$$

where $RecoveryRate_{k,i,c,t}$ denotes the bank's on asset type k securing a loan to borrower i in country c, originated at time t. α_c, α_t, and α_j are country, time, and industry fixed effects, absorbing unobserved confounding characteristics. $Movable_k$ is a $0/1$ variable indicating the type of collateral, while $Firm_{i,t}$ includes firm characteristics. The estimate, β_1, measures the difference in recovery rates within the same country and should be negative when movable collateral is identified with a dummy equal to 1.

A second specification measures how this coefficient varies across low-enforcement versus high-enforcement countries:

$$\begin{aligned} RecoveryRate_{k,i,c,t} &= \alpha_c + \alpha_t + \alpha_j + \beta_1 Movable_k + \\ &+ \beta_2 Movable_k * CreditorRights_c + \gamma_1 Firm_{i,t} + \epsilon_{k,i,c,t} \end{aligned} \tag{5.9}$$

Here, $CreditorRights_c$ is a dummy equal to one for a high-creditor-rights country and zero for a low-creditor-rights country. As above, β_1 should be negative, if recovery rates differ between movable and non-movable collateral, but β_2 should be positive, as this difference should be less pronounced in high-enforcement countries.

There are, however, two assumptions underlying these specifications. First, that omitted country factors affect in the same way movable and non-movable collateral. But, they could indeed affect movable and immovable collateral differently. And second, that firms borrowing against movable collateral are similar to firms borrowing against non-movable collateral. However, borrowers could self-select into loans with each type of collateral, as a result of unobservable individual characteristics. To support the first assumption, Degryse et al. (2016) include an interaction term between each country's GDP and the collateral type.

To provide empirical support for the second assumption, they employ a within-borrower framework:

$$RecoveryRate_{k,i,c,t} = \alpha_i + \alpha_j + \beta_1 Movable_k + \\ + \beta_2 Movable_k * CreditorRights_c + \gamma_1 Firm_{i,t} + \epsilon_{k,i,c,t} \quad (5.10)$$

where α_i are borrower-fixed effects.

The results confirm the hypothesis that the value of movable collateral is lower than the value of non-movable collateral, and that this is especially true in emerging markets. Across the different estimations, the authors document consistently that the liquidation values for movable assets are on average 30.7 percentage points higher relative to the liquidation value for other assets, in countries with strong creditor protection relative to countries with weak credit protection.

The lower recovery rates on loans with movable collateral are reflected in significantly higher interest rates. In specifications with time and borrower-fixed effects, where the comparison is made between loans granted to the same borrower while also controlling for changes in loan and borrower characteristics, the interest rates are on average 31.8 bps higher on loans backed by movable collateral relative to loans backed by immovable collateral. Moreover, this negative relationship between expected recovery values and interest rates prevails only in countries with weak enforcement of creditor rights.

But while many emerging countries have passed legal reforms that facilitate the repossession and deployability of movable collateral, there is less consensus that this should also be the case for patent collateral. It is unclear whether stronger credit rights to patents stimulate or hurt investment in innovation. On the one hand, stronger creditor rights will increase collateral value and loan-to-value ratios. On the other hand, they can also discourage risk-taking by allocating more bargaining power to creditors in the event of financial distress. While this is true for other types of collateral, the downsides are plausibly more important in innovative industries, where higher risks are other rewarder with the right to monetize the patent for many years. Using quasi-experimental evidence from court decisions that strengthened creditor rights for patenting firms incorporated in Delaware, Mann (2018) shows that stronger law enforcement on patents is also associated with increases in debt and investment at affected firms.

The study investigates these outcomes at mature firms that hold patents. The sample comes from the Compustat firms that also appear in the Patent Assignment Dataset from the United States Patent and Trademark Office (USPTO). The data set included information on which patents are used as collateral. To study the relationship between collateral patents and the financing of innovations, Mann (2018) exploits four court decisions, from 2002, 2003, 2007, and 2009, that limited the cases in which federal patent law supersedes state-level property law in the US. While these changes did not have a big impact for most of the US, prior to this, the state of Delaware has relatively stronger pro-creditor property rights. The court decisions reinforced the latter, thus effectively strengthening creditor rights for patent collateral.

Using difference-in-differences specifications on firms incorporated in Delaware versus firms incorporated elsewhere, the author finds that the total debt at the former rose by $1 on average for every $100 of total book assets in the two years on average following a court decision. This increase in access to finance for innovative firms appears to have translated into higher investment levels. Over the same period, R&D spending at treated firms rose by $0.17 for every $100 of total assets on average, following a court decision. Moreover, the estimates show no effect on investment in tangible capital, which provides support to the hypothesis that increasing the collateral value of patents alleviates credit constraints particularly for investment in R&D.

5.5 Conclusion

A large fraction of individual and commercial loans are backed by some type of collateral, which, from a revealed preference perspective, suggests that financing frictions are still important to alleviate ex ante and ex post frictions in credit markets. The empirical banking literature has long struggled to formally establish the existence of these frictions, but recent years have seen significant progress in this direction. The main hurdle came from the difficulty to establish causality due to the simultaneity of financial constraints and economic growth. Recent contributions reviewed here faced this hurdle with great creativity: by instrumenting real estate collateral with local housing supply elasticities, combining microdata with legal interventions, or by exploiting discontinuities in loan contract terms. The findings from these studies robustly suggest that the availability of both real estate and movable collateral greatly facilitate credit flows, especially in informationally opaque markets.

There are still several frontiers in this literature that are worth pushing. One of them concerns the role of patent collateral, particularly for innovative start-ups that are supported less by tangibles and more by the intangible know-how of the entrepreneurs. While there has been some progress in this direction, the challenge is still to find robust ways to capture the monetary value and pledgeability of this type of intangible assets. Another avenue to explore is related to the role of FinTech lenders, which are platforms that intermediate lending flows between final investors and borrowers. So far, this credit innovation has been able to function without relying on collateral. The last chapter of this book offers a thorough review of the interaction between FinTech and lending. Finally, there is a whole dimension of collateral in banking that is beyond the scope of this book: central bank collateral as a new tool for monetary policy. The massive provision of liquidity by central banks in the aftermath of the 2008 financial crisis was backed by banking collateral. To access the liquidity operations, commercial banks have built large stocks of securitized assets, sovereign or commercial bonds, or loan portfolios. In this set-up, it is indispensable to understand to what extent collateral types and cut-offs set by central banks have influenced the production of assets in the economy.

CHAPTER 6

Global Banking

The degree to which the global banking system is integrated has important consequences for the transmission of monetary policy and economic shocks between monetary areas. Further, it has implications for firms' access to finance and potentially the real economy, other than the country where the shocks originate (host countries). Hence, the integration of the global banking system has implications for the stability of the global financial system. It is important for policymakers to have an understanding of these effects, so that they are better able to design policy that has its desired impact. Further, these policies may "spill over" across borders, potentially implying a need for international coordination in local prudential policy-making.

While there is evidence of financial disintegration of European countries since the 2008 financial crisis and the subsequent sovereign debt crisis (Chakraborty et al. 2017), Member States have since agreed to the creation of a Banking Union, further integrating the EU banking system (European Commission 2017). Financial disintegration impairs firms' access to capital which results in lower output. Chakraborty et al. (2017) model the cost of financial disintegration since the financial crisis to be a 0.54% drop in output in Europe, a significant loss to the economy. However, there are risks associated with financial integration and the speed at which financial integration occurs, such as its effect on financial stability (Popov and Ongena 2011). Understanding this trade-off is important in designing

A. Bilan et al., *Banking and Financial Markets*, Palgrave Macmillan Studies in Banking and Financial Institutions,
https://doi.org/10.1007/978-3-030-26844-2_6

regulation that fosters the benefits of financial integration while limiting the costs.

The earlier literature used the foreign spillovers to identify credit supply effects. Some of the earlier papers found evidence that shocks to the Japanese financial system were transmitted to the US bank lending market (Peek and Rosengren 1997), and this had an impact on the real economy in the US (Peek and Rosengren 2000). However, the literature only truly developed following the financial crisis. Its aim has been to understand the implications of global banking for cross-border economic shock transmission, including monetary policy (Bräuning and Ivashina 2017; Morais et al. 2019; Buch et al. 2019), and other economic shocks (Cetorelli and Goldberg 2012b; Ongena et al. 2015, 2018). From a regulatory viewpoint, the concept of "cross-border lending" was not mentioned in regulatory guidelines until 2006 (Aiyar et al. 2014).

Global banking models have evolved from relatively straightforward exporting of local impulses (Peek and Rosengren 1997) to more complex models involving global loan portfolios and liquidity management (Cetorelli and Goldberg 2012a; Giannetti and Laeven 2012). They borrow heavily from the bank lending channel literature (Kashyap and Stein 2000), and incorporate foreign exchange, through FX Swaps (Bräuning and Ivashina 2017), as well as study real effects (Ongena et al. 2015; Morais et al. 2019).

In the sections that follow, we begin by providing an overview of the main concepts in the literature and the different channels of economic shock transmission. We then review the data and methodologies employed in the global banking literature. Following this, we provide an in-depth analysis on a selection of papers. Particularly, we focus on the papers that seek to answer questions such as: How does (interbank) integration affect borrowing constraints, loan rates, and output? How and why do banks establish foreign affiliates (branches and subsidiaries)? How do the assets of a local bank's foreign affiliates affect their sensitivity to local funding shocks? How do banks change their local lending in response to shocks to their foreign funding sources (inward transmission)? How do banks change their foreign lending in response to shocks to their local funding sources (outward transmission)? How do foreign banks adjust their central bank reserves in response to local monetary policy changes? Finally, how does global banking interact with macroprudential regulation?

6.1 The International Transmission of Financial Shocks

The main concept in the literature is that global banks have global balance sheets which can be shocked by monetary policy changes (Cetorelli and Goldberg 2012a; Buch et al. 2019) or other economic shocks (Cetorelli and Goldberg 2012b; Ongena et al. 2015), in their home countries or the host (foreign) countries of their affiliates (branches and subsidiaries). In the global banking context monetary shocks can be distinguished as being transmitted either inward or outward. An inward transmission defined as foreign monetary policy affecting domestic banks' lending, foreign affiliate lending to local firms, and cross-border lending to local firms. Similarly, an outward transmission of monetary policy occurs when local monetary policy affects the lending of local banks' foreign affiliates, foreign banks in their local markets, and local banks' cross-border lending. These shocks, in turn, affect the allocation of capital between the head office and affiliates, impacting loan supply in both home and host country.

The altering of individual banks' home and host country loan portfolios impacts the proportion of loans granted by global banks, as a whole, in the host country. Thus, shocks in the home country have the potential to affect the credit cycle in host countries (Giannetti and Laeven 2012). Lastly, the decision to readjust an international loan portfolio and liquidity management (central bank deposits) also takes into account the FX market and the cost of hedging (Bräuning and Ivashina 2017). Figure 6.1 provides a stylized diagram of the mechanisms in the global banking literature.

The literature that focuses on (international) monetary policy transmission through global banks identifies two main channels: the bank lending channel and the balance sheet channel. These transmission channels focus on different frictions which banks face. While the bank lending channel relies on the friction of the funding costs of banks, the balance sheet channel works through altering the risk structure of banks' assets. Hence, while focusing on different frictions the bank lending channel is often said to be more narrow but still comprised in the bank balance sheet channel.

According to the bank lending channel, the impact of monetary policy works through changing banks liquidity constraints and short-term funding costs. Here an increase in the monetary policy rate causes a reduction in deposits in the banking system. The reduction in deposits is purported to be a result of either a direct change to reserves which determines the amount of deposits, or by altering the relative yields of deposits and other assets. This altering of relative yields modifies the households demand for

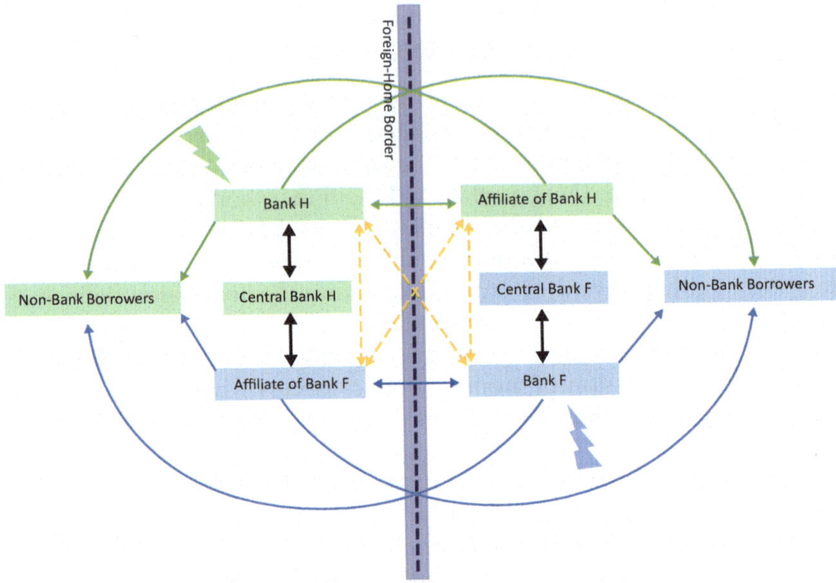

Fig. 6.1 Stylized global banking system diagram
Note: This stylized diagram of the global banking system includes the mechanisms which the global banking literature seeks to understand. Here, blue represents effects originating in the home country banks or the foreign affiliates of these banks. Green represents the same for foreign banks or local affiliates of foreign banks. The yellow arrows represent the global interbank market where home banks lend to other local banks, foreign banks, and local affiliates of foreign banks. An inward transmission of monetary policy is represented as follows: the arrows from the foreign central bank, Central Bank F, to the affiliate of the home bank, Affiliate of Bank H, and the foreign bank, Bank F, represent the transmission of monetary policy through these banks. These banks then transmit this foreign monetary policy to Non-Bank Borrowers in the home country, in green. This is done directly through cross-border flows (the curved arrows) or through home banks, Bank H, or local affiliates of foreign banks, Affiliate of Bank F. The diagram also shows the outward transmission of the monetary policy. This follows a similar path as the inward transmission but where the monetary policy originates from the home central bank, Central Bank H. The dashed vertical line depicts the boarded between the home country and the foreign country. The area around this dashed line represents the friction of foreign exchange. Finally, the lightning bolts represent shocks to the foreign bank, blue, or the home bank, green. Here “shocks” can either be shocks to the assets of these banks or changes in macroprudential policy

deposits. Banks which are not able to frictionlessly substitute the reduction in deposits with other sources of financing, reduce their loan supply.

Disyatat (2011) proposes the reverse view in which loans drive deposits. The author models monetary policy as working through increasing the external finance premium that banks face, which is determined by their balance sheet strength and risk perception. Here the potency of monetary policy is determined by the banks' reliance on market-based funding, where a greater reliance results in a more potent monetary policy mechanism.

Both views rely on banks' access to (market-based) funding. Therefore, banks will have a heterogeneous response to monetary policy if they differ in their liquidity, reliance on deposit funding, and reliance on wholesale funding. Hence, the capital ratio of banks, their access to liquidity from affiliated banks, and their size, which measures their access to funding, is expected to affect banks' response to monetary policy

The balance sheet channel of monetary policy proposes a different, broader mechanism, through which monetary policy affects the supply of loans in an economy. Under the balance sheet channel, monetary policy alters borrowers' balance sheet strength, and banks' sensitivity to borrowers' balance sheets. For example, a contractionary monetary policy reduces the creditworthiness of borrowers and causes banks to contract their loan supply. In the global banking literature, this may be viewed as a reduction in the collateral values of home country borrowers. Global banks respond to the reduction in local collateral values by shifting their loan supply to foreign borrowers, with safer assets. To measure the impact of this channel, the literature measures how the change in potency of monetary policy varies with banks characteristics such as their size, capitalization, and the riskiness of their assets: the ratio of securities to total assets and international asset holdings to total assets.

Further frictions may be important to the international transmissions of monetary policy that do not relate directly to the traditional channels. Firstly, related to the bank lending channel, global banks' access to the liquidity of their affiliates, or the other way around, may impact the potency of monetary policy, as well as its transmission across borders. Secondly, banks engaging in global banking are faced with foreign exchange frictions, and the costs and access to foreign exchange may impact the potency of cross-border monetary policy transmission. Thirdly, while the effect of regulation, particularly capital regulation, may be explained by the traditional frictions, different regulatory requirements imposed on banks in different countries may affect the potency of local monetary policy and its cross-border transmission. This is particularly relevant as Basel III introduces counter-cyclical capital buffers. If business cycles are asynchronous, this implies that the required counter-cyclical capital buffer will differ across countries. This may cause banks to shift their loan portfolios to countries whose banks are facing capital constraints as a result of these counter-cyclical buffers. Further, it may reduce the efficacy of capital regulation if foreign banks are able to pick up the slack from local banks.

6.2 Data

Global banking requires data across countries. For instance, the "perfect" data set to test the international transmission of monetary policy through banks would be a multi-country credit registry, combined with detailed data on banks and firms, and potentially enhanced with loan applications.[1] This unfortunately does not exist yet, due to the confidential nature of credit registries. However, the European System of Central Banks has set up a project, AnaCredit, with the aim of creating a multi-country credit registry dataset.[2] Although the data set is still under development, Altavilla et al. (2018) make use of the preparatory phase data set of AnaCredit in a multi-country study of the role of banking supervision for banks' risk-taking and its interaction with changes in monetary policy and the macroeconomic conditions in a country.

As a result, the data sets most frequently used for country-level studies are the Bank of International Settlements Locational Banking Statistics and, more recently, their Consolidated Banking Statistics. The Locational Banking Statistics database contains data on the composition of banks' balance sheets by currency, and a geographical breakdown for their counterparties. The Consolidated Banking Statistics database contains data on the worldwide consolidated country risk exposure of internationally active banks, with headquarters in countries which report to Bank for International Settlements.[3] In addition, information on bank lending

[1] See Jiménez et al. (2012) for the use of loan application data in identifying the bank balance sheet channel of monetary policy transmission.

[2] These countries are Austria, the Czech Republic, Belgium, France, Germany, Ireland, Italy, Lithuania, Latvia, Malta, Portugal, Romania, Slovenia, Slovakia, and Spain.

[3] Cerutti (2015) notes two criticisms of these datasets. Firstly, the level of borrow country credit exposures is often overstated due to the use of balance sheets claims as they do not represent the parent bank's legal exposure. Cerutti (2015) argues that this would be

behaviour across countries is sometimes available from surveys (an example being the Bank Lending Survey, carried out by the Eurosystem). However, aggregation at the country level (or even the bank level) requires the strong assumption of homogeneous loan demand across banks. It is therefore crucial to control for borrower characteristics to avoid having to make this assumption.

Thus, a tension between internal and external validity is present in the global banking literature, even at the level of data comprehensiveness. To include the additional dimension of borrower information, the global banking literature has had to sacrifice coverage. For example, Morais et al. (2019) use the Mexican credit registry in order to identify the international credit channel of monetary policy. The data is rich enough to allow them to employ time-varying bank and firm effects, which benefits identification. Further, the granularity of the data allows the authors to test for heterogeneous real effects at the firm level. The ability to measure real effects is important, as the transmission of monetary policy or other economic shocks only matters if there are real effects. All this consolidates the internal validity of their study. However, the use of this data confines the analysis to a single country, which limits its external validity.

Syndicated loan data sets resolve this issue as they contain bank-firm data covering multiple countries. However, they have a different weakness. Although the data is sufficiently granular, syndicated loans tend to be large loans given to large firms. Using this data can hide credit supply effects on small and medium-sized firms. Further, a key requirement for monetary policy to have real effects is imperfect substitutability between bank lending and other financing sources. Large firms are likely to have better access to outside financing. Thus, an analysis using this data is likely to underestimate the real effects of the bank lending channel.[4]

Authors have found other ways to combine these data sets in ways that alleviate the tension between external and internal validity. Although not a multi-country credit registry, Ongena et al. (2015) employ granular data across countries and currency areas, combining multiple data sets to

better represented by the capital incorporated in the subsidiaries of the borrowing countries. Secondly, subsidiaries in borrower countries funding models are often dominated by local residents' deposits and are thus not necessarily dependent on parent bank/foreign funding sources.

[4] Aggregated bank or country-level data also suffers from this vulnerability, as lending to large firms drives aggregate loan volumes.

obtain bank-firm data on SMEs, across 13 countries.[5] This allows for the identification of the international bank lending channel and the analysis of its real effects, across a heterogeneous sample of firms. Popov and Ongena (2011) use the Business Environment and Enterprise Performance Survey (BEEPS), to create a synthetic panel dataset that can be merged with interbank market rates from the Global Financial database. This level of granularity in a panel structure allows for the modelling of the effects of financial integration on firms' access to bank credit (borrowing constraints) and the cost of bank credit (loan rates).

The choice of the monetary policy indicator is non-trivial, and is not always simply the central banks' policy rate. The correct measure depends on the currency area and time period under analysis. For example, the 3-month Euro Interbank Offered Rate (3m EURIBOR) is a common choice in studies of Eurozone countries, while the Bernanke and Mihov (1998) measure is often used for US studies. Further, the time period under analysis will affect the choice of the monetary policy indicator, where a distinction between periods of conventional and unconventional monetary policy affects this choice.

The shadow policy rate is an interest rate that captures the fact that the unconventional monetary policy can affect the long end of the yield curve and general liquidity conditions. The shadow rate has many advantages over policy rates in times of unconventional monetary policy. Firstly, shadow rates reflect changes to banks' funding conditions that are not reflected in the policy rate, such as quantitative easing. Moreover, as central banks' policy rate has a floor at zero, known as the zero lower bound, banks' funding conditions would appear unchanged if measured by the policy rate during this period. Additionally, shadow rates allow for the comparison between times of conventional and unconventional monetary policy as it translates unconventional monetary policy into a comparable nominal interest rate.

A common choice of shadow rate is the shadow rates calculated by Krippner (2016) which they provide on their website (Buch et al. 2019;

[5] They combine the bank-ownership database compiled by Claessens and van Horen (2014), bank funding data using Dealogic, bank balance sheet information from Bankscope, firm balance sheet information from Amadeus, and bank-firm connection information from Kompass. Note: Bureau van Dijk's Bankscope has been replaced by Moody's Analytics BankFocus.

Temesvary et al. 2018).[6] Krippner (2019) notes that authors should be cautious in selecting a particular shadow rate as there is no one correct shadow rate. This is because shadow rates are generated from shadow/lower-bound term structure models and are sensitive to minor choices in their estimation. The author recommends a process to evaluate shadow rates, in particular focusing on how well different shadow rates proxy for the Federal Funds Rate in periods where the policy rate is near the zero lower bound.

For unified measures of macroprudential policies, researchers have employed the database developed by the International Banking Research Network and International Monetary Fund. This database includes macroprudential policy instruments from 64 countries for the period 2000 to 2014. The macroprudential instruments include loan-to-value ratio limits, concentration on limits, interbank exposure limits, changes in reserve requirements, and capital requirements.[7]

6.3 Methodologies

In terms of econometric methodology, the global banking literature uses a range of panel data econometric techniques to aid in uncovering the transmission channels. These techniques, along with what makes them useful in a global banking context, are discussed below.

As in the bank lending channel literature, if researchers want to be able to say anything about a shock transmission through banks, they need to disentangle loan demand from loan supply. This is because we view an equilibrium outcome. Initial work on the bank lending channel literature (Kashyap and Stein 2000) relied on proxies for time-varying loan demand, such as GDP growth, and on the assumption that all banks face homogeneous loan demand. Recent literature on the bank lending channel and on global banking have employed more sophisticated approaches, such as using time-varying country/firm effects (Altunbas et al. 2010; Bräuning and Ivashina 2017) or explicitly modelling firm heterogeneity (Ongena et al. 2015).

[6] The python code used to estimate the shadow rate in Krippner (2016) is available at: www.github.com/as4456/Leo_Krippner_SSR.

[7] See Cerutti et al. (2017) for a detailed description of the database.

The interaction of time and country fixed effects (e.g., country-year fixed effects) is used to control for country-level loan demand and other time varying country-level effects (omitted variables). This fixed effect specification absorbs factors such as the demand for bank debt in a particular country, at a particular time. By including these country-level effects, researchers are able to make statements about effects at the bank level, that is, how changes in the supply of bank loans vary by banks' characteristics. Put differently, the inclusion of these fixed effects allows researchers to analyse within-country variation.

Another fixed effect specification is the use of both bank-year fixed effects and firm-year fixed effects. The former controls for bank factors that vary with time, such as the shock to Japanese banks documented in Peek and Rosengren (1997), cause an overall contraction in lending by these banks at that particular time. The latter controls for loan demand factors at the borrower level.[8] Bräuning and Ivashina (2017) are able to use this fixed effect specification because they employ data from the syndicated loan market in which loans involve multiple banks and where banks lend to multiple firms, that is, bank-firm-level data. As a result, the authors are able to make statements about bank-firm-level factors (e.g., the probability of firm i obtaining a loan from bank j in time t), while controlling for time-varying bank and firm-specific effects.

However, the use of fixed effects does not come without its disadvantages, as Khwaja and Mian (2008) make clear. With loan-level (bank-firm-level) data, the use of firm-level fixed effects can effectively exclude parts of the sample and potentially diminish external validity. This occurs as many firms, especially SMEs, have a relationship with only one bank (Degryse et al. 2009). A solution is to control for observable key firm characteristics. Khwaja and Mian (2008) show that after controlling for firm characteristics, including firm-level fixed effects has little impact on the estimated coefficient. In Ongena et al. (2015), this problem is particularly relevant as their data set contains mainly SMEs, and the inclusion of firm-level fixed effects would have excluded two-thirds of their sample. They resolve this issue by following the solution of Khwaja and Mian (2008), while employing higher-level fixed effects (country and industry).

[8] The use of this fixed effect specification, in the global banking literature, often includes the country-time effects, or explicit controls for macro-effects at country level, for example GDP growth rates.

In addition, the literature often makes use of lags of the dependent variable. The number of lags used varies and depends on the frequency of the data (4 lags for quarterly; 12 lags for monthly). Such dynamic panel data models are constructed to allow for dynamics in changes of the loan supply. They reflect the fact that changes in monetary policy takes time to percolate into the banking system. However, the inclusion of dynamics in what is often a fixed effects regression causes inconsistency in the parameter estimates (Nickell 1981).

Once demand and supply have been disentangled, the traditional bank lending channel literature explains heterogeneous changes to banks' loan supply by differences in banks' characteristics, such as size (Kashyap and Stein 2000). This raises a potential issue of simultaneity bias as a bank's loan growth affects its size. To resolve this issue, the traditional literature uses bank size in the previous period, as it is unlikely to be determined by its growth in loans in the current period. As a precaution, the literature tends to lag all bank characteristics, whether the potential for simultaneity bias is clear or not. The global banking literature has used the same approach (Cetorelli and Goldberg 2012a).

The potential for independent variables to be endogenous and the problem of Nickell bias in these dynamic panel data models has led the bank lending channel literature to adopt estimation techniques that specifically address these issues, such as the Generalized Method of Moments (GMM) estimators developed by Arellano and Bond (1991) and extended by Arellano and Bover (1995) and Blundell and Bond (1998).[9] Once again, the global banking literature has borrowed from the traditional bank lending channel literature and has used these estimation techniques (Wu et al. 2011; Cerutti 2015).

In the sections that follow, we discuss a selection of papers and highlight their methodologies, data, and their findings.

[9] See Ehrmann et al. (2001) for an early use of these estimators in the traditional bank lending channel literature.

6.4 How Does Interbank Integration Affect Borrowing Constraints, Loan Rates, and Output?

Before discussing the international transmission of financial shocks through global banks, we discuss its precursor, financial integration, and its effect on borrowing constraints, loan rates, and economic output (Fig. 6.2). Chakraborty et al. 2017 develop a general equilibrium model to quantify the impact of financial integration on the level and distribution of economic activity, through the trade-off of bank lending and systemic risk. They calibrate their model using data from 15 European Union countries to reflect the change in financial integration in the region since the global financial crisis. The model suggests that the decrease in financial integration in the European Union lead to a 0.54% decrease in GDP.

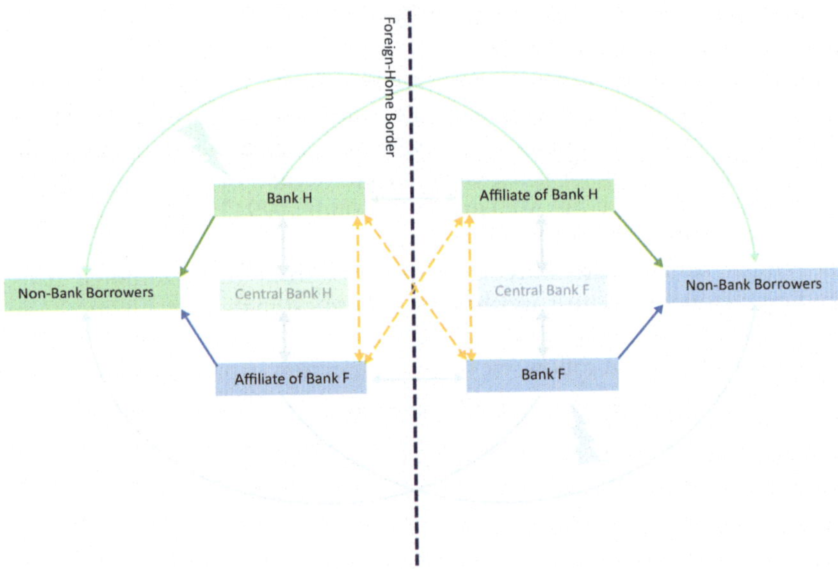

Fig. 6.2 Stylized global banking system diagram-Interbank Integration
Note: See Fig. 6.1 for a description of the mechanisms depicted. The bold parts are the mechanisms considered in this section; the opaque parts are not considered

While the majority of the literature does not explicitly model the degree of financial integration, Popov and Ongena (2011) do measure the degree of integration in the interbank market in a first-stage regression. Their measure is the co-integration (Engle and Granger 1987) between the rates in the domestic interbank market and the rates in a benchmark market (Germany). By basing the relationship of interbank lending rates on an error correction model, they are able to disentangle the long-run co-movement of the interbank rates from the short-run adjustment towards the equilibrium. They then use the coefficient estimates from this first-stage regression as an explanatory variable in later regressions measuring the impact of interbank integration on borrowing constraints and loan rates.

The authors combine the 2004 & 2005 version of BEEPS, transform the data from a cross-sectional to a synthetic panel dataset, and combine it with interbank market rates from the Global Financial database. The resulting data set includes 6407 firms from January 1998 to December 2005, active across 14 countries. This level of granularity in a panel structure allows for the implicit modelling of the effects of the degree of financial integration on firms access to bank credit (borrowing constraints), and the cost of bank credit (loan rates), while taking the structure (competition) of the local banking industry into account.

Popov and Ongena (2011) find that an increase in the degree of financial integration results in lower loan rates and less-stringent borrowing constraints. These effects are stronger for firms in competitive banking sectors. Here, competition is measured by the Herfindahl-Hirschman Index (HHI), which is calculated as the sum of the squared shares of total assets held by each individual bank in the country. Their alternative measure for competition "C3" is calculated as the share of banking sector assets held by the three largest banks in the country.

Competition affects the speed at which banks pass changes to their funding costs onto borrowers. That is, in less-competitive banking sectors, banks are slower to pass on a decrease in their cost of funding to their borrowers, while in competitive banking sectors, banks will reduce the loan rates for firms faster for fear of losing market share. Specifically, the authors find an increase in the degree of integration by two standard deviations, in a competitive banking sector, decreases loan rates by 121 basis points, after selection bias is accounted for. Lastly, the authors find evidence that the pace of integration matters for firms' financial stability as rapid integration is associated with firms becoming substantially over-leveraged.

In constructing the measure of financial integration in the interbank market, Popov and Ongena (2011) measure the co-integration (Engle and Granger 1987) between the nominal rates in the domestic interbank markets and the rates in a benchmark market (Germany). To compute a time-varying measure of the degree of integration, a simple model could be used:

$$r_t^j = \alpha^j + \beta^j r_t^b + \epsilon_t \tag{6.1}$$

where r_t^j is the nominal yield to maturity at time t in country j and r_t^b is the corresponding rate in the benchmark country (Germany). In integrated markets, the co-integration parameter $\beta^j = 1$, as idiosyncratic shocks are diversified away and prices are mainly driven by common shocks. A large β^j would correspond to a disintegrated state. The β^j can then be calculated over a rolling period.

The problem with computing the measure using Eq. (6.1) is that there will be serial correlation in the standard errors of each of the β^j's, resulting in inflated t-statistics. This is an issue as the β^j's are used as explanatory variables in their main regressions. A solution is to compute the following model:

$$r_t^j = \alpha^j + (\beta_0^j + \beta_1^j t + \beta_2^j t^2) \cdot r_t^b + u_{jt} \tag{6.2}$$

In Eq. (6.2), the β^js are calculated over the whole sample, not over a rolling window, as in Eq. (6.1). Computing the β^js using Eq. (6.2) resolves the serial correlation problem while still producing time-varying estimates.

Further, in order to disentangle the long-run co-movement of the interbank rates from the short-run adjustments towards the equilibrium, the authors base the relationship between the yields on an error correction model. This is done by estimating the degree of convergence in the differenced series, Eq. (6.3), as well as the level series, Eq. (6.2).

$$\Delta r_t^j = \theta^j u_{jt-1} + (\eta_0^j + \eta_1^j t + \eta_2^j t^2) \cdot \Delta r_t^b + v_{jt} \tag{6.3}$$

where Δr_t^j is the time-series differenced yields at time t in country j and Δr_t^b is the corresponding differenced rate in the benchmark country (Germany). Equation (6.3) includes an error correction term, $\theta^j u_{jt-1}$, where θ^j is the average correction coefficient towards the long-run equilibrium.

Popov and Ongena (2011) then use the estimates from Eq. (6.2) ($\beta^j = \beta_0^j + \beta_1^j + \beta_2^j$) and from Eq. (6.3) ($\eta^j = \eta_0^j + \eta_1^j + \eta_2^j$) as a measure of interbank market integration for each country j, in later regressions.

The authors make use of a three-stage Tobit scheme, following Heckman (1979), in order to account for a double-selection bias. This bias arises from the fact that loan rates are only observed conditional on firms not being credit constrained, and firm credit constraints are only observed when they have a positive credit demand. The correction has been used for similar purposes in studies on consumer debt, where this method is used to differentiate between desired and actual debt (Hayashi 1982; Cox and Jappelli 1993). Popov and Ongena (2011) assume that the observed loan rates, Y_{ijt}^*, are a linear function of time-varying firm-specific variables, X_{it}, and time-varying country-specific factors Z_{jt}. Equation (6.4) represents this assumption:

$$\begin{aligned} Y_{ijt}^* &= \beta_1 X_{1it} + \beta_2 Z_{jt} + \epsilon_{1ijt} \\ \epsilon_{1ijt} &\sim (0, \sigma_1^2) \end{aligned} \tag{6.4}$$

They then account for any selection bias by using information on firms without bank loans. These are firms that either do not have a positive demand for bank loans, Eq. (6.5) or have a positive demand but are credit constrained, Eq. (6.6). Firms' credit demand is modelled using Eq. (6.5) and estimated using the whole sample.

$$\begin{aligned} q &= \gamma_1 X_{2it} + \gamma_2 Z_{jt} + \epsilon_{2it} \\ \epsilon_{2it} &\sim (0, \sigma_2^2) \end{aligned} \tag{6.5}$$

where $Q = 1$ if a firm has demand for credit ($q > 0$) and 0 otherwise. X_{2it} contains the variables of X_{1it} as well as other variables that potentially affect firm's demand for credit. These include variables such as firm size, and measures of integration, such as the β^j's from Eq. (6.2). Further, the equation includes year and country fixed effects to account for unobserved time-varying macroeconomic and country characteristics that drive demand for bank credit.

To model firms' credit constraints, the authors use Eq. (6.5) and estimate it using the subsample of firms that have a positive demand for bank credit.

$$c = \delta_1 X_{3ijt} + \delta_2 Z_{jt} + \sigma_1 \rho_{23} \frac{\phi(q)}{\Phi(q)} + \epsilon_{3ijt}$$
$$\epsilon_{3ijt} \sim (0, \sigma_3^2) \tag{6.6}$$

where $C = 1$ if a firm is unconstrained ($c > 0$) and 0 otherwise, and $\frac{\phi(q)}{\Phi(q)}$ is the inverse Mill's ratio estimated from Eq. (6.5). Here, X_{3ijt} proxies for characteristics of the banking sector in country j at time t, and further contains variables that may determine the demand for debt. Using Eqs. (6.4) to (6.6), the expectation of the cost of bank credit for firms which have a positive demand for credit and are unconstrained ($Q = 1, C = 1$) is:

$$E(Y^*_{ijt} | X_i, Z_j, Q = 1, C = 1) =$$
$$\beta_1 X_{1it} + \beta_2 Z_{jt} + E(\epsilon_{1ijt} | X_i, Z_j, Q = 1, C = 1) \tag{6.7}$$

The distributions of the error terms defined in Eqs. (6.4) to (6.6) are then used to simplify Eq. (6.7). The result, Eq. (6.8), is estimated using the subsample of firms that have a positive demand for bank credit while incorporating the information from the two selection equations, Eqs. (6.5) and (6.6).

$$Y^*_{ijt} = \beta_1 X_{1it} + \beta_2 Z_{jt} + \sigma_1 \rho_{13} \frac{\phi(c)}{\Phi(c)} \tag{6.8}$$

Here, ρ_{13} is the correlation between error terms from Eqs. (6.4) and (6.6), ϵ_1 and ϵ_3. Further, Eq. (6.8) includes $\frac{\phi(q)}{\Phi(q)}$, the inverse Mill's ratio estimated from Eq. (6.6). Finally, the authors account for the structure of the banking sector by incorporating measures for the degree of competition in the banking industry in country j. Here, bank sector concentration $BC = 1$ if either of the competition measures in country j at time t are below the median ($BC = 0$ if above).

$$Y_{ijt} = \alpha_0 + \alpha_1 \beta_t^j \cdot BC_{jt} + \alpha_2 \beta_t^j + \alpha_3 BC_{jt} + \alpha_4 X_i + \alpha_5 D_j + \alpha_6 D_t + \sigma_1 \rho_{13} \frac{\phi(c)}{\Phi(c)} + \epsilon_{ijt} \tag{6.9}$$

where Y_{ijt} is either the loan rate granted to firm i in country j at time t or the firms' capital structure. D_t and D_j represent time and country fixed effects, respectively. The specification includes controls for firm and loan characteristics X_i. Lastly, β_t^j is the estimated interbank market integration, calculated using Eq. (6.2).

The estimates of interest are α_1, the coefficient of $\beta_t^j \cdot BC_{jt}$), and α_2, the coefficient of β_t^j. The expected sign of α_1 is positive as interest rates are expected to be higher for low banking sector concentration and higher integration. Similarly, the expected sign of α_2 is positive in specifications which exclude competition, as a higher value of β_t^j implies less integration. Using this specification, i.e., accounting for selection bias, the authors find that in a competitive banking sector an increase in the degree of integration by two standard deviations leads to a decrease in loan rates by 121 basis points.

6.5 How and Why Do Banks Establish Foreign Affiliates: Branches or Subsidiaries?

While one measure of the integration of banking systems is the degree to which local interbank markets are integrated, another, potentially complementary, measure is the establishment affiliates in host countries (Fig. 6.3). The choice of affiliate organizational form has important implications as it may affect the competitiveness of the local banking system differently. Further, the type of affiliate may have differential effects on the stability of the local banking system and the efficacy of local macroprudential policy (Aiyar et al. 2014).

Cerutti et al. (2007) seek to uncover why banks establish foreign affiliates and what determines their choice of the type of affiliate to establish, that is, branches or subsidiaries. To do so, the authors combine multiple data sets which include data from Bankscope, the Bankers Almanac, and data from national central banks. They construct a data set that includes data on parent and affiliate bank characteristics operating in Latin America and Eastern Europe. They further supplement this data by including information on home and host country characteristics. In their final sample, the choice of establishing a subsidiary appears to dominate that of establishing a branch, as subsidiaries make up 82% of foreign affiliates in Eastern Europe and 65% in Latin America.

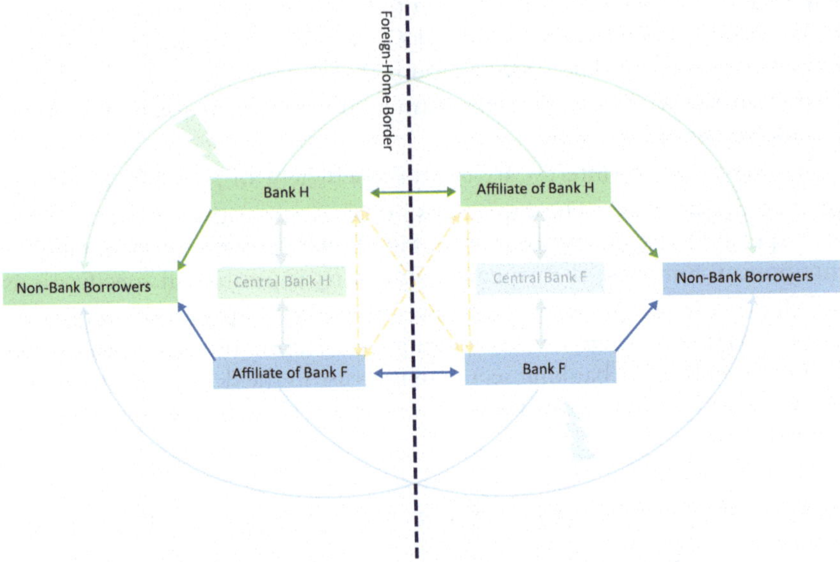

Fig. 6.3 Stylized global banking system diagram-Banking Affiliates
Note: See Fig. 6.1 for a description of the mechanisms depicted. The bold parts are the mechanisms considered in this section; the opaque parts are not considered

The authors begin by investigating the choice of affiliate type by estimating Eq. (6.10):

$$\begin{aligned} Organizational\ Form_{ijk} = & \alpha_0 + \beta_1 Parent\ Bank\ Characteristics_{ij} \\ & + \beta_2 Affiliate\ Bank\ Characteristics_i \\ & + \beta_3 Home\ Country\ Regulations_j \\ & + \beta_4 Host\ Country\ Factors_k + \epsilon_{ijk} \end{aligned} \tag{6.10}$$

where $Organizational\ Form_{ijk}$ is an indicator variable that is equal to 1 if the parent bank, i, from home country, j, operates a branch in host country, k, and is equal to 0 if it operates a subsidiary. The vectors $Parent\ Bank\ Characteristics_{ij}$ and $Affiliate\ Bank\ Characteristics_i$

include variables that account for ownership-specific factors, including parent size, business orientation, international strategy of the parent bank, affiliate size, if the affiliate was acquired through an acquisition, and the year in which the affiliate was established. $Home\ Country\ Regulations_j$ includes variable to account for restriction on foreign banks' foreign operations imposed on them by their home regulators. Finally, $Host\ Country Factors_k$ include characteristics of the host country, including country size, level of development, country risk (political, economic, and investment), local banking regulations, and corporate taxation.

The authors find that banks are more likely to establish a branch as opposed to a subsidiary in countries with lower regulatory restrictions on bank entry and on foreign branches, wealthier (per capita) and which have higher corporate tax rates. Further, branches are the dominant organizational form where the affiliate was not acquired through an acquisition and where their operations are smaller in scope and size. Additionally, parent banks are more likely to establish a branch in countries with high economic risk. Cerutti et al. (2007) argue that this is due to the shield provided by the limited liability of subsidiaries being stronger than ring-fencing provisions of branches. Finally, they find that parent banks are more likely to establish a branch in countries with higher political risk.

The decision to establish a branch or subsidiary is a nested one. That is, the first stage of the decision is to establish foreign operations, and the second is the choice between establishing a branch or subsidiary. The authors only observe parent banks that have established foreign operations. Hence, failure to account for the nested nature of this decision might lead to a sample selection bias. While the authors focus their attention on the latter choice, they take the nested nature of the decision into account in a robustness test. They do so by using a Heckman probit model where, in a first stage, they estimate the selection equation, Eq. (6.11):

$$\begin{aligned} Foreign\ Bank\ Presence_{ijk} =& \alpha_0 + \beta_1 Parent\ Bank\ Characteristics_{ij} \\ &+ \beta_2 Affiliate\ Bank\ Characteristics_i \\ &+ \beta_3 Home\ Country\ Regulations_j \\ &+ \beta_4 Host\ Country\ Factors_k \\ &+ \beta_5 Home - Host\ Proximity_{j,k} + \epsilon_{ijk} \end{aligned} \tag{6.11}$$

where $Foreign\,Bank\,Presence_{ijk}$ is an indicator variable that is equal to 1 if the parent bank, i, from home country, j, operates a branch or subsidiary in host country, k, and is equal to 0 if it does not operate in the host country. $Home-Host\,Proximity_{j,k}$ includes variables which are common to gravity models in the trade literature. These include the amount of bilateral trade, the geographical distance, and whether or not the countries share colonial ties, a common language, or common legal origins.

Cerutti et al. (2007) find that parent banks are more likely to establish operations in countries which are geographically closer, trade more, share a common language, and which have colonial ties with its home country. Hence, the relevance criteria are met. They argue that these variables meet the exclusion restriction as these variables did not affect the second-stage equation. In a second stage, they estimate Eq. (6.10) and find that their results are largely unchanged, and concluded that their results are robust to sample selection bias.

In order to account for the nested nature of the decision to establish a branch or subsidiary, an alternative approach would be to use a nested logit model. In this model, the first decision level is the decision to establish operations or not, and the second is the decision to operate as a subsidiary or branch. Cerutti et al. (2007) argue that this approach would limit their ability to measure the effect of affiliate characteristics on this decision, as these characteristics are only observable if the choice in the first stage is to establish operations. They state that, in unreported results, using a nested logit model for the remaining characteristics yields similar findings.

6.6 How Does a Bank's Global Activity Affect Its Sensitivity to Local Funding Shocks?

Cetorelli and Goldberg (2012a) conduct a two-step Kashyap and Stein (2000) style analysis to test for differences in the response of US banks to monetary policy, based on whether banks have foreign operations or not (Fig. 6.4). This is done by first estimating Eq. (6.12):

$$\Delta log(Y_{i,t}) = \sum_{j=1}^{4} \alpha_{tj} \cdot \Delta log(Y_{i,t-j}) + \beta_t \cdot X_{i,t-1} + Controls + \epsilon_{i,t} \qquad (6.12)$$

where $\Delta log(Y_{i,t})$ is the change in the total lending of bank, i, in quarter, t. $X_{i,t-1}$ is the log of the bank's liquidity ratio. Control variables include

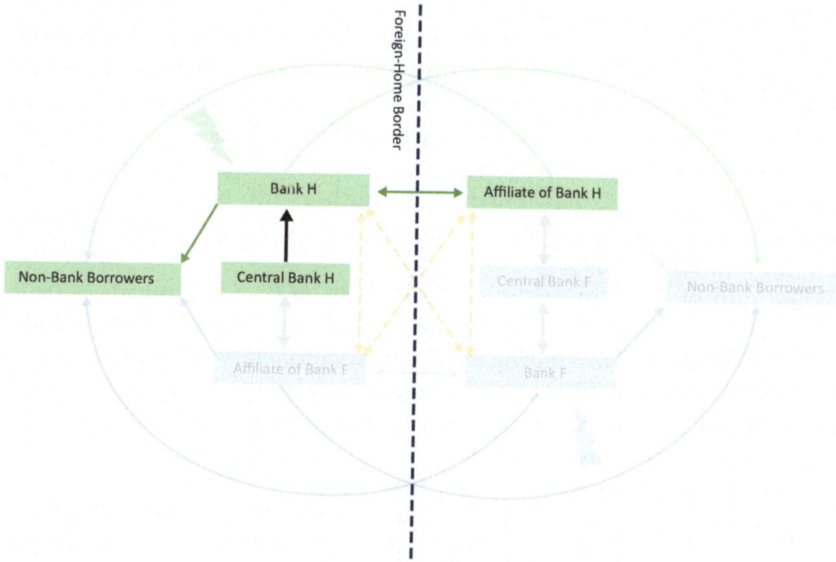

Fig. 6.4 Stylized Global Banking System Diagram-Global Banks-Local Funding Shocks
Note: See Fig. 6.1 for a description of the mechanisms depicted. The bold parts are the mechanisms considered in this section; the opaque parts are not considered

banks' capitalization ratios, size, and non-performing loans, following the bank lending channel literature. The first lag of $X_{i,t}$ and the controls are used in order to avoid simultaneity bias.[10] Further, state and metropolitan area fixed effects are included to account for unobserved loan demand factors. Equation (6.12) is estimated for each quarter, resulting in a time series of β_t estimates, which are used in the next step.

The second step of the analysis uses the β_t's estimated from Eq. (6.12) as the dependent variable, to determine how the sensitivity of bank lending to bank balance sheet characteristics, in this case liquidity, varies with monetary policy changes. This is estimated using Eq. (6.13):

$$\hat{\beta}_t = \eta + \sum_{j=1}^{n} \phi_j \cdot MP_{t-j} + \delta \cdot Controls + u_t \tag{6.13}$$

[10] For example, banks may be large due to experiencing high loan growth.

where MP_{t-j} is an indicator of monetary policy, for which an increase corresponds to a tightening of monetary policy. The authors select a lag, n, of eight quarters to capture a slow response of lending to monetary policy conditions. Controls include GDP growth, as well as its lags, to account for business cycle fluctuations. Time fixed effects are also included. Equation (6.13) is run separately for a sample of large domestic banks, and for large global banks. Further, the authors use Newey-West robust standard errors to account for autocorrelation in the standard errors (Newey and West 1987).

The sign of the sum of the coefficients of MP_{t-j} is positive, as bank lending is expected to be more dependent on liquidity during tight monetary policy and less during expansionary monetary policy. By splitting the sample into global banks and domestic banks, the authors are able to test if the ϕ_j's are significantly different from zero in each specification. They then draw conclusions about the bank lending channel's flow through global or domestic banks.

Cetorelli and Goldberg (2012a) find, contrary to the traditional bank lending channel literature (Kashyap and Stein 2000), that large banks are sensitive to monetary policy if they are not global. Similarly, the authors find that small banks affiliated with large global banks are less sensitive to monetary policy shocks than small banks affiliated with large domestic banks. They argue that this is due to large global banks being able to use foreign liquidity to insulate the loan supplies of their affiliates.

6.7 How Do Banks Change Their Local Lending in Response to Shocks to Their Foreign Funding Sources? (Inward Transmission)

Ongena et al. (2015) take a more traditional view of the bank as a local entity, but determine its global operations in terms of its funding sources. They use a unique combination of databases and exploit the Lehman failure to test for the existence of the international bank lending channel. Then, the authors measure real effects at both firm and country levels. They find supporting evidence for the existence of the international bank lending channel, where foreign-owned, or internationally borrowing domestic banks contract their loan supply more than locally funded domestic banks, after the shock (Fig. 6.5).

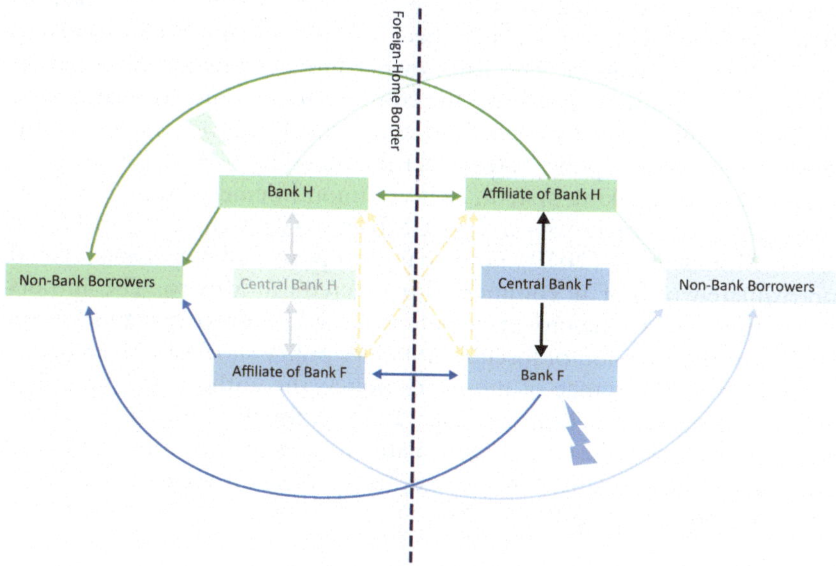

Fig. 6.5 Stylized Global Banking System Diagram-Inward Transmission
Note: See Fig. 6.1 for a description of the mechanisms depicted. The bold parts are the mechanisms considered in this section; the opaque parts are not considered

When looking at firm-level effects, the authors find that credit-dependent firms, which borrow from foreign banks or internationally borrowing domestic banks, experience negative financial and real effects. These effects are especially pronounced when a firm has a relationship with only one bank, is small, or it has limited tangible assets.

As mentioned previously, Ongena et al. (2015) do not include firm fixed effects in their specification as doing so would have effectively excluded two-thirds of their sample. They address this issue by including key firm characteristics as control variables, along with higher-level fixed effects.

Lastly, at the country level, Ongena et al. (2015) find that firms more reliant on foreign funding, from countries with slow contract enforcement and a low level of financial development, were especially affected by the Lehman failure.

To identify the international credit and risk-taking channel of monetary policy, Morais et al. (2019) employ Mexican supervisory datasets. These data sets include detailed information on business loans from 2001 to 2018, combined with firm balance sheet information and bank ownership and funding information. The bank ownership and funding information is key in this study as it allows the authors to identify foreign banks, specifically banks owned by US, Eurozone, and UK investors, and test if their home monetary policy rates affect their lending to Mexican firms.

The Mexican banking system, as is common in emerging markets, has a strong presence of European and US banks (Claessens and van Horen 2014). Morais et al. (2019) note that European and US banks extend approximately 60% of all commercial bank credit in Mexico. The authors analyse the effect of the monetary policy of the US, Eurozone and UK on the inward transmission of foreign monetary policy shocks in Mexico.

To measure the stance of monetary policy, the authors use the policy rates of the respective countries (e.g., EONIA for the Eurozone and the Fed Funds rate for the US). They isolate changes in the monetary policy rates that are not explained by changes to the business cycle of a currency area. They do this using Eq. (6.14):

$$MP_{k,t} = \beta_1 \Delta Real\ GDP_{k,t} + \beta_2 CPI_{k,t} + \epsilon_{k,t} \tag{6.14}$$

where $MP_{k,t}$ is monetary policy rates in currency area, k, at time, t, $\Delta Real\ GDP_{k,t}$ is the real GDP growth in currency area k and $CPI_{k,t}$ is the inflation rate. Further, where $MP_{k,t}$ is the Mexican policy rate, the authors include the Mexican GDP growth rate and inflation rate, as well as the US GDP growth rate and inflation rate to account for the large affect the US economy has on the Mexican economy. Morais et al. (2019) use the residual, $\epsilon_{k,t}$, as the measure of monetary policy for a currency area in their main regressions. Further, they show that the residual monetary policy rates are only moderately correlated, reducing concerns about the multicollinearity of monetary policies. As a measure of unconventional monetary policy, they use the change in the central bank's balance sheet as a share of GDP, where the central bank is determined by the location of the parent bank.

Morais et al. (2019) begin by first analysing whether foreign monetary policy affects the credit supply from foreign banks to local firms. Second, they analyse whether expansive foreign monetary policy induces banks to reach for yield and, hence, induces risk-taking (risk-taking channel). They employ loan-level data at the monthly frequency with firm, or firm-month fixed effects to account for loan demand. Since 79% of firms in their data set borrow from a single bank, the use of firm-month fixed effects will exclude a large part of their sample. Hence, the authors employ firm-bank fixed effects with state-industry-month fixed effects. This allows for the inclusion of single bank borrowers while still controlling for demand side effects at the state-industry level.

The authors find that foreign banks increase their loan supply in response to an expansionary monetary policy at home. For example, the Eurozone monetary policy rate affects the credit supply in Mexico through foreign banks with parents in the Eurozone. Specifically, they find that a one standard deviation reduction in foreign monetary policy rates increases credit supply by foreign banks in Mexico by approximately 2.1% and increases the loan maturity by 6.7%.

Further, the authors identify the risk-taking channel of monetary policy, both in terms of liquidity and credit risk. They find that a one standard deviation reduction in foreign monetary policy rates increases the probability of loan default, over the following year, by 9.8%. Further, they find that foreign banks increase their liabilities, particularly short-term and foreign liabilities, in response to an expansionary monetary policy in their home countries. Hence, foreign banks increase their short-term funding and fragile foreign funding while increasing the duration of the credit they provide. Thus, foreign banks increase both their credit risk and liquidity risk in response to an expansionary monetary policy in their home countries.

Additionally, Morais et al. (2019) find that the international transmission of monetary policy shocks has real effects. The authors analyse the effects on Mexican firms' investment, employment, loan defaults, and the dynamics of their assets. They find that a one standard deviation decrease in foreign monetary policy results in an increase in net investments of 0.5%, employment of 0.4%, future defaults rates of 5.3%, average loan maturity of 4.9%, bank credit volume of 1.5%, firm liabilities of 1.2%, total assets of 0.7%, and a decrease of 0.1% in loan interest rates.

Finally, the authors show a differential effect of unconventional and conventional monetary policy. They find that unconventional monetary policy tends to have a smaller effect, in terms of economic magnitude, than conventional monetary policy. For example, they find that a one standard deviation increase in the Fed Funds rate increases the credit supply of US banks by 6% and extends the maturity by 9.9%. In contrast, a one standard deviation increase in the Federal Reserve's balance sheet as a proportion of US GDP, their measure of unconventional monetary policy, increases credit supply by only 2.5% and maturity by only 7.1%. Further, unconventional monetary policy also appears to flow through the risk-taking channel, as a one standard deviation increase in the balance sheet of the Federal Reserve is associated with a 6.5% increase in future loan defaults, at the firm level. However, the authors find no significant evidence of real effects of unconventional monetary policy.

The results of Morais et al. (2019) are consistent with the inward transmission of foreign monetary policy through the credit and risk-taking channels. Here, when foreign policy rates are lower, foreign banks experience an increase in their liquidity but also reduced yields in their home markets. This leads them to reach for yield by increasing their credit supply to emerging markets with higher credit and liquidity risk. This creates a credit boom in the local markets. However, when foreign policy rates increase, foreign banks decrease their lending supply to emerging markets. This increases the financing constraints of local firms and results in firm-level real effects.

Given the granularity and depth of their data, Morais et al. (2019) were able to analyse the inward transmission of foreign monetary policy transmission in detail. Hence, they were able to maximize the internal validity of their study, but as it is limited to one country, the external validity cannot be tested. To this end, Buch and Goldberg (2017) conducted a meta-analysis of a multi-study initiative of the International Banking Research Network on the inward and outward transmission of monetary policy.[11] In this study, the research network analysed the spillovers of monetary policy from the US, the UK, Japan, and the Eurozone. The research network in this study consisted of central banks from 17 countries.[12] They designed the empirical studies to be very similar as each team used the same baseline model.[13] Setting up the meta-analysis in this way removes the issue of publication bias which can affect meta-analyses. Each team conducted a test

[11] The International Banking Research Network is a group of researchers from central banks and institutions from around the world. The network conducts coordinated research on issues related to global banks and their activities internationally.

[12] These countries include Austria, Canada, Chile, France, Germany, Hong Kong, Ireland, Italy, the Netherlands, Poland, Portugal, Russia, South Korea, Spain, Switzerland, the UK, and the US.

[13] The papers that contributed to this study are: Argimon et al. (2019); Auer et al. (2019); Avdjiev et al. (2018); Barbosa et al. (2018); Gajewski et al. (2019); Gräb and Żochowski (2017); Hills et al. (2019); Kruglova and Styrin (2018); Lindner et al. (2019); Schmidt et al. (2018).

on either the inward transmission, or the outward transmission of monetary policy, depending on the idiosyncrasy of their respective economies.[14]

To analyse the inward transmission, researchers from different central banks used their respective confidential bank-level data. Each team used a common regression model, Eq. (6.15):

$$\Delta Y_{b,t} = \alpha_0 + \sum_{crty} \left(\sum_{k=0}^{K} \left(\alpha_{1,k}^{ctry} \cdot \Delta MP_{t-K}^{ctry} \cdot Channel_{b,t-K-1}^{ctry} \right) + \alpha_2^{ctry} \cdot Channel_{b,t-K-1}^{ctry} \right) + \alpha_3 X_{b,t-1} + f_b + f_t + \epsilon_{b,t} \tag{6.15}$$

where $\Delta Y_{b,t}$ is the log change of lending to the private non-bank sector by bank, b, at time, t. The vector $X_{b,t-1}$ contains time-varying bank control variables. ΔMP_{t-K}^{ctry} measures the change in the foreign monetary policy. The foreign country was chosen by each central bank based on the countries that are most financially connected to their respective economies. The common specifications include a subset of the monetary policies from the Eurozone, the US, the UK, and Japan. As the monetary policy rates from these four currency areas are highly correlated, the teams included multiple foreign currency rates in order to disentangle the different currency areas' monetary policy rates from each other. $Channel_{b,t-K-1}^{ctry}$ includes bank-level variables which the authors include to explain the transmission of monetary policy through different frictions (e.g., net cross-border liabilities to total assets, short-term funding ratio, and tier 1 capital ratio) Finally, f_b and f_t are bank and time fixed effects, respectively, where the time fixed effects control for other domestic and global time-varying effects.

This meta-analysis finds the inward transmission of monetary policy to be statistically significant across all studies under analysis. Some countries reported a positive impact of monetary policy (i.e., an increase in foreign rates leads to an increase in the domestic local loan supply), while others found the opposite. Further, the countries differed in terms of the frictions that matter for inward monetary policy transmission, implying

[14] The following countries participated in the inward transmission analysis: Austria, Chile, France, Germany, Hong Kong, Ireland, Italy, Portugal, South Korea, Switzerland, and the UK. Outward transmission analysis was conducted by teams from Canada, Germany, the Netherlands, Spain, and the US.

the relevance of transmission channels varies across countries. The most frequently important frictions were funding structures, capitalization, and cross-border positions. Finally, the transmission of US monetary policy appears to be the most relevant with nearly all countries reporting statistically significant results. The monetary policy of the other countries under analysis (Eurozone, the UK, and Japan) were less relevant for most countries.

Additionally, the study contributes to the debate about the appropriate measurement of unconventional monetary policy. Buch et al. (2019) compare two measures of unconventional monetary policy: central banks' balance sheets to GDP, and the shadow rate, as calculated by Krippner (2016). They find that the shadow rate generates more evidence of the international transmission of monetary policy, during unconventional monetary policy, while the distinction is less clear during times of conventional monetary policy.

6.8 How Do Banks Change Their Foreign Lending in Response to Shocks to Their Local Funding Sources? (Outward Transmission)

Along with their analysis of the inward transmission of monetary policy, (Buch et al. 2019) conduct a meta-analysis of the outward transmission (Fig. 6.6). Here, the specification that each central bank used as well as the teams involved in this part of the study are different from the inward analysis. The specification changed to measure the outward transmission, Eq. (6.16):

$$\begin{aligned}\Delta Y_{b,j,t} =& \alpha_0 + \sum_{k=0}^{K} \left(\alpha_{1,k}^{domestic} \cdot \Delta MP_{t-K}^{domestic} \cdot Channel_{b,j,t-K-1}^{ctry}\right) \\ &+ \alpha_2^{ctry} \cdot Channel_{b,j,t-K-1}^{ctry} \\ &+ \alpha_3 X_{b,t-1} + f_b + f_{j,t} + \epsilon_{b,j,t}\end{aligned} \tag{6.16}$$

where $\Delta Y_{b,t}$ is the log change in lending by the affiliate of domestic bank, b, in country, j, at time, t. $\Delta MP_{t-K}^{domestic}$ is the change in the

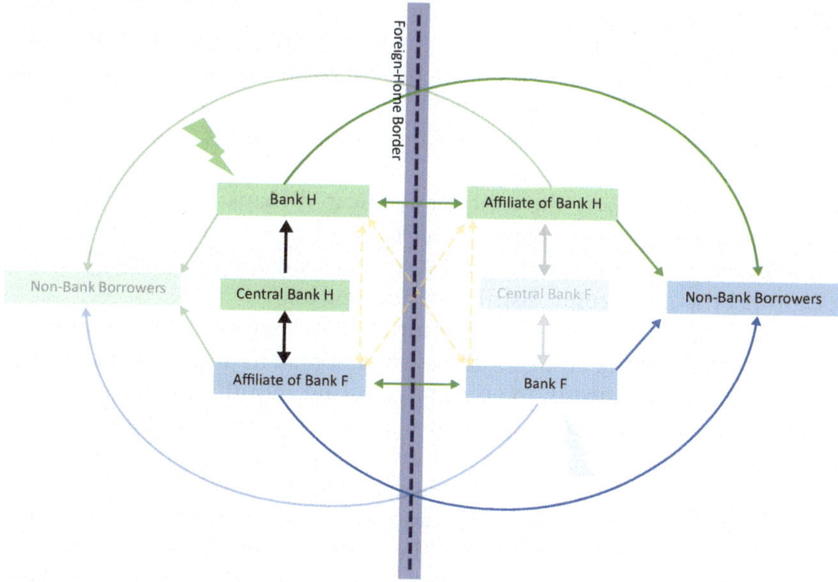

Fig. 6.6 Stylized Global Banking System Diagram-Outward Transmission
Note: See Fig. 6.1 for a description of the mechanisms depicted. The bold parts are the mechanisms considered in this section; the opaque parts are not considered

domestic monetary policy rate. In inward transmission specification, they included time fixed effects; here, they include country-time fixed effects, $f_{j,t}$, to account for time-varying country-level effects such as loan demand and monetary policy changes in the destination country. The remaining variables have the same meaning as in the inward specification, Eq. (6.15). Buch et al. (2019) find statistically significant evidence for the outward transmission channel occurring through both cross-border lending and the lending by hosted foreign branches, across most countries in the study.

Similarly, Giannetti and Laeven (2012) find that global banks redistribute their loan portfolios based on their funding conditions at home. During good times (low-funding costs), global banks tend to redistribute their loan portfolio in favour of foreign markets (flight abroad), and when home funding conditions are poor, they tend to favour their home country (flight home). Furthermore, the authors show that the globalization of banking activities affects the amplitude of credit cycles and that banks export home-grown shocks to host markets.

Giannetti and Laeven (2012) test their first hypothesis, that global banks redistribute their loan portfolio based on their funding conditions at home, by analysing the behaviour of the coefficient α_1 in Eq. (6.17):

$$Loan\ Share_{ijt} = \alpha_0 + \alpha_1 Funding\ Conditions_{i,t-1} + \Gamma X_{ijt} + \epsilon_{ijt} \quad (6.17)$$

where $Loan\ Share_{ijt}$ is the ratio of syndicated loans originated to borrowers in country j, by bank i, in year-month t to total loan supply. $Loan\ Share_{ijt}$ cannot be affected by overall loan supply shocks, because it captures the geographic distribution of new loans.

$Funding\ Conditions_{i,t-1}$ is measured by either the median ratio of market equity to book equity or the average spread in the interbank market over the overnight spread, in country i, during month-year t. Firms have a lower cost of issuing equity when market valuations are higher, which is captured by a higher market-to-book equity ratio (Pagano et al. 1998; Baker et al. 2009). The interbank spread measures banks' short-term funding conditions. Because the study uses syndicated loan data, and multiple banks lend to multiple firms within the same country, identification relies on host country-year fixed effects, X_{ijt}. This controls for time-varying host country variability, such as host country loan demand.

The authors find that a one standard deviation increase in banks' market-to-book equity ratios (or one standard deviation decrease in interbank spreads) increases (decreases) the proportion of foreign loans by close to 5%. The authors stress that these findings are distinct from a flight to quality (a preference for lower-risk assets in tighter funding conditions). They do so by including interactions between funding conditions and a variable measuring creditor rights in the host country. Then, they show that the flight abroad is stronger for countries with strong creditor rights (perceived as safe), ruling out the flight to quality argument.

Giannetti and Laeven (2012) proceed by testing their second hypothesis that the degree of globalization of banking activities in a host country affects the impact of home economic shocks on the credit cycles of the host country. Changes to bank funding conditions impact the degree of their home bias in issuing new loans, with an effect on the aggregate supply of credit in the host countries where they operate. The authors show that this home bias varies over time.

Adding the volatility of home bias to a host country's credit cycle should increase its overall volatility. This increase in volatility of the host country loan supply is determined by its exposure to foreign-funded loans, as represented in Eq. (6.18):

$$Vol(Loan\ Supply)_{jt} = \alpha_0 + \alpha_1 \frac{Loans\ from\ Foreign_{jt}}{Total\ Loans_{jt}} + \alpha_2 \frac{Loans\ to\ Foreign_{jt}}{Total\ Loans_{jt}} + \eta_{ijt} \tag{6.18}$$

where $Vol(LoanSupply)_{jt}$ is measured as the deviations in a country's real credit per capita from its trend. The use of real credit allows for a country's credit cycles to be disconnected from the dynamics of its GDP.

The authors find that the proportion of foreign loans in a host country explains between 20% and 40% of the volatility of credit, depending on the specification used. They conclude that countries dominated by foreign banks should have highly volatile business credit. Further, they argue that banks are more inclined to adjust their foreign loans when funding conditions change. As a result, home countries of international banks should experience less variation in their supply of loans.

Cetorelli and Goldberg (2012b) take the perspective of the foreign branch by employing US call report data on the activity of foreign banks in the US. The authors leverage a funding shock to the foreign parent bank to test for internal capital markets. This shock is measured as the degree to which the parent was exposed to Asset Back Commercial Paper conduits as a proportion of its equity capital, as of 31 December 2006. The authors find that higher internal capital transfers for branches with parents are subject to larger funding shocks, the largest effects being amongst the biggest branches. The median-sized bank (total assets of $1B), with a parent ABCP exposure ratio equal to 1, would have experienced an internal fund withdrawal (transfer to parent) of $343 million more than a parent bank without Asset Back Commercial Paper exposure. This is approximately 12% of the average level of internal balance at the branch, an economically significant effect.

Further, the authors document a positive and significant link between changes in net internal borrowing and branch credit supply. Specifically, they estimate that, for the median sized branch, a $1 decrease in internal funding would result in a $40c to $50c decrease in total domestic lending. This is again an economically significant effect. Lastly, they show that the loan supply of larger branches is less sensitive to changes in internal funds.

This might be due to increased access to alternative funding sources, which are not available to smaller branches.

Bräuning and Ivashina (2017) focus on the hedging costs arising from currency mismatches between global banks' funding and investment activities. The authors argue that if currency flows are large enough, the cost of hedging will increase, which will decrease the return on lending in the foreign currency. They show that an increase in the monetary policy interest rate differential, between two currency areas, decreases foreign lending, leading to a redeployment of capital through the global balance sheet and an increase in local lending. At the bank level, they document a reallocation of loan volumes, as an increase in the $IOER_{US-HQ}$ leads to a 1% decrease in lending in the foreign currency. The effects are particularly strong for lowly capitalized banks.

Additionally, at the firm level, Bräuning and Ivashina (2017) find that increasing the $IOER_{US-HQ}$ by 0.25% leads to a 1% lower probability of a particular bank lending to a particular firm in a given period (extensive margin), as well as an associated 3% decline in the lending volume (intensive margin). Lastly, they show that, at the aggregate domestic credit supply level, firms that had a larger share of foreign global banks in their syndicate, which subsequently experienced monetary easing in the country of their headquarters, faced a stronger contraction in credit. Specifically, a one standard deviation increase in the past share of foreign global banks in the syndicate leads to a 6.5% decrease in the probability of obtaining a loan and a 4% drop in volume of granted loans, after an expansionary monetary policy in the home of the foreign bank.

At the aggregate macro level, Bräuning and Ivashina (2017) show that there is a positive relationship between foreign bank reserve holdings and the difference between the overnight rate on excess reserves ($IOER_{US-HQ}$). Specifically, they find that an increase in the $IOER_{US-HQ}$ of 0.25% leads to a 6% increase in deposits with the US Federal Reserve (with the funds transferred from their foreign offices) and a 2.5% decrease in lending to US firms. They also document an increase in banks' FX swapping activity into high-yield currencies, as well as an increase in the cost of hedging in response to a decrease in the monetary policy rate in the home country.

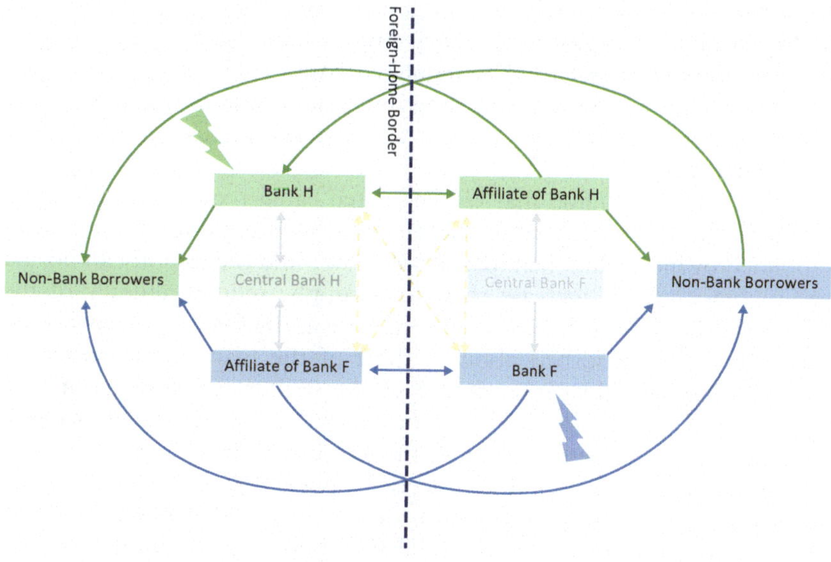

Fig. 6.7 Stylized Global Banking System Diagram-Macroprudential Regulation
Note: See Fig. 6.1 for a description of the mechanisms depicted. The bold parts are the mechanisms considered in this section; the opaque parts are not considered

6.9 How Does Global Banking Interact with Macroprudential Regulation?

In an alternative strand of the global banking literature, researchers have analysed the effects of cross-border prudential policy spillovers as an additional source of impulse to local banking systems.[15] These shocks occur when a change in home country macroprudential policies affects banks' behaviour in host countries, and the other way around (Fig. 6.7).

Aiyar et al. (2014) investigate the effects of UK macroprudential policy on bank credit supply in the UK. The authors use quarterly data from 1998 to 2007 on minimum capital requirements, and other bank

[15] Examples of such policies include limits on loan-to-value ratios, debt-to-income ratios, credit growth, as well as reserve and capital requirements. See Claessens et al. (2013) for a detailed discussion of the different macroprudential policies.

characteristics, from the regulatory databases of the Bank of England and the Financial Services Authority. They employ bank-specific, time-varying capital requirements set for UK-regulated banks (UK-owned banks and resident foreign subsidiaries) to determine the effect of the policies on bank credit supply and how the efficacy of these policies is affected by unregulated banks.

Aiyar et al. (2014) find that UK-regulated banks reduced their lending in response to tighter capital requirements, while hosted foreign branches responded by increasing their loan supply. They find the response of hosted foreign branches, to increase their loan supply, reduces efficacy of the policies by about a third. That is, the increase in the loan supply by hosted foreign branches absorbed about a third of the loan supply reduction that otherwise would have resulted from the tighter capital requirements. This suggests that foreign branches, or banks that are not subject to local regulation, may reduce the efficacy of macroprudential policy.

As in Buch et al. (2019), Buch and Goldberg (2017) conducted a meta-analysis of a multi-study initiative of the International Banking Research Network. In this study, 15 central banks and 2 international organizations conducted country-level analyses on the international spillovers of prudential policy for bank lending.[16] The network developed a new database, described in Cerutti et al. (2017), to measure macroprudential regulation. The use of a unified database across countries enhanced the comparability of results in this meta-analysis. Buch and Goldberg (2017) find that while these spillovers sometimes occur, they are not large on average. Further, the effects vary across prudential instruments, while bank-specific characteristics, such as business models and balance sheet conditions, impact the size and direction of the spillovers.

6.10 Conclusion

The degree to and manner in which the global banking system is integrated has important consequences for firms' access to credit, the transmission of monetary and macroprudential policy, as well as economic shocks between

[16] These countries are Canada, Chile, France, Germany, Hong Kong, Italy, Mexico, the Netherlands, Poland, Portugal, South Korea, Switzerland, Turkey, the UK, and the US. The two international organizations are the Bank for International Settlements and the European Central Bank.

monetary areas. The global banking literature has shown that financial integration improves firms' access to credit and affects their investment and employment decisions. Further, global banks transmit foreign economic shocks to home economies, inward transmission, as well as transmit local shocks to foreign economies, outward transmission. There appears to be no single answer to how global banks transmit economic shocks as the literature has shown that the effects of financial integration differ across countries and depend on their particular idiosyncrasies. Hence, policymakers in each country should be aware of how the integration of their banking system affects their economy in particular and cannot rely on the findings from other countries.

Additionally, the literature has shown that the efficacy of macroprudential policy may be impeded by the presence of foreign banks' branches. Further, financial integration affects the volatility of countries business cycles, where countries dominated by foreign banks experience highly volatile business cycles. These findings suggest macroprudential policymakers need to take into account the presence of foreign banks when setting regulation, particularly regulation linked to the countries business cycle, for example counter-cyclical capital buffers. Finally, these findings suggest the need for policymakers from different currency areas to coordinate their policies.

There are three important issues the literature has yet to fully address. Firstly, at a data level, there is a tension between internal and external validity, while detailed country-level analyses maximize the former, meta-analyses maximize the latter. Here, a multi-currency area credit registry would assist in reducing this tension but such a data set does not exist yet. Secondly, a key assumption in the literature of international monetary policy transmission is that the monetary policy of foreign countries is exogenous to the domestic environment. If foreign monetary policy responds to domestic monetary policy, the effects found in the literature may be a result of the domestic policy, and, hence, the findings of an international monetary policy transmission channel may be spurious. Finally, further distinction between branches and subsidiaries is warranted as the banks' choice to set up a branch or subsidiary may have important consequences, for example the efficacy of local macroprudential policy. Table 6.1 offers a compact overview of the papers reviewed in this chapter.

Table 6.1 Global banking

Paper	*Research question*	*Data*	*Methodology*	*Main findings*
Popov and Ongena (JBF, 2011)	How does (interbank) **integration** affect borrowing constraints, loan rates, and output?	Business Environment and Enterprise Performance Survey (2004 and 2005) combined with interbank market rates from the Global Financial database.	**Engle-Granger Cointegration:** to measure integration of the interbank markets. **Three-Equation generalized Tobit model:** to adjust for selection bias as loan rates are only observed for firms which are not credit constrained and have a positive credit demand. **Fixed effects:** control for time and country fixed effects, as well as firm observables, to disentangle the supply from the demand effect.	An increase in the degree of integration by two standard deviations, in a competitive banking sector, decreases loan rates by 121 basis points, after selection bias is accounted for. Rapid integration is associated with firms becoming substantially over-leveraged.

Cerutti et al. (JBF, 2007)	How and why do banks **establish** foreign **affiliates?**	Multiple data sets covering Latin America and Eastern Europe, obtained from Bankscope,* the Bankers Almanac, and national central banks amongst other sources.	**Probit model:** for the probability of a foreign bank establishing a branch as opposed to a subsidiary which is explained by country, parent bank, and affiliate bank observables. **Heckman correction:** to account for the decision to establish an affiliate.	Banks are more likely to establish a branch as opposed to a subsidiary in countries with higher economic risk, lower political risk, lower regulatory restrictions on bank entry and on foreign branches, and countries which have higher corporate tax rates and are wealthier (per capita). Branches are the dominant organizational form where the affiliate was not acquired through an acquisition and where their operations are smaller in scope and size.

(*continued*)

Table 6.1 (continued)

Paper	*Research question*	*Data*	*Methodology*	*Main findings*
Cetorelli and Goldberg (JF, 2012b)	How do the **assets** of a local bank's **foreign affiliates'** affect their sensitivity to **local funding** shocks?	Quarterly US Call Report Data and weekly data on the assets and liabilities of commercial banks in the US (H.8 Statistical Release).	**Two-Step Regression Approach**: following Kashyap and Stein (AER, 2000). The sample is split along some dimension (e.g., global/domestic), then in the first-stage regression, the change in credit is explained by bank some bank characteristic (e.g., liquidity). The coefficients from the first-stage regression on bank characteristic over time are used as the dependent variable in the second stage where changes in monetary policy is used to explain the coefficients from the first stage. Differences in the results of the second stage according to implies difference in response to monetary policy along that dimension.	Large banks are sensitive to monetary policy if they are not global. Small banks affiliated with large global banks are less sensitive to monetary policy shocks than small banks affiliated with large domestic banks.

Ongena et al. (IMF Economic Review,2015)	How do banks change their **local lendingin response to shocks to their foreign funding sources? (Inward Transmission)**	Bank-ownership database compiled by Claessens and van Horen (JMCB, 2014), bank funding data using Dealogic, bank balance sheet information from Bankscope,* firm balance sheet information from Amadeus, and bank-firm connection information from Kompass.	**Difference-in-differences:** Exploiting the intensity of exposure to the Lehman shock, where banks which are foreign-owned or obtain foreign funding, or firms which lend from these banks, are exposed to the shock.	Foreign-owned, or internationally borrowing domestic banks, contract their loan supply more than locally funded domestic banks, after the Lehman shock. Credit-dependent firms, which borrow from foreign banks or internationally borrowing domestic banks, experience negative financial and real effects. Small firms with only one banking relationship, with limited tangible assets, which are more reliant on foreign funding, from countries with slow contract enforcement and a low level of financial development, were especially affected.

(*continued*)

Table 6.1 (continued)

Paper	*Research question*	*Data*	*Methodology*	*Main findings*
Morais et al. (JF, 2019)		Mexican supervisory data sets.	**Exogenous Variation:** foreign monetary policy is exogenous to Mexican macroeconomic conditions. **Correlations and cross-sectional variation:** across banks with exposures to different foreign monetary policies based on their foreign ownership.	A one standard deviation reduction in foreign monetary policy rates increases credit supply by foreign banks in Mexico by approximately 2.1%, loan maturity by 6.7%, and the probability of loan default, over the following year, by 9.8%. Foreign banks increase their short-term and foreign liabilities in response to an expansionary monetary policy in their home countries. Unconventional monetary policy tends to have a smaller effect, in terms of economic magnitude, than conventional monetary policy.

Buch et al. (JIMF, 2019)		Researchers from different central banks used their respective confidential bank-level data.	**Meta-analysis:** of a multi-study initiative of the International Banking Research Network on the inward and outward transmission of monetary policy where each country team employed similar regression models to reduce publication bias.	The inward transmission of monetary policy is statistically significant across all studies in the analysis, with some countries reporting a positive impact of monetary policy, while others found the opposite. The most frequently important frictions were funding structures, capitalization, and cross-border positions. The transmission of US monetary policy appears to be the most relevant with nearly all countries reporting statistically significant results. Statistically significant evidence for the outward transmission channel occurring through both cross-border lending and the lending by hosted foreign branches, across most countries in the study.

(continued)

Table 6.1 (continued)

Paper	*Research question*	*Data*	*Methodology*	*Main findings*
Giannetti and Laeven (AER, 2012)	How do banks change their **foreign lending** in response to shocks to their **local funding sources?** (Outward Transmission)	Syndicated loan data from Dealogic, systemically important banking crises dates from Laeven and Valencia (IMF WP, 2010), stock market returns from DataStream, amongst other data sets.	**Correlations and cross-sectional variation:** across banks with exposures to different foreign funding conditions. **Fixed effects:** include host country-time fixed effects to account for differences in demand across country.	A one standard deviation increase in banks' market-to-book equity ratios (or one standard deviation decrease in interbank spreads) increases (decreases) the proportion of foreign loans by close to 5%. The proportion of foreign loans in a host country explains between 20% and 40% of the volatility of credit, depending on the specification used.

Cetorelli and Goldberg (AER, 2012b)	US Call Report data	**Difference-in-differences:** Exploiting the intensity of exposure to parent bank pre-crisis exposure to asset bank commercial paper. **Two-Step Regression Approach:** in first stage, the change in branch net internal borrowing is explained by parent bank's pre-crisis exposure to asset bank commercial paper. In a second stage, the change in branch loan supply is explained from the estimated net internal borrowing from the first stage.	The median-sized bank (total assets of $1B), with a parent asset-backed commercial paper exposure ratio equal to 1, would have experienced an internal fund withdrawal (transfer to parent) of $343 million more than a parent bank without Asset Back Commercial Paper exposure. A $1 decrease in internal funding , for the median-sized branch, would result in a $40c to $50c decrease in total domestic lending. The loan supply of larger branches is less sensitive to changes in internal funds.

(*continued*)

Table 6.1 (continued)

Paper	*Research question*	*Data*	*Methodology*	*Main findings*
Bräuning and Ivashina (WP, 2017)	How do foreign banks adjust their **central bank reserves** in response to **local monetary policy** changes?	DealScan syndicated loan data, combined with US Call Reports data, reserve data from 16 other central banks, and BIS Consolidated Banking Statistics and Locational Banking Statistics.	**Correlations and within-group variation:** banks with exposures to different foreign funding conditions. **Fixed effects:** include firm-time and borrower-time fixed effects to account for demand and bank-time-varying responses to home country economic conditions	An increase in the overnight interest rate differential on central bank reserves of 0.25%, leads to a 1% decrease in lending in the foreign currency, a 1% lower probability of a particular bank lending to a particular firm in a given period (extensive margin), as well as an associated 3% decline in the lending volume (intensive margin). A one standard deviation increase in the past share of foreign global banks in the syndicate leads to a 6.5% decrease in the probability of a firm obtaining a loan and a 4% drop in volume of granted loans, after an expansionary monetary policy in the home of the foreign bank.

		Correlations and within-group variation: a bank's reserve holdings across time explained by the overnight interest rate spread between the banks' headquarters and the rate in the US. **Fixed effects**: include time and bank fixed effects to account for changes in the composition banks and common time-varying factors.	Specifically, they find that a 0.25% increase in the overnight interest rate differential on central bank reserves leads to a 6% increase in deposits with the US Federal Reserve and a 2.5% decrease in lending to US firms. Increase in banks' FX swapping activity into high-yield currencies, as well as an increase in the cost of hedging in response to a decrease in the monetary policy rate in the home country.

(*continued*)

Table 6.1 (continued)

Paper	*Research question*	*Data*	*Methodology*	*Main findings*
Aiyar et al. (JMCB, 2014)	How does **global banking** interact with **macroprudential** regulation?	Minimum capital requirements and other bank characteristics from the regulatory databases of the Bank of England and the Financial Services Authority	**Correlations and cross-sectional variation:** the change in loan supply explained by change in banks' capital requirements, where banks' capital requirements changes were staggered throughout the sample period.	UK-regulated banks reduced their lending in response to tighter capital requirements, while hosted foreign branches responded by increasing their loan supply. The increase in foreign branch lending reduces efficacy of the policies by about a third.
Buch and Goldberg (IJCB, 2017)		Researchers from different central banks used their respective confidential bank-level data combined with the macroprudential regulation database, described in Cerutti et al. (ICJB, 2007).	**Meta-analysis:** of a multi-country initiative international spillovers of prudential policy changes and their effects on bank lending growth where each country team employed the same data set on macroprudential policy.	While macroprudential spillovers sometimes occur, they are not large on average. The effects vary across prudential instruments, while bank-specific characteristics, such as business models or balance sheet conditions, impact the size, and direction of the spillovers.

*Note: Bureau van Dijk's Bankscope has been replaced by Moody's Analytics BankFocus

CHAPTER 7

FinTech and the Future of Banking

"FinTech" is a popular term that captures technological changes in the financial sector. Philippon (2016) defines it as "digital innovations and technology-enabled business model innovations in the financial sector". While banking has been a sector with a relatively mild penetration of new technologies (one could only think, for example, of automated teller machines, wire transfers, and online banking), this recent technological wave is the result of combined technological advances impacting business models and of increasing bank regulation.

IMF (2019) provides an overview of the FinTech experience so far on financial services. Their proposed Fig. 7.1 maps users' needs for different financial services (pay, save, borrow, manage risks, and get advice) to traditional solutions and emerging fintech solutions. In doing so, it flags the key gaps that technology seeks to fill, and which new technologies are applied in different services. The authors also indicate the expected impact of various technological innovations (high H, medium M, and low L) and the ongoing FinTech solutions. In this chapter, we mainly focus on recent research dealing with the box "borrow".

FinTech lenders have emerged as new companies with an increasing market share. They are mainly start-ups (LendingClub, Prosper, and Funding Circle in the US or Auxmoney in Germany) but also technological

A. Bilan et al., *Banking and Financial Markets*, Palgrave Macmillan Studies in Banking and Financial Institutions,
https://doi.org/10.1007/978-3-030-26844-2_7

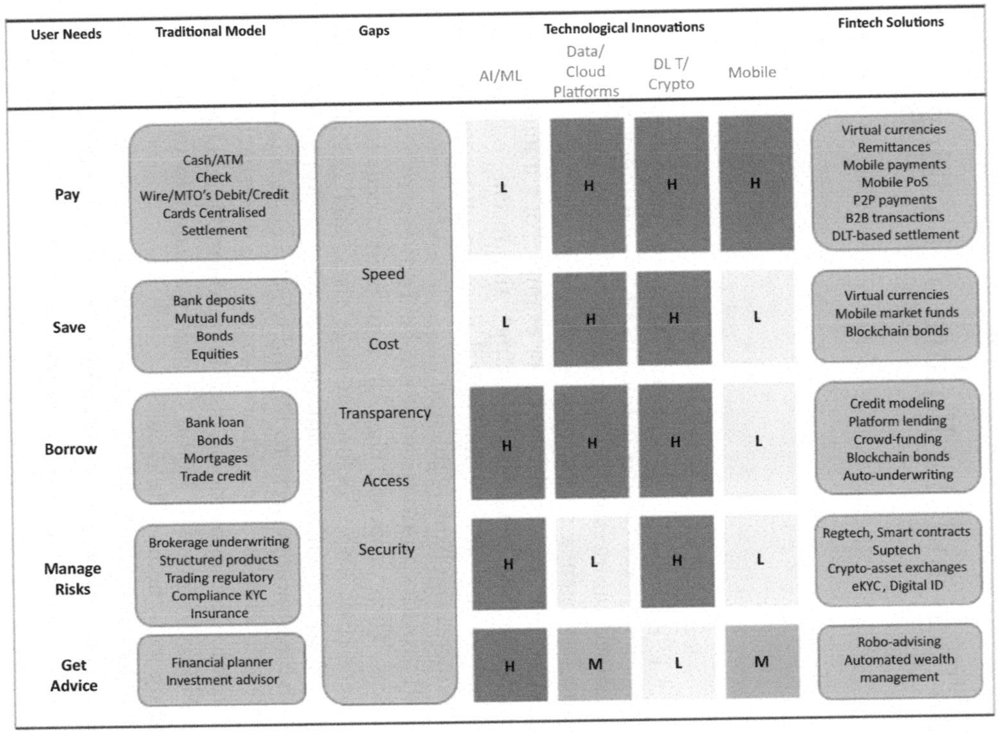

Fig. 7.1 The evolution of financial services
Note: Source: IMF (2019) This figure outlines the needs of consumers for financial services, disaggregated by traditional and fintech services

incumbents, all competing in a market that was traditionally reserved to banks.[1]

While FinTech players typically cannot match banks' lower cost of funding since their liabilities are mainly equity and they have no access to insured deposits, FinTech lenders gain margins by leveraging a higher ability to exploit new technologies, without the need to reorganize their existing organizational structure. In particular, this advantage originates in the ability of FinTech firms to process loans applications entirely online, to read default-relevant borrower information from their customers' digital footprint, or to adjust credit supply to demand more flexibly. While the FinTech phenomenon is relatively recent, it has the potential to invigorate a lending market characterized by an inexplicably high and persistent cost of intermediation.[2]

In this chapter, we review the very recent academic literature that has developed to understand and explain the potential and the pitfalls of FinTech lending. We start by discussing the data (Sect. 7.1) and methodologies (Sect. 7.2) employed by these studies. Section 7.3 then analyses the interplay between technology and recent bank regulations in driving the rise of FinTech firms. Subsequently, Sect. 7.4 looks more closely into whether these newcomers act as competitors or complements to traditional bank lending. Section 7.5 discusses the liability side of the FinTech lenders and the behaviour of their investors. Finally, Sect. 7.5.1 concludes. Table 7.1 offers a compact overview of the papers reviewed.

7.1 Data

Data on FinTech lending volumes and on the composition of loan portfolios of FinTech firms has become only recently available. Some of the largest lending platforms today make their data public or are willing to share it with researchers. This has contributed to advancing this branch of the literature

[1] According to IBIS World Industry Report OD4736: Peer-to-Peer Lending Platforms in the US (2016) loans issued by FinTech firms represent one-third of the volume of unsecured consumer loans. Fuster et al. (2019) note that in the home mortgage market, FinTech lending has grown annually by 30% from US$34 billion of total originations in 2010 (2% of market) to US$161 billion in 2016 (8% of market).

[2] Philippon (2016) observes that the unit cost of financial intermediation in the US and other developed economies has remained particularly high for the past 130 years and despite the recent financial crisis.

Table 7.1 Fintech and lending

Paper	*Research question*	*Data*	*Methodology*	*Main findings*
Berg et al. (RFS, 2018)	*What are the drivers behind the recent rise in FinTech lending?*	New data set covering around 250,000 purchases with buyer characteristics from an E-Commerce company located in Germany. The company gathers credit-relevant data both online, by recording the digital footprint of their customers, and also by accessing information from private credit bureaus.	Univariate and multivariate **credit scoring models** enhanced with explanatory variables extracted from the buyer's digital footprint.	When including digital footprint variables, the Area-Under-Curve (AUC) metric for measuring the power of credit score models improves from 68.3% to 73.6%. Therefore, technology can improve screening for defaults.
Fuster et al. (RFS, 2019)		Loan, applications, and borrower characteristics from the US mortgage lending market, collected under the Home Mortgage Disclosure Act (HMDA). The data includes bank and non-bank lenders. Enhanced with information on riskier loans insured by the Federal Housing Administration (FHA).	**OLS specifications** with proxies for lending frictions as main variables: loan processing times, likelihood of default, likelihood to refinance. The share of FinTech lending is the main explanatory variable.	FinTech innovations have improved the efficiency of the US mortgage market in terms of shorter processing times with no negative effect on defaults, increased elasticity of the supply of loans, and more efficient refinancing.

Buchak et al. (JFE, 2018)		Mortgage lending data from Home Mortgage Disclosure Act (HMDA) as in Fuster et al. (2019). Enhanced with loan performance data from Fannie Mae and Freddie Mac, as well as Federal Housing Administration data on loans granted to risky borrowers. For measures of bank regulation, bank call reports as well as information from lawsuit settlements.	**Difference in differences** models at both country and loan levels, around major changes in bank regulation.	Bank regulation appears to also drive the rise of FinTech. Shadow banks gained market share and expanded lending in countries whose banks were more exposed to increases in regulatory burdens.
De Roure et al. (WP, 2018)	*And banks and FinTech lenders substitutes or complements?*	New consumer loans granted by savings and cooperative German banks, as well as loans granted by Auxmoney, Germany's largest FinTech platform	**Quasi-experimental:** unexpected increase in capital that was required by the European Banking Authority following its stress tests in 2011 and which affected two large Landesbanken and their savings banks in Germany	FinTech lending raises more in those states with affected savings banks and most of the effect comes from high-risk borrowers. Banks and FinTech lenders appear to be substitutes for infra-marginal borrowers

(*continued*)

Table 7.1 (continued)

Paper	*Research question*	*Data*	*Methodology*	*Main findings*
Tang (RFS, 2019)		Merges bank financial data with lending data sourced from a large FinTech platform, the Lending Club. Bank balance sheets are extracted from call reports. The Lending Club provides loan-level data on volumes, borrower applications, and borrower characteristics.	**Quasi-experimental:** Exploits a shock to US bank lending originating in the introduction of a new regulation by the Financial Accounting Standards Board. Statistical tests for changes in the distribution of new FinTech borrowers as a result of the shock.	Banks and FinTech lending platforms are substitutes for infra-marginal borrowers and complements for small borrowers.
Vallee and Zeng (RFS, 2019)	*Are non-bank, FinTech investors able to competitively screen for loan performance?*	Data on borrower and loan characteristics from the Lending Club, as well as private data on investor sophistication from LendingRobot, a robo-advisor for retail investors on lending marketplaces	**OLS specifications** comparing the performance of loans screened by investors with heterogenous levels of sophistication	Sophisticated FinTech investors are able to screen directly for loan performance without the need of bank intermediation

on empirical banking. Lending Club, Prosper, are all FinTech lending platforms that have shared their lending data, including loan applications and loan outcomes, volumes of lending, borrower characteristics, and loan performance. Such data can then be merged with loan portfolios from commercial banks, with the purpose of studying any differences. Academics have also exploited regulatory data sets, such as the database on US mortgage lending compiled under the Home Mortgage Disclosure Act (HMDA), which includes both bank and non-bank (often FinTech) lenders. Finally, any firm with an online presence can gather information on the digital footprint of their potential customers. Such information can be useful to study to what extent digital footprints are relevant for predicting borrower creditworthiness and the probability of default. This is precisely the type of information where FinTech lenders enjoy a competitive advantage in compiling and interpreting.

7.2 Methodology

While this recent literature on FinTech has innovated through its ability to raise and answer relevant questions and source new data for this purpose, the research designs employed have been more conventional. Some of the studies reviewed below have relied on comparing the strength of correlations across the portfolios of FinTech lenders and banks, or across the behaviour of investors (Fuster et al. 2019; Vallee and Zeng 2019). Other authors have recycled credit shocks from the existing literature on banking and applied them to study possible substitution patterns between Fintech platforms and banks (Buchak et al. 2018; Tang 2019; De Roure et al. 2018). Finally, Berg et al. (2018) have enhanced existing credit scoring models with new variables of borrowers' digital footprints, in order to see how predictions of the models change.

7.3 Technology, Bank Regulation, and the Rise of FinTech

7.3.1 *Technological Advances*

One of the main reasons why banks exist has to do with their superior ability to access and process information relevant for the screening and the monitoring of borrowers (Boot and Thakor 2000; Berger et al. 2005). This is fundamental to reduce concerns of information asymmetries between savers and investors. Recent *technological advances* however have the potential to affect this function of the banking sector. Nowadays, accessing technology reveals significantly more information about users than in the past. This may lead to a collection of more hard information but also soft information about borrowers could be more substantiated and hardened (Liberti and Petersen 2019). Some of this information can be predictive of borrower default.

In their recent work, Berg et al. (2018) seek to understand precisely to what extent borrower default can be predicted by their digital footprint-the information that borrowers leave online simply by accessing or registering on a website. If digital footprints have significant predictive power for defaults, then FinTech firms that learn how to exploit this data can thwart the informational advantage of traditional financial intermediaries and challenge their business models.

To address this question, the authors rely on a new data set covering around 250,000 purchases from an E-Commerce company located in Germany. The company is concerned with the creditworthiness of their customers, as they first deliver the merchandises and only two weeks later charge the customers. Consequently, they gather credit-relevant data both online, by recording the digital footprint of their customers, and also by accessing information from a private credit bureau. This E-commerce company granted access to all this information, at borrower level, to the authors.

The digital footprint indicators from the data set contain ten variables that are easily accessible to any firm operating online. These variables include the borrower's device type (desktop, tablet, mobile), the operating system they use (Windows, IOS, Android), and their email provider. A second type of digital information is the channel through which the customer has visited the E-commerce firm's homepage, such as paid clicks, direct (customers browsing directly to the URL of the E-commerce company), affiliate (customers coming from an affiliate site that links to the E-commerce company's webpage such as a price comparison site), and organic (from the non-paid results of a search engine). Personal characteristics (such as self-control or care for reputation) can also be inferred from the timing of the purchase or from whether the customer has used an email address containing their full name. Finally, the credit bureau data includes credit scores at borrower level. The horizon of the analysis in Berg et al. (2018) expands between October 2015 and December 2016.

The empirical approach starts with a univariate analysis, in which Berg et al. (2018) test whether the previous characteristics, taken one at a time, exhibit discriminatory power for the borrower's probability of default. The authors subsequently undertake a multivariate analysis which consists in estimating the predictive probability of all the digital footprint variables and the credit bureau score on a borrower-level default dummy. The precise econometric specification used is a logistic regression. Taking the two groups of explanatory variables separately and jointly, the authors calculate and report the Area-Under-Curve (AUC), which is a common metric to judge the discriminatory power of credit scores (Stein 2002).[3]

Interestingly, the reveals that the digital footprint variables indeed predict borrower probability of default. The variables that proxy for income and wealth reveal significant differences in payment behaviour. Orders from mobile phones are three times as likely to default than orders from desktop or orders from tablets. Moreover, orders from the Android operating systems are almost twice as likely to default as orders from iOS systems-consistent with the idea that customers purchasing an iPhone are usually wealthier than customers purchasing other smartphones. Information on people's character also has discriminatory power. Customers arriving on the homepage through adds exhibit the largest default rate among all other arriving channels, while customers purchasing between noon and 6 pm are approximately half as likely to default as customers purchasing from midnight to 6 am. Reputation also seems to matter, as customers who use their name in their email address are relatively less likely to default.

In the , a model that uses only the digital footprint variables has an AUC of 69.6%, 1.3 percentage points higher than the AUC of the model using only the credit bureau scores (68.3%). The most striking feature of this result lies in the fact that the digital data set only contains information that is easily accessible to any firm with an online presence. When the variables are considered jointly, the AUC of the combined model (credit bureau score and digital footprint) jumps to 73.6%, which suggests that the digital footprint is not only predictive on its own, but it is also complementary to the traditional screens for borrower default. These results imply that barriers to entry in financial intermediation might be lower in a digital world and that digital footprints are useful to increase the efficiency of

[3] The AUC ranges from 50% (purely random prediction) to 100% (perfect prediction).

credit markets. Accessing digital information can improve the accuracy of standard credit score models.

Fuster et al. (2019) provide further support for this hypothesis of increased efficiency in credit markets driven by FinTech firms. In particular, they study whether FinTech platforms have increased innovation in the US residential mortgage market as compared to banks. The authors define innovations in the context of mortgage markets as reductions in frictions such as lengthy loan processing, capacity constraints, inefficient refinancing, and limited access to finance. FinTech platforms are those lenders that offer an application process that occurs completely online. This particular business model-the authors conjecture-could indeed lead to reductions in frictions, but at the possible cost of increasing risk-taking. Fuster et al. (2019) set out to investigate whether this is the case in the US mortgage market.

Using data on both bank and non-bank lenders, the authors measure how prevalent lending frictions are in the online versus the traditional mortgage market. Information on residential lending is collected in the US under the Home Mortgage Disclosure Act (HMDA). HMDA data capture characteristics of individual residential mortgage applications and loan originations from the majority of US banks and non-bank financial intermediaries. These characteristics include the identity of the lenders, the loan amounts as well as a set of property and borrower indicators such as property location, borrower income, race, and gender. This chapter follows loans for which the applications were lodged between 2010 and 2016.

Fuster et al. (2019) start by examining the effect of FinTech lending on loan outcomes and risk. They focus on how long it takes platforms versus traditional banks to originate a loan, and whether the difference in processing times has any implications for the risk of the mortgages. Ex ante, the authors argue, it is not entirely clear whether Fintech lenders should automatically improve efficiency in the loan granting process. They may indeed be faster at processing loans than traditional lenders because online processing is automated, centralized, and with less scope for human error. At the same time, this highly automated approach might be less effective at screening borrowers for soft information (in contrast to Berg et al. (2018)), therefore resulting in higher defaults and increased ex post costs. This is why efficiency is viewed as the conjunction between processing times and riskiness in loan outcomes.

To measure the interaction between these two outcomes, a first OLS regression employed is:

$$ProcessingTime_{ijct} = \delta_{ct} + \beta FinTech_j + \gamma Controls_{ijct} + \epsilon_{ijct} \quad (7.1)$$

where $ProcessingTime_{ijct}$ is the time it takes to approve loan i, issued by lender j, in census tract c, and for an application received in month t. $FinTech_j$ is an indicator variable equal to one for FinTech lenders and zero otherwise. γ_{ct} is a vector of census-tract-month fixed effects. $Controls_{ijct}$ include loan and borrower controls.

A second regression looks at whether there are any simultaneous changes in loan risk. The authors restrict the analysis to a group of mortgages that are insured by the Federal Housing Administration (FHA) and which represent the riskiest segment of the US mortgage market. Then they estimate the following regression:

$$Default_{ijst} = \alpha + \beta FinTech_j + \gamma Controls_{ijst} + \epsilon_{ijst} \quad (7.2)$$

$Default_{ijst}$ on loan i by lender j in state s originated in month t is an indicator variable equal to one if a loan becomes delinquent for 90 days or longer over the observation period, $FinTech_j$ is an indicator variable equal to one for FinTech issuers, and $Controls_{ijst}$ is a broad set of control variables such as origination month or state-by-origination month fixed effects, loan purpose fixed effects, borrower FICO scores, loan-to-value (LTV) ratios, and debt-to-income (DTI) ratios.

A second way to assess whether frictions in mortgage lending are heterogeneous in the banking technology is to see whether FinTech lenders are better able to accommodate sudden changes in mortgage demand. By automating, centralizing, and standardizing the underwriting process, FinTech lenders may conceivably increase the elasticity of lending supply to demand shocks. To empirically identify differential demand elasticities across lenders, Fuster et al. (2019) use changes in nationwide application volume as a source of exogenous variation in local mortgage demand. Then, they trace out the correlations with loan processing times.

Using the same loan-level HMDA data, the precise regressions employed are as follows:

$$ProcessingTime_{ijct} = \gamma Applications_t + \beta Applications_t * FinTech_j + $$
$$+\theta Controls_{it} + \alpha_j + \sigma_c + \epsilon_{ijct} \quad (7.3)$$

where $ProcessingTime_{ijct}$ is the number of days between application and closing for mortgage i from lender j in census tract c and application month t, $Applications_t$ is the log of aggregate mortgage applications in month t, and $FinTech_j$ is an indicator variable equal to one for FinTech lenders. α_j and σ_c are vectors of lender and census-tract fixed effects, while $Controls_{it}$ include borrower and loan controls.

Finally, the authors look at whether FinTech mortgage lending affects a borrower's propensity to refinance. Existing research has shown that many borrowers refinance too little or at the wrong times. To capture refinancing behaviour, the authors use data from Equifax's Credit Risk Insight Servicing McDash (CRISM), which provides the standard loan and borrower characteristics, but also is borrower identifier, allowing them to track borrowers across loans. To measure the effect of FinTech lending on monthly refinancing propensities, they use the following OLS regression:

$$RefiPropensity_{ct} = \alpha_c + \alpha_t + \beta FinTechShare_{c,t-s} + \theta Controls_{ct} + \epsilon_{ct} \tag{7.4}$$

where $RefiPropensity_{ct}$ is the share of mortgages in county c in month t that are refinanced and $FinTechShare_{c,t-s}$ is the one-quarter-lagged four-quarter moving average market share of FinTech mortgage lenders amount refinance loans in a county. The specifications include county fixed effects,α_c, to control for fixed unobservable differences in refinancing speeds across counties and month fixed effects, α_t to control for aggregate conditions. The time-varying controls include average FICO scores, average combined-loan-to-value ratios, the average interest rate on outstanding loans, and the share of outstanding loans that are high-risk.

The findings of Fuster et al. (2019) suggest that FinTech innovations have indeed improved the efficiency of the US mortgage market. Specifically, the authors first document that processing times for mortgage applications decrease substantially, with no negative effect on risk-taking. FinTech lenders process mortgages faster than traditional lenders, measured by total days from the submission of a mortgage application until the closing. In particular, FinTech processing times are lower by about ten days, or 20% of the average processing time. Crucially, default rates on FinTech mortgages are about 25% lower than those for traditional lenders, even when controlling for detailed loan characteristics. Moreover, there is no significant difference in interest rates for similar loans granted by the platforms or by traditional banks. These results speak against a "lax screening" hypothesis and, instead, indicate that FinTech lending technologies might help attract and screen for less risky borrowers.

Second, the authors show that FinTech lending is indeed more elastic to changes in demand, and hence it is likely to attenuate capacity constraints in credit markets. These specifications show that a doubling of the applications volume raises the loan processing time by 13.5 days (or 26%) for traditional lenders, compared to only 7.5 days for FinTech lenders. FinTech lenders also appear to reduce denial rates relative to other lenders when application volumes rise, suggesting that their faster processing is not simply due to credit rationing during peak periods.

Third, Fintech lending also reduces refinancing frictions. Borrowers are more likely to refinance in counties with a larger FinTech lender presence (controlling for county and time fixed effects). An 8 percentage points increase in the lagged market share of FinTech lenders raises the likelihood of refinancing by about 10% of the average. Importantly, by reducing such refinancing frictions, FinTech lending increases the pass-through of market interest rates to households.

All in all, Fuster et al. (2019) show that the technology used by FinTech platforms is disruptive in that it improves the efficiency of the credit market. This complements Phillipon's (2016) observation that FinTech has the potential to decrease the unit cost of financial intermediation.

7.3.2 *Bank Regulation*

Aside from their ability to use technology to screen loans faster and more efficiently, another main driver of the recent growth in Fintech lending appears to be related to the increasing pace of *bank regulation*. Buchak et al. (2018) study whether regulatory differences have indeed contributed to the growth of the shadow banking sector, a sector in which Fintech platforms have a large size.

The authors approach this question by studying changes in the market share of banks and shadow banks around significant changes in banking regulation. They focus on the impact of four types of events: increases in capital requirements, the tightening of mortgage servicing rights, the outcomes of mortgage-related lawsuits, and the movement of supervision to the Office of Comptroller and Currency (OCC) following the closure of the Office of Thrift Supervision (OTC). The latter considered to be a lax regulator.

The empirical analysis is carried out in a difference-in-differences setting at both country and loan levels. The authors combine four sources of data. First, they gather mortgage application data collected under the Home Mortgage Disclosure Act (HMDA), which is also the main data source in Fuster et al. (2019). This is enhanced with loan performance data from Fannie Mae and Freddie Mac, as well as Federal Housing Administration data on loans granted to borrowers with particularly low credit scores. To measure changes in bank regulatory burden associated with the four regulatory events mentioned previously, Buchak et al. (2018) extract financial indicators from bank call reports as well as recent lawsuit settlements brought against banks, lenders, and mortgage servicers.

The first findings show that shadow banks are more likely to serve riskier, less credit-worthy borrowers and areas with larger minority populations. Since several enforcement actions that increased regulatory burden particularly targeted banks' treatment of such riskier borrowers, the evidence appears consistent with shadow banks expanding in segments where the regulatory burden has risen the most. Regarding the pricing of loans, Buchak et al. (2018) document negligible differences in traditional and shadow bank interest rates. Finally, tests that exploit the four regulatory events mentioned above reveal that indeed shadow banks gained market share and expanded lending in countries whose banks were more exposed to increases in regulatory burdens.

Taken together, the finding in Buchak et al. (2018) suggest that the recent rise in the market share of the shadow banking, and in particular of Fintech platforms, is not only a by-product of technological progress, but also a result of increasingly regulating the traditional banking sector.

7.4 Banks vs. FinTech: Substitutes or Complements

Another part of the recent literature on Fintech lending has been concerned with the precise place that the platforms have come to occupy in the credit market. Do FinTech lenders serve the same customer segments as traditional banks, or do they take niche positions on particular segments of the market? Are Fintech lenders substitutes or complements to traditional banks? Technological advances could, in fact, stimulate the financial inclusion of new borrowers and thus allow FinTech lenders to become complementary to banks and serve new customers. Or, technology could simply decrease the intermediation costs, thus turning FinTech lenders into stronger competitors for bank borrowers. Or, both could happen at the same time. Similarly, new banking regulations could raise the intermediation costs for traditional banks.

Tang (2019) investigates this precise question: whether FinTech platforms are substitutes or complements to traditional bank lending in consumer credit markets. To tackle the lack of loan application data at individual level, Tang (2019) studies how a negative shock to bank credit changes the distribution of borrower quality on a FinTech platform by pushing borrowers away from the affected banks and towards the platforms. The economic reasoning behind her analysis is as follows. After a negative credit shock, banks tighten their lending criteria, with a resulting excess of borrowers whose loan applications are rejected. Some of these borrowers will search for loans at the FinTech providers. If the platforms are substitutes to traditional banks, then they will face an increase in lower-quality customers previously rejected by the affected banks. In this case and assuming the platforms were indeed interested in this lower-quality demand, in equilibrium the distribution of borrower quality on lending platforms would shift towards riskier loans. On the contrary, if lending platforms were to complement traditional bank lending, then their customer distribution should become less risky, as better bank customers would be joining the platforms in response to the credit shock.

To test empirically whether lending platforms and banks are substitutes or complements, the author exploits a shock to US bank lending originating in the introduction of a new regulation, FAS 166/167, by the Financial Accounting Standards Board. This regulation required banks to consolidate onto their balance sheet off-balance sheet assets which had been securitized. As a result, those banks targeted by the regulation were required to impose new risk weights on these assets. Tang (2019) borrows this regulatory event from previous literature (Dou 2017; Dou et al. 2018). The treatment is designed so as to exploit heterogeneity among banks. The banks with the highest pre-existing amounts of securitized assets were affected the most. This treatment is then applied at county level: treated counties are defined as those with at least one treated bank; the counties with no treated bank are allocated to the control group.

The study merges bank financial data with lending data sourced from a large FinTech platform, the Lending Club. Bank balance sheets come from the Call Reports and they cover 59 banks. The Lending Club provides loan-level data on volumes, borrower applications, and borrower characteristics. The horizon covered by the study is 2009-2012. To identify the effect of the regulatory shock on FinTech lending, Tang (2019) estimates the following equation:

$$y_{c,t} = \beta Treated_c * Post_t + Controls_{c,t} + \gamma_c + \sigma_t + \epsilon_{c,t} \quad (7.5)$$

where c denotes counties and t indexes quarters or years, depending on the model. $Treated_c$ equals one for treated counties and zero otherwise, while $Post_t$ takes value one from 2011 onwards-the post-event period. The dependent variable y_c changes progressively to study the volume and distribution of FinTech lending. $Controls_{c,t}$ includes control variables that account for the time-varying structure of local banking markets.

When using either FinTech application volumes or FinTech loan origination volumes, β is always positive, suggesting that after the regulatory shock applications and lending volumes at the FinTech provider increased significantly in treated versus control counties. While these results are necessary for the rest of the analysis, to actually distinguish between the opposite hypotheses of substitutes or complements, in the remaining part of the study y_c captures statistical measures for changes in the distribution of borrowers. These include measures of average borrower quality (FICO scores) as well as the quantiles of the borrower quality distribution. The analysis then reveals that both the ten quantiles and the mean of the average borrower distribution decrease simultaneously in treated versus control counties. This supports the hypothesis that banks and FinTech lending platforms are substitutes. Further frequency tests holding the FICO thresholds constantly suggest that most of the effect comes from infra-marginal borrowers, that is, from those borrowers of relatively lower quality. This is because the frequency of borrowers is larger in low FICO ranges, for FinTech firms, in the post-event period.

Lastly, Tang (2019) goes on to show that FinTech platforms operate also as complements to banks, but only on the borrower segment which is most reliant on small loans. This result is derived by applying the same borrower distribution and frequency tests as above, but to the size of the loans in the sample, rather than to their numbers. In fact, borrowers that migrate from banks to FinTech lenders apply for larger loans than did the existing FinTech borrowers. Relative to the control group, the average FinTech loan size in treated counties increases by over US$1000 in the post-event period and across most quantiles of the distribution. Taken jointly, these two results suggest that infra-marginal bank borrowers (substitutes) and small borrowers (complements) are the most likely to benefit from the expansion of FinTech lending.

In contemporaneous work, De Roure et al. (2018) also study the interaction between bank and FinTech lending, using German regulatory data on bank and FinTech commercial lending. They start by developing a simple theoretical model in which banks and Fintech platforms compete locally, for the same customers. The model is useful to determine whether FinTech lenders attracts the best bank customers ("cream-skimming") or the riskiest ("bottom-fishing"). The equilibrium in this lending market is disturbed by a rise in regulatory constraints on banks. As banks are financed with both equity and deposits, they tend to have a cost advantage over the platforms, which are generally only funded through equity. However, when capital constraints are raised for banks, this relative competitive advantage decreases and some borrowers shift to the FinTech platforms. Following this economic rationale, the model generates three empirical predictions. First, following exogenous increases in regulatory costs, banks in aggregate should lose loan market share to FinTech lenders. Second, the loans that migrate to the platforms should be riskier than the average bank loans, as they should require larger capital charges. And, third, the risk-adjusted interest rates on P2P loans should be lower than those on bank loans, as there are no capital charges.

The authors then test these predictions with data on new consumer loans granted by savings and cooperative German banks, and loans granted by Auxmoney, Germany's largest FinTech platform. To measure the effects of tighter bank capital requirements, De Roure et al. (2018) rely on an unexpected increase in capital that was required by the following its stress tests in 2011. Two large Landesbanken in Germany were found to hold insufficient capital and were required to adjust within few months. The Landesbanken are associated with local savings banks, which, in turn, used loanable funds to purchase equity in their respective Landesbank. Other local savings and cooperative banks were not affected, and are used in the study as controls. Using this event, the authors document that FinTech lending raises more in those states with an affected savings bank and that this market share shift is largest when the unaffected banks in the region are financially weaker.

Moreover, most of the shift comes from the riskiest borrowers, leading the authors to conclude that FinTech lenders are "bottom-fishing" or capturing the weakest borrowers. These findings are consistent with the results of Tang (2019), regarding the substitutability in loan providers for infra-marginal borrowers.

7.5 The Liability Side of FinTech

While banks are the main intermediaries responsible for screening and monitoring loans, lending platforms leave a significant part of these tasks to their investors. Vallee and Zeng (2019) study this fundamental difference between banks and lending platforms in a theoretical and empirical framework where investors are the ones who put effort in loan screening and in producing information. Their model features a lending platform which functions similarly to Lending Club or Prosper. The platform gathers some initial hard information on the borrowers and it constructs risk buckets to which it allocates each borrower. This information is then distributed to two types of investors: sophisticated investors and non-sophisticated investors. Sophisticated investors are able to use additional technology to screen loans based on the indicators made available by the platform, while non-sophisticated investors strictly follow the suggestions of the platform. As a result, the model predicts that sophisticated investors will generally outperform unsophisticated ones. Moreover, because of their ability to find profitable loans and finance them when the platforms algorithms might suggest otherwise, sophisticated investors also boost lending volumes on the platform.

There is, however, a contrary effect on volumes. Because the sophisticated investors are able to identify and cherry-pick the best loans, non-sophisticated investors might in response reduce their lending volumes as they expect to match with loans of a lower quality. This is a standard adverse selection scenario which, if severe enough, might push non-sophisticated investors out of the market completely. Hence, the platform needs to permanently trade off these two forces: allowing sophisticated investors to trade and collect the information they produce, but only up to the point where its own screening algorithms become powerful enough to maximize lending volumes.

In the second part of their study, Vallee and Zeng (2019) test empirically the implications of their model. They use publicly available data on borrower and loan characteristics from the Lending Club, as well as private data on investor sophistication from LendingRobot, a robo-advisor for retail investors on lending marketplaces. LendingRobot offers different investment menus to its clients, ranging from unsophisticated "monitor-only" to "robot" and "advanced" accounts, which give investors access to a sophisticated screening tools and to increased speed of execution.

Over a horizon spanning 2014 to 2017, Vallee and Zeng (2019) first study whether more sophisticated investors screen differently than less sophisticated ones. They run linear probability regressions looking at the correlation between the different account types and borrower characteristics, as follows:

$$Prob(TypeAccount_i = 1) + \beta * BorrowerCharacteristics + \sum_{j=1}^{n} *IR_j + \\ + \sum_{t=1}^{T} *m_t + +\epsilon_i \tag{7.6}$$

The explained variable is equal to 1 in turn for the three type of accounts $RobotAccount_i$, $AdvancedAccount_i$ and $MonitoredOnlyAccount_i$. $BorrowerCharacteristics$ are collected by the lending platform, IR_j are fixed effects for the n distinct levels of interest rate paid to investors at loan issuance, m_t are month fixed effects and e_i is the error term. If the model showed that different borrower characteristics have different explanatory power across the three account types, that could be consistent with different screening intensity by the investors behind these accounts.

Second, the authors test whether sophisticated investors hold portfolios that significantly outperform unsophisticated investors. For this, they measure performance at the loan level, using an indicator variable when the loan is in default or chargedoff. This performance indicator is then regressed on indicator variables for participation by different types of investors:

$$Prob(ChargedOff = 1)_i = \beta_1 * \mathbb{1}_{TypeAccount} + \sum_{j=1}^{n} *IR_j + \sum_{t=1}^{T} *m_t + +\epsilon_i \tag{7.7}$$

where $\mathbb{1}_{TypeAccount}$ takes, in turn, the value of one for the three types of investor account provided by the LendingRobot: monitored-only, robot, and advanced.

In a third step, Vallee and Zeng (2019) investigate the relationship between a platform's incentives to provide information and investor screening activities. For this, they use a difference-in-differences methodology. The research design exploits Lending Club's decision to remove from the investor information set half of the 100 variables on borrower characteristics, starting from November 7, 2014. While the shock affected all investors, the authors contend that it should have reduced the outperformance of informed investors, since they had less variables to screen on. To test whether there is any evidence of a reduction in the performance of informed investors following this event, the authors rely on the following specification:

$$
\begin{aligned}
Prob(ChargedOff = 1)_i = {} & \beta_1 * \mathbb{1}_{robot} + \beta_2 * \mathbb{1}_{robot} * Post \\
& + \beta_3 * \mathbb{1}_{advanced} + \beta_4 * \mathbb{1}_{advanced} * Post \\
& + \beta_5 * \mathbb{1}_{monitor} + \beta_6 * \mathbb{1}_{monitor} * Post \\
& + \sum_{j=1}^{n} * IR_j + \sum_{t=1}^{T} * m_t + \epsilon_i
\end{aligned}
$$

where $\mathbb{1}_{robot}$ is an indicator variable equal to one if at least two robot accounts are invested in loan i, $\mathbb{1}_{advanced}$ is an indicator variable equal to one if at least two advanced accounts are invested in the loan, and $\mathbb{1}_{monitor}$ is an indicator variable equal to one if at least two monitor-only accounts are invested in the loan. $Post$ is an indicator variable for being in the sample in the period after the shock to the information set, while IR_j and m_t are interest rate and month fixed effects.

The first results show that indeed more sophisticated investors rely on different loan characteristics to finance loans than non-sophisticated investors. This points to the fact that they process and produce information differently. In fact, loans selected by sophisticated investors have a significantly lower probability of default, and this appears to hold true across all risk buckets. Specifically, loans selected by sophisticated investors have a default rate on average 3 percentage points lower than the average loan, corresponding to a reduction of more than 20% of the average default risk. Finally, using the Lending Club's decision to alter the number of variables disclosed as a way to generate exogenous variation in investors' information set, confirms the hypothesis that sophisticated investors produce information. Vallee and Zeng (2019) find that sophisticated investor outperformance drops by more than half at the time of the reduction.

7.5.1 *Conclusion*

FinTech, a proxy for a recent technological wave in the financial services industry, has the potential to change the banking sector. IMF (2019) provides an overview of the FinTech experience so far on financial services, and indicates the key gaps technology could fill to satisfy different consumer needs regarding financial services.

Our review regarding FinTech lending shows that FinTech is not only the result from technological developments but also from tighter bank regulation. FinTech lenders compete with banks by gathering more customer information, possibly quicker processing of information, quicker decision-making, and lighter regulation. FinTech lenders have emerged as new kids on the block with an increasing market share. Mostly they are start-ups but also technological incumbents that compete in a market that was traditionally reserved to banks.

FinTech can contribute to financial inclusion and complement banks in this way to enrich financial development. FinTech can also function as a substitute to banks. Both changes may generate impacts on bank-risk-taking. Initial results indicate that information collected by FinTech firms about consumers' digital footprint helps in predicting loan defaults. FinTech also seems to lead to a reduction in frictions and greater efficiency as revealed in shortened processing times for loan approval, and improved consumer behaviour in the mortgage market. The jury on whether FinTech complements or substitutes for banks is still out there. Most likely, different segments of the borrower population will be differentially affected. Initial results seem to suggest that FinTech lenders are "bottom-fishing" or capturing the weakest borrowers.

In any case, academic research on this topic is blossoming and more research is warranted as banks business models will continue to be challenged by new FinTech developments. More broadly, FinTech could also have implications for credit bureaus and credit registries. In order to remain valuable, these information-sharing mechanisms could consider to incorporate FinTech-generated information in the calculation of credit scores.

CHAPTER 8

Conclusion

The goal of this book was to review the data sets, empirical methodologies, and findings regarding the role of banks and financial technology in current financial markets. It should be clear by now that the modern banking industry goes much further than their initial purpose of transferring funds from savers to investors, and, in this way, screen and monitor borrowers, provide liquidity, and perform maturity transformation.

Several key features of loan contracts are affected through derivatives that allow to transfer risks to other players in financial markets. We considered different aspects of the loan contract including amounts via loan securitization, interest rate, credit risk, collateral, currency, and technology (i.e., FinTech).

The review of the literature shows that many new data sets have become available over time and that empirical research in this area is blossoming. Researchers have combined several data sets to address important questions. Researchers rely more and more on (quasi-)natural experiments to come to identification, employing empirical methodologies such as difference-in-difference methods.

The different chapters of the book lead to a number of key findings regarding the implications of the interaction between banks and financial markets. A first key takeaway is that the presence of derivatives allows banks to hedge and thus transfer risk to other market players, but also to add risks to their loan portfolio. This has both costs and benefits for banks and their borrowers. The benefit is that banks may enhance the

A. Bilan et al., *Banking and Financial Markets*, Palgrave Macmillan Studies in Banking and Financial Institutions,
https://doi.org/10.1007/978-3-030-26844-2_8

features of loan contracts not only to the benefit of existing borrowers but also to reach out to new borrowers locally as well as globally. This still while banks perform the function of screening, monitoring, and liquidity provision. The downside is that banks' incentives to screen and monitor could be undermined. Banks could also be exposed to shocks stemming from the functioning of derivative markets and regulatory modifications on those markets. Loan securitization, for example, clearly contributed to the global financial crisis of 2008-2009: fast ex ante bank screening combined with low ex post monitoring led to the drop in investor confidence that precipitated the crisis. Another example are credit default swaps that may give rise to the empty creditor problem.

Second, regulatory pressure on banks and unconventional monetary policy shape the incentives for banks to employ derivatives markets and determine the screening and monitoring function of banks. Following the global financial crisis, regulation has required banks to consolidate securitized off-balance sheet assets onto their balance sheet. Also unconventional monetary policies have allowed banks to obtain liquidity against securitized loan portfolios. These interventions have enhanced the screening and monitoring of bank loans.

Third, a key takeaway concerns banks' usage of information in screening and monitoring loans and technological progress. While traditionally banks needed local presence to obtain soft information about their clients, the reliance on credit bureaus and credit registries implied that banks could also employ externally available hard and soft information in loan granting decisions. Recent technological advances touch the boundaries of privacy as they allow to gather digital footprints of customers and to harden this soft information. FinTechs may leverage on this information more than banks do. Banks and FinTech could complement each other and lead to financial inclusion. Tighter regulation imposed on banks could also lead FinTechs to substitute for banks and to gain market share. An important unanswered question is how the industrial organization of banks and FinTechs will evolve. Will banks and FinTechs specialize in segments of the markets, or will they compete for the same borrowers across the board? How does regulation affect all of this?

Fourth, despite the improvements in collecting information and monitoring, collateral is a key feature of bank loan contracts. Collateral allows to further mitigate ex ante information asymmetries and reduces ex post moral hazard. Improvements in legal institutions have broadened the scope of collateral that can be pledged and enforced. An example concerns the role of patent collateral, particularly for innovative start-ups that are supported less by tangibles and more by the intangible know-how of the entrepreneurs. A greater reliance on collateral may increase banks sensitivity to swings in collateral values and bank behaviour can amplify these swings. The presence of substitutes like FinTech which have been able to function without relying on collateral may therefore become more important.

Fifth, banks have grown internationally and become more exposed to international regulation as well as cross-border impacts of monetary and macroprudential policies.

From the book, it should be clear that the interaction between banks, financial markets, and new FinTech players is leading to a new financial ecosystem. More research is needed to advocate a financial ecosystem that serves society.

References

Abad, J., I. Aldasoro, C. Aymanns, M. D'Errico, L. Fache Rousová, P. Hoffmann, S. Langfield, M. Neychev, and T. Roukny (2016). Shedding light on dark markets: First insights from the new EU-wide OTC derivatives dataset. Technical Report 11, European Systemic Risk Board (ESRB).

Acharya, V. V., and T. C. Johnson (2007). Insider Trading in Credit Derivatives. *Journal of Financial Economics 84*(1): 110–141.

Acharya, V. V., P. Schnabl, and G. Suarez (2013). Securitization Without Risk Transfer. *Journal of Financial Economics 107*(3): 515–536.

Adrian, T., and H. S. Shin (2010). Liquidity and Leverage. *Journal of Financial Intermediation 19*(3): 418–437.

Aiyar, S., C. Calomiris, and T. Wieladek (2014). Does Macro-Prudential Regulation Leak? Evidence from a UK Policy Experiment. *Journal of Money, Credit and Banking 46*(s1): 181–214.

Albertazzi, U., M. Bottero, L. Gambacorta, and S. Ongena (2016). Asymmetric information and the securitization of sme loans.

Albertazzi, U., F. Fringuellotti, and S. Ongena (2018). Fixed rate versus adjustable rate mortgages: evidence from euro area banks. *Bank of Italy Temi di Discussione (Working Paper) No. 1176.*

Allen, F., and E. Carletti (2006). Credit Risk Transfer and Contagion. *Journal of Monetary Economics 53*: 89–111.

Allen, F., and D. Gale (2009). *Understanding financial crises.* Oxford University Press.

A. Bilan et al., *Banking and Financial Markets*, Palgrave Macmillan Studies in Banking and Financial Institutions,
https://doi.org/10.1007/978-3-030-26844-2

Altavilla, C., M. Boucinha, J. Peydró, and F. Smets (2018). Banking Supervision, Monetary Policy and Risk-Taking: Big Data Evidence from 15 Credit Registers. *European Central Bank Memeo.*

Altunbas, Y., L. Gambacorta, and D. Marques-Ibanez (2010). Bank Risk and Monetary Policy. *Journal of Financial Stability 6*(3): 121–129.

Amiram, D., W. H. Beaver, W. R. Landsman, and J. Zhao (2017). The Effects of Credit Default Swap Trading on Information Asymmetry in Syndicated Loans. *Journal of Financial Economics 126*(2): 364–382.

Arellano, M., and S. Bond (1991). Some Tests of Specification for Panel Data: Monte Carlo Evidence and an Application to Employment Equations. *The Review of Economic Studies 58*(2): 277–297.

Arellano, M., and O. Bover (1995). Another Look at the Instrumental Variable Estimation of Error-Components Models. *Journal of Econometrics 68*(1): 29–51.

Argimon, I., C. Bonner, R. Correa, P. Duijm, J. Frost, J. de Haan, L. de Haan, and V. Stebunovs (2019). Financial Institutions' Business Models and the Global Transmission of Monetary Policy. *Journal of International Money and Finance 90*: 99–117.

Arping, S. (2014). Credit Protection and Lending Relationships. *Journal of Financial Stability 10*(1): 7–19.

Ashcraft, A. B. (2006). New Evidence on the Lending Channel. *Journal of Money, Credit and Banking 38*(3): 751–775.

Ashcraft, A. B., and J. A. Santos (2009). Has the CDS Market Lowered the Cost of Corporate Debt? *Journal of Monetary Economics 56*(4): 514–523.

Asriyan, V., L. Laeven, and A. Martin (2018). Collateral booms and information depletion.

Auer, S., C. Friedrich, M. Ganarin, T. Paligorova, and P. Towbin (2019). International Monetary Policy Transmission through Banks in Small Open Economies. *Journal of International Money and Finance 90*: 34–53.

Avdjiev, S., C. Koch, P. McGuire, and G. von Peter (2018). Transmission of Monetary Policy through Global Banks: Whose Policy Matters? *Journal of International Money and Finance 89*: 67–82.

Badarinza, C., J. Y. Campbell, and T. Ramadorai (2018). What Calls to ARMs? International Evidence on Interest Rates and the Choice of Adjustable-Rate Mortgages. *Management Science 64*(5): 2275–2288.

Baker, M., C. F. Foley, and J. Wurgler (2009). Multinationals as Arbitrageurs: The Effect of Stock Market Valuations on Foreign Direct Investment. *The Review of Financial Studies 22*(1): 337–369.

Ball, R., R. M. Bushman, and F. P. Vasvari (2008). The Debt-Contracting Value of Accounting Information and Loan Syndicate Structure. *Journal of Accounting Research 46*(2): 247–287.

Barbosa, L., D. Bonfim, S. Costa, and M. Everett (2018). Cross-Border Spillovers of Monetary Policy: What Changes During a Financial Crisis? *Journal of International Money and Finance 89*: 154–174.

Barro, R. J. (1976). The Loan Market, Collateral, and Rates of Interest. *Journal of Money, Credit and Banking 8*(4): 439–456.

Bartram, S. M., J. S. Conrad, J. Lee, and M. G. Subrahmanyam (2018). Credit default swaps around the world: investment and financing effects. *Warwick Business School Working Paper* (April).

Basel Committee on Banking Supervision (2004). Principles for the management and supervision of interest rate risk. Technical report, Bank for International Settlements.

Basel Committee on Banking Supervision (2006). International convergence of capital measurement and capital standards: A revised framework. Technical report, Bank for International Settlements.

Basel Committee on Banking Supervision (2016). Interest rate risk in the banking book. Technical report, Bank for International Settlements.

Basten, C., B. Guin, and C. Koch (2018). How do banks and households manage interest rate risk? Evidence from mortgage applications and banks ' responses. *Bank of England, Staff Working Paper No. 733.*

Bedendo, M., L. Cathcart, and L. El-Jahel (2016). Distressed Debt Restructuring in the Presence of Credit Default Swaps. *Journal of Money, Credit and Banking 48*(1): 165–201.

Benmelech, E., J. Dlugosz, and V. Ivashina (2012). Securitization Without Adverse Selection: The Case of Clos. *Journal of Financial Economics 106*(1): 91–113.

Berg, T., V. Burg, A. Gombović, and M. Puri (2018). On the rise of fintechs–credit scoring using digital footprints. Technical report, National Bureau of Economic Research.

Berger, A. N., W. S. Frame, and V. Ioannidou (2011). Tests of Ex Ante Versus Ex Post Theories of Collateral Using Private and Public Information. *Journal of Financial Economics 100*(1): 85–97.

Berger, A. N., N. H. Miller, M. A. Petersen, R. G. Rajan, and J. C. Stein (2005). Does Function Follow Organizational Form? Evidence from the Lending Practices of Large and Small Banks. *Journal of Financial Economics 76*(2): 237–269.

Bernanke, B., and M. Gertler (1990). Financial Fragility and Economic Performance. *The Quarterly Journal of Economics 105*(1): 87–114.

Bernanke, B., and I. Mihov (1998). Measuring Monetary Policy. *The Quarterly Journal of Economics 113*(3): 869–902.

Bester, H. (1985). Screening vs. Rationing in Credit Markets with Imperfect Information. *American Economic Review 75*(4): 850–855.

Bester, H. (1987). The Role of Collateral in Credit Markets with Imperfect Information. *European Economic Review 31*(4): 887–899.

Beyhaghi, M., N. Massoud, and A. Saunders (2016). Why and How do Banks Lay off Credit Risk? The Choice Between Retention, Loan Sales and Credit Default Swaps. *Journal of Corporate Finance 42*: 335–355.

Blanchflower, D. G., and A. J. Oswald (1998). What Makes an Entrepreneur? *Journal of Labor Economics 16*(1): 26–60.

Blundell, R., and S. Bond (1998). Initial Conditions and Moment Restrictions in Dynamic Panel Data Models. *Journal of Econometrics 87*(1): 115–143.

Bolton, P., and M. Oehmke (2011). Credit Default Swaps and the Empty Creditor Problem. *The Review of Financial Studies 24*(8): 2617–2655.

Bonaccorsi di Patti, E., and E. Sette (2016). Did the Securitization Market Freeze Affect Bank Lending During the Financial Crisis? Evidence from a Credit Register. *Journal of Financial Intermediation 25*: 54–76.

Boot, A. W., and A. V. Thakor (2000). Can Relationship Banking Survive Competition? *The Journal of Finance 55*(2): 679–713.

Boot, A. W., A. V. Thakor, and G. F. Udell (1991). Equilibrium Analysis, Policy Implications. *The Economic Journal 101*(406): 458–472.

Bräuning, F., and V. Ivashina (2017). Monetary policy and global banking. *National Bureau of Economic Research Working Paper w23316.*

Brunnermeier, M., and Y. Koby (2018). The reversal interest rate. *NBER Working Paper Series No. 25406.*

Brunnermeier, M., and Y. Sannikov (2016). The I theory of money. *NBER Working Paper Series No. 22533.*

Buch, C. M., M. Bussierè, L. Goldberg, and R. Hills (2019). The International Transmission of Monetary Policy. *Journal of International Money and Finance 91*: 29–48.

Buch, C. M., and L. Goldberg (2017). Cross-Border Prudential Policy Spillovers: How Much? How Important? Evidence from the International Banking Research Network. *International Journal of Central Banking 13*(S1): 505–558.

Buchak, G., G. Matvos, T. Piskorski, and A. Seru (2018). Fintech, Regulatory Arbitrage, and the Rise of Shadow Banks. *Journal of Financial Economics 130*(3): 453–483.

Caglio, C., R. M. Darst, and E. Parolin (2018). Half-Full or Half-Empty? Financial Institutions, CDS Use, and Corporate Credit Risk.

Calomiris, C. W., M. Larrain, J. Liberti, and J. Sturgess (2017). How Collateral Laws Shape Lending and Sectoral Activity. *Journal of Financial Economics 123*(1): 163–188.

Campbell, J. Y. (2013). Mortgage Market Design. *Review of Finance 17*(1): 1–33.

Campello, M. (2002). Internal Capital Markets in Financial Conglomerates: Evidence from Small Bank Responses to Monetary Policy. *The Journal of Finance 57*(6): 2773–2805.

Campello, M., and M. Larrain (2015). Enlarging the Contracting Space: Collateral Menus, Access to Credit, and Economic Activity. *The Review of Financial Studies 29*(2): 349–383.

Carbo-Valverde, S., H. Degryse, and F. Rodríguez-Fernández (2015). The Impact of Securitization on Credit Rationing: Empirical Evidence. *Journal of Financial Stability 20*: 36–50.

Catherine, S., T. Chaney, Z. Huang, D. A. Sraer, and D. Thesmar (2018). Quantifying reduced-form evidence on collateral constraints.

Cerqueiro, G., S. Ongena, and K. Roszbach (2016). Collateralization, Bank Loan Rates, and Monitoring. *The Journal of Finance 71*(3): 1295–1322.

Cerutti, E. (2015). Drivers of Cross-Border Banking Exposures During the Crisis. *Journal of Banking and Finance 55*: 340–357.

Cerutti, E., R. Correa, E. Fiorentino, and E. Segalla (2017). Changes in Prudential Policy Instruments-A New Cross-Country Database. *International Journal of Central Banking 13*(S1): 477–503.

Cerutti, E., G. Dell'ariccia, and M. S. Martínez Pería (2007). How Banks Go Abroad: Branches or Subsidiaries? *Journal of Banking and Finance* (31): 1669–1692.

Cetorelli, N., and L. Goldberg (2012a). Banking Globalization and Monetary Transmission. *The Journal of Finance 67*(5): 1811–1843.

Cetorelli, N., and L. Goldberg (2012b). Follow the Money: Quantifying Domestic Effects of Foreign Bank Shocks in the Great Recession. *The American Economic Review 102*(3): 213–218.

Chakraborty, I., R. Hai, H. A. Holter, and S. Stepanchuk (2017). The Real Effects of Financial (Dis)Integration: A Multi-Country Equilibrium Analysis of Europe. *Journal of Monetary Economics*.

Chan, Y.-S., and A. V. Thakor (1987). Collateral and Competitive Equilibria with Moral Hazard and Private Information. *The Journal of Finance 42*(2): 345–363.

Chaney, T., D. Sraer, and D. Thesmar (2012). The Collateral Channel: How Real Estate Shocks Affect Corporate Investment. *American Economic Review 102*(6): 2381–2409.

Chang, X., Y. Chen, S. Q. Wang, K. Zhang, and W. Zhang (2017). Credit Default Swaps and Corporate Innovation. *Forthcoming, Journal of Financial Economics*.

Chava, S., and M. R. Roberts (2008). How Does Financing Impact Investment? The Role of Debt Covenants. *The Journal of Finance 63*(5): 2085–2121.

Chiappori, P.-A., and B. Salanié (2000). Testing for Asymmetric Information in Insurance Markets. *Journal of political Economy 108*(1): 56–78.

Claessens, S., S. R. Ghosh, and R. Mihet (2013). Macro-Prudential Policies to Mitigate Financial System Vulnerabilities. *Journal of International Money and Finance 39*: 153–185.

Claessens, S., and N. van Horen (2014). Foreign Banks: Trends and Impact. *Journal of Money, Credit and Banking 46*(s1): 295–326.

Cloyne, J., K. Huber, E. Ilzetzki, and H. Kleven (2017). The effect of house prices on household borrowing: a new approach. Technical report, National Bureau of Economic Research.

Colonnello, S., M. Efing, and F. Zucchi (2016). Empty Creditors and Strong Shareholders: The Real Effects of Credit Risk Trading. *Forthcoming, Journal of Financial Economics*.

Cox, D., and T. Jappelli (1993). The Effect of Borrowing Constraints on Consumer Liabilities. *Journal of Money, Credit and Banking 25*(2): 197–213.

Danis, A. (2016). Do Empty Creditors Matter? Evidence from Distressed Exchange Offers. *Management Science 63*(5): 1285–1301.

Danis, A., and A. Gamba (2018). The Real Effects of Credit Default Swaps. *Journal of Financial Economics 127*(1): 51–76.

Das, S., M. Kalimipalli, and S. Nayak (2014). Did CDS Trading Improve the Market for Corporate Bonds? *Journal of Financial Economics 111*(2): 495–525.

Davydenko, S. A., and J. R. Franks (2008). Do Bankruptcy Codes Matter? A Study of Defaults in France, Germany, and the UK. *The Journal of Finance 63*(2): 565–608.

De Roure, C., L. Pelizzon, and A. Thakor (2018). P2p lenders versus banks: Cream skimming or bottom fishing?

Degryse, H., Y. Gündüz, K. O'Flynn, and S. Ongena (2019). Identifying Empty Creditors with a Shock and Micro-Data. *KU Leuven Memeo.*

Degryse, H., V. Ioannidou, J. M. Liberti, and J. Sturgess (2016). When do laws and institutions affect recovery rates on collateral?

Degryse, H., M. Kim, and S. Ongena (2009). *Microeconometrics of Banking: Methods, Applications, and Results.* Oxford University Press.

Demyanyk, Y., and O. Van Hemert (2009). Understanding the Subprime Mortgage Crisis. *The Review of Financial Studies 24*(6): 1848–1880.

Diamond, D. W., and R. G. Rajan (2005). Liquidity Shortages and Banking Crises. *The Journal of finance 60*(2): 615–647.

Diamond, D. W., and R. G. Rajan (2012). Illiquid Banks, Financial Stability, and Interest Rate Policy. *Journal of Political Economy 120*(3): 552–591.

Disyatat, P. (2011). The Bank Lending Channel Revisited. *Journal of Money, Credit and Banking 43*(4): 711–734.

Dou, Y. (2017). The spillover effect of consolidating securitization entities on small business lending. *Available at SSRN 2727958.*

Dou, Y., S. G. Ryan, and B. Xie (2018). The Real Effects of Fas 166/167 on Banks' Mortgage Approval and Sale Decisions. *Journal of Accounting Research 56*(3): 843–882.

Drechsler, I., A. Savov, and P. Schnabl (2018). Banking on deposits: Maturity transformation without interest rate risk. *NBER Working Paper Series No. 24582.*

Duffee, G. R., and C. Zhou (2001). Credit Derivatives in Banking: Useful Tools for Managing Risk? *Journal of Monetary Economics 48*(1): 25–54.

Ehrmann, M., L. Gambacorta, J. Martínez-Pagés, P. Sevestre, and A. Worms (2001). Financial systems and the role of banks in monetary policy transmission in the Euro area. *ECB Working Paper Series No. 105.*

Ehrmann, M., and M. Ziegelmeyer (2017). Mortgage Choice in the Euro Area: Macroeconomic Determinants and the Effect of Monetary Policy on Debt Burdens. *Journal of Money, Credit and Banking 49*(2–3): 469–494.

Engle, R., and C. Granger (1987). Co-Integration and Error Correction: Representation, Estimation, and Testing. *Econometrica 55*(2): 251.

English, W. B., S. J. V. D. Heuvel, and E. Zakraj (2018). Interest Rate Risk and Bank Equity Valuations. *Journal of Monetary Economics 98*: 80–97.

Esposito, L., A. Nobili, and T. Ropele (2015). The Management of Interest Rate Risk During the Crisis: Evidence from Italian Banks. *Journal of Banking & Finance 59*: 486–504.

European Commission (2017). European financial stability and integration review. Technical report.

Evans, D. S., and B. Jovanovic (1989). An Estimated Model of Entrepreneurial Choice Under Liquidity Constraints. *Journal of Political Economy 97*(4): 808–827.

Evans, D. S., and L. S. Leighton (1989). Some Empirical Aspects of Entrepreneurship. *The American Economic Review 79*(3): 519–535.

Flannery, M. J., and C. M. James (1984a). Market Evidence on the Effective Maturity of Bank Assets and Liabilities. *Journal of Money, Credit and Banking 16*(4): 435–445.

Flannery, M. J., and C. M. James (1984b). The Effect of Interest Rate Changes on the Common Stock Returns of Financial Institutions. *The Journal of Finance 39*(4): 1141–1153.

Froot, K. A., D. S. Scharfstein, and J. C. Stein (1993). Risk Management: Coordinating Corporate Investment and Financing Policies. *The Journal of Finance 48*(5): 1629–1658.

Fuster, A., M. Plosser, P. Schnabl, and J. Vickery (2019). The Role of Technology in Mortgage Lending. *The Review of Financial Studies 32*(5): 1854–1899.

Fuster, A., and J. Vickery (2015). Securitization and the Fixed-Rate Mortgage. *Review of Financial Studies 28*(1): 176–211.

Gajewski, K., A. Jara, Y. Kang, J. Mok, D. Moreno, and D. Serwa (2019). International Spillovers of Monetary Policy: Lessons from Chile, Korea, and Poland. *Journal of International Money and Finance 90*: 175–186.

Giannetti, M., and L. Laeven (2012). Flight Home, Flight Abroad, and International Credit Cycles. *The American Economic Review 102*(3): 219–224.

Goetzmann, W., and K. G. Rouwenhorst (2008). The History of Financial Innovation. In *Carbon Finance, Environmental Market Solutions to Climate Change*, Chapter 1, pp. 18–43. Yale School of Forestry and Environmental Studies.

Gomez, M., A. Landier, D. Sraer, and D. Thesmar (2016). Banks exposure to interest rate risk and the transmission of monetary policy. *NBER Working Paper Series No. 18857.*

Gorton, G., and A. Metrick (2012). Securitized Banking and the Run on Repo. *Journal of Financial economics 104*(3): 425–451.

Gorton, G. B., and G. G. Pennacchi (1995). Banks and Loan Sales Marketing Nonmarketable Assets. *Journal of monetary Economics 35*(3): 389–411.

Gräb, J., and D. Żochowski (2017). The International Bank lending channel of unconventional monetary policy. *ECB Working Paper Series No 2109.*

Gündüz, Y., S. Ongena, G. Tümer-Alkan, and Y. Yu (2016). CDS and Credit: Testing the Small Bang Theory of the Financial Universe with Micro Data. *Deutsche Bundesbank Discussion Paper.*

Hannan, T. H., and A. N. Berger (1991). The Rigidity of Prices: Evidence from the Banking Industry. *The American Economic Review 81*(4): 938–945.

Hart, O., and J. Moore (1994). A Theory of Debt Based on the Inalienability of Human Capital. *The Quarterly Journal of Economics 109*(4): 841–879.

Hasan, I., and D. Wu (2017). Credit default swaps and bank loan sales: evidence from bank syndicated lending. *Gabelli School of Business Working Paper.*

Hayashi, F. (1982). The Permanent Income Hypothesis: Estimation and Testing by Instrumental Variables. *Journal of Political Economy 90*(5): 895–916.

Heckman, J. (1979). Sample Selection Bias as a Specification Error. *Econometrica 47*(1): 153.

Hellwig, M. (1994). Liquidity Provision, Banking, and the Allocation of Interest Rate Risk. *European Economic Review 38*(7): 1363–1389.

Hills, R., K. Ho, D. Reinhardt, R. Sowerbutts, E. Wong, and G. Wu (2019, feb). The International Transmission of Monetary Policy through Financial Centres: Evidence from the United Kingdom and Hong Kong. *Journal of International Money and Finance 90*: 76–98.

Hirtle, B. (2009). Credit Derivatives and Bank Credit Supply. *Journal of Financial Intermediation 18*(2): 125–150.

Hochberg, Y. V., C. J. Serrano, and R. H. Ziedonis (2018). Patent Collateral, Investor Commitment, and the Market for Venture Lending. *Journal of Financial Economics 130*(1): 74–94.

Hoffmann, P., S. Langfield, F. Pierobon, and G. Vuillemey (2018). Who Bears Interest Rate Risk? *Forthcoming, Review of Financial Studies*: 1–62.

Holmstrom, B., and J. Tirole (1997). Financial Intermediation, Loanable Funds, and the Real Sector. *the Quarterly Journal of economics 112*(3): 663–691.

Holtz-Eakin, D., D. Joulfaian, and H. S. Rosen (1994). Entrepreneurial Decisions and Liquidity Constraints. *The Rand Journal of Economics*: 334–347.

Hu, H. T., and B. Black (2008a). Debt, Equity and Hybrid Decoupling: Governance and Systemic Risk Implications. *European Financial Management 14*(4): 663–709.

Hu, H. T., and B. Black (2008b). Equity and Debt Decoupling and Empty Voting II: Importance and Extensions. *University of Pennsylvania Law Review 156*(3): 625–739.

Hurst, E., and A. Lusardi (2004). Liquidity Constraints, Household Wealth, and Entrepreneurship. *Journal of Political Economy 112*(2): 319–347.

Iacus, S. M., G. King, and G. Porro (2012). Causal Inference Without Balance Checking: Coarsened Exact Matching. *Political Analysis 20*(1): 1–24.

IMF (2019). Fintech: The experience so far. *IMP Policy paper*, 73.

Ioannidou, V., S. Ongena, and J.-L. Peydró (2014). Monetary Policy, Risk-Taking, and Pricing: Evidence from a Quasi-natural Experiment. *Review of Finance 19*(1): 95–144.

ISDA (2003). The 2003 ISDA credit derivatives definitions. Technical report.

ISDA (2009a). Standard European corporate CDS contract specification. Technical report.

ISDA (2009b). Standard North American corporate CDS contract specification. Technical report.

Jiménez, G., S. Ongena, J.-L. Peydró, and J. Saurina (2012). Credit Supply and Monetary Policy: Identifying the Bank Balance-Sheet Channel with Loan Applications. *American Economic Review 102*(5): 2301–2326.

Jiménez, G., S. Ongena, J.-L. Peydró, and J. Saurina (2014). Hazardous Times for Monetary Policy: What Do Twenty-Three Million Bank Loans Say About the Effects of Monetary Policy on Credit Risk-Taking? *Econometrica 82*(2): 463–505.

Kashyap, A., and J. C. Stein (2000). What Do a Million Observations on Banks Say About the Transmission of Monetary Policy? *The American Economic Review 90*(3): 407–428.

Keys, B. J., T. Mukherjee, A. Seru, and V. Vig (2010). Did Securitization Lead to Lax Screening? Evidence from Subprime Loans. *The Quarterly Journal of Economics 125*(1): 307–362.

Khwaja, A. I., and A. Mian (2008). Tracing the Impact of Bank Liquidity Shocks: Evidence from an Emerging Market. *The American Economic Review 98*(4): 1413–1442.

Kiyotaki, N., and J. Moore (1997). Credit Cycles. *Journal of Political Economy 105*(2): 211–248.

Krippner, L. (2016). Documentation for Measures of Monetary Policy. *Reserve Bank of New Zealand* (mimeo): 1–19.

Krippner, L. (2019). A Note of Caution on Shadow Rate Estimates. *Journal of Money, Credit and Banking*, jmcb.12613.

Kruglova, A., and K. Styrin (2018). Transmission of foreign monetary shocks to a small open economy under structural instability : the case of Russia. *Bank of Russia Working Paper Series No. 38*.

Li, F., K. L. Morgan, and A. M. Zaslavsky (2018, jan). Balancing Covariates via Propensity Score Weighting. *Journal of the American Statistical Association 113*(521): 390–400.

Li, J. Y., and D. Y. Tang (2016, jun). The Leverage Externalities of Credit Default Swaps. *Journal of Financial Economics 120*(120): 491–513.

Liberti, J. M., and M. A. Petersen (2019). Information: Hard and Soft. *The Review of Corporate Finance Studies 8*(1): 1–41.

Lindner, P., A. Loeffler, E. Segalla, G. Valitova, and U. Vogel (2019). International Monetary Policy Spillovers through the Bank Funding Channel. *Journal of International Money and Finance 90*(13): 161–174.

Loutskina, E. (2011). The Role of Securitization in Bank Liquidity and Funding Management. *Journal of Financial Economics 100*(3): 663–684.

Maddala, G. S., and F. D. Nelson (1974). Maximum Likelihood Methods for Models of Markets in Disequilibrium. *Econometrica: Journal of the Econometric Society*, 1013–1030.

Maddaloni, A., and J.-L. Peydró (2011). Bank risk-taking, securitization, supervision, and Low Interest Rates: Evidence from the Euro-Area and the US Lending Standards. *The Review of Financial Studies 24*(6): 2121–2165.

Mann, W. (2018). Creditor Rights and Innovation: Evidence from Patent Collateral. *Journal of Financial Economics 130*(1): 25–47.

Markit (2009a). The CDS Big Bang: Understanding the changes to the global CDS contract and North American conventions. Technical report.

Markit (2009b). The CDS Small Bang: Understanding the global contract & European convention changes. Technical report.

Mayordomo, S., J. I. Pena, and E. S. Schwartz (2014, sep). Are All Credit Default Swap Databases Equal? *European Financial Management 20*(4): 677–713.

Mian, A., and A. Sufi (2009). The Consequences of Mortgage Credit Expansion: Evidence from the US Mortgage Default Crisis. *The Quarterly Journal of Economics 124*(4): 1449–1496.

Minton, B. A., R. Stulz, and R. Williamson (2009). How Much Do Banks Use Credit Derivatives to Hedge Loans? *Journal of Financial Services Research 35*(1): 1–31.

Morais, B., J.-L. Peydró, J. Roldán Peña, and C. Ruiz Ortega (2019). The International Bank Lending Channel of Monetary Policy Rates and Quantitative Easing. *The Journal of Finance LXXIV*(1): 55–90.

Newey, W., and K. West (1987). A Simple, Positive Semi-Definite, Heteroskedasticity and Autocorrelation Consistent Covariance Matrix. *Econometrica 52*: 345–380.

Nickell, S. (1981). Biases in Dynamic Models with Fixed Effects. *Econometrica 49*(6): 1417.

Oehmke, M., and A. Zawadowski (2015). Synthetic or Real? the Equilibrium Effects of Credit Default Swaps on Bond Markets. *The Review of Financial Studies 28*(12): 3303–3337.

Oehmke, M., and A. Zawadowski (2017). The Anatomy of the CDS Market. *The Review of Financial Studies 30*(1): 80–119.

Ongena, S., J.-L. Peydró, and N. van Horen (2015). Shocks Abroad, Pain at Home? Bank-Firm-Level Evidence on the International Transmission of Financial Shocks. *IMF Economic Review 63*(4): 698–750.

Ongena, S., G. Tumer-Alkan, and N. von Westernhagen (2018). Do Exposures to Sagging Real Estate, Subprime, or Conduits Abroad Lead to Contraction and Flight to Quality in Bank Lending at Home? *Review of Finance 22*(4): 1335–1373.

Pagano, M., F. Panetta, and L. Zingales (1998). Why Do Companies Go Public? An Empirical Analysis. *The Journal of Finance 53*(1): 27–64.

Parlour, C. A., and G. Plantin (2008). Loan Sales and Relationship Banking. *The Journal of Finance 63*(3): 1291–1314.

Parlour, C. A., and A. Winton (2013). Laying Off Credit Risk: Loan Sales Versus Credit Default Swaps. *Journal of Financial Economics 107*(1): 25–45.

Peek, J., and E. Rosengren (1997). The International Transmission of Financial Shocks: The Case of Japan. *The American Economic Review 87*(4): 495–505.

Peek, J., and E. Rosengren (2000). Collateral Damage: Effects of the Japanese Bank Crisis on Real Activity in the United States. *The American Economic Review 90*(1): 30–45.

Pennacchi, G. G. (1988). Loan Sales and the Cost of Bank Capital. *The Journal of Finance 43*(2): 375–396.

Petersen, M. A., and R. G. Rajan (1994). The Benefits of Lending Relationships: Evidence from Small Business Data. *The Journal of Finance 49*(1): 3–37.

Petersen, M. A., and S. R. Thiagarajan (2000). Risk Measurement and Hedging: With and Without Derivatives. *Financial Management 29*(4): 5–29.

Philippon, T. (2016). The fintech opportunity. Technical report, National Bureau of Economic Research.

Popov, A., and S. Ongena (2011). Interbank Market Integration, Loan Rates, and Firm Leverage. *Journal of Banking & Finance 35*: 544–559.

Purnanandam, A. (2007). Interest Rate Derivatives at Commercial Banks: An Empirical Investigation. *Journal of Monetary Economics 54*(6): 1769–1808.

Purnanandam, A. (2010). Originate-to-Distribute Model and the Subprime Mortgage Crisis. *The Review of Financial Studies 24*(6): 1881–1915.

Rajan, R. G. (2006). Has Finance Made the World Riskier? *European Financial Management 12*(4): 499–533.

Rampini, A. A., and S. Viswanathan (2010). Collateral, Risk Management, and the Distribution of Debt Capacity. *The Journal of Finance 65*(6): 2293–2322.

Rampini, A. A., S. Viswanathan, and G. Vuillemey (2019). Risk management in financial institutions. *Duke University Mimeo 33*.

Saretto, A., and H. E. Tookes (2012). Corporate Leverage, Debt Maturity and Credit Supply: The Role of Credit Default Swaps. *The Review of Financial Studies 26*(972): 1190–1247.

Schmalz, M. C., D. Sraer, and D. Thesmar (2017). Housing Collateral and Entrepreneurship. *The Journal of Finance 72*(1): 99–132.

Schmidt, J., M. Caccavaio, L. Carpinelli, and G. Marinelli (2018). International Spillovers of Monetary Policy: Evidence from France and Italy. *Journal of International Money and Finance 89*: 50–66.

Smith, C. W., and R. M. Stulz (1985). The Determinants of Firms' Hedging Policies. *The Journal of Financial and Quantitative Analysis 20*(4): 391.

Stein, R. M. (2002). Benchmarking default prediction models: Pitfalls and remedies in model validation. *Moody's KMV, New York 20305*.

Stiglitz, J. E., and A. Weiss (1981). Credit Rationing in Markets with Imperfect Information. *The American Economic Review 71*(3): 393–410.

Streitz, D. (2016). The Impact of Credit Default Swap Trading on Loan Syndication. *Review of Finance 20*(1): 265–286.

Subrahmanyam, M. G., D. Y. Tang, and S. Q. Wang (2014). Does the Tail Wag the Dog?: The Effect of Credit Default Swaps on Credit Risk. *The Review of Financial Studies 27*(10): 2926–2960.

Subrahmanyam, M. G., D. Y. Tang, and S. Q. Wang (2017). Credit Default Swaps, Exacting Creditors and Corporate Liquidity Management. *Journal of Financial Economics 124*(2): 395–414.

Sufi, A. (2007, apr). Information Asymmetry and Financing Arrangements: Evidence from Syndicated Loans. *The Journal of Finance 62*(2): 629–668.

Tang, H. (2019). Peer-to-Peer Lenders Versus Banks: Substitutes or Complements? *The Review of Financial Studies 32*(5): 1900–1938.

Temesvary, J., S. Ongena, and A. L. Owen (2018). A Global Lending Channel Unplugged? Does U.S. Monetary Policy Affect Cross-Border and Affiliate Lending by Global U.S. Banks? *Journal of International Economics 112*: 50–69.

Townsend, R. M. (1979). Optimal Contracts and Competitive Markets with Costly State Verification. *Journal of Economic Theory 21*(2): 265–293.

Vallee, B., and Y. Zeng (2019). Marketplace Lending: A New Banking Paradigm? *The Review of Financial Studies 32*(5): 1939–1982.

Wu, J., A. Luca, and B. N. Jeon (2011). Foreign Bank Penetration and the Lending Channel in Emerging Economies: Evidence from Bank-Level Panel Data. *Journal of International Money and Finance*.

Index

A

Affiliates, 149

Asset sensitive, 44

B

Bank failure, 41

Banking competition, 145

Banking deposits

  duration, 36, 39

Bank regulation, 191

Bank run, 27

Branches, 149

C

Co-integration, 145

Collateral, 105

  collateral channel, 119

  financing constraints, 116

  intangible assets, 125

  legal framework, 126

  movable assets, 122

  non-tradeable collateral, 113

  real estate collateral, 113

Commitment device, 81

Credit cycles, 162

Credit default swaps, 63

  bank monitoring, 76

  Big Bang, 65, 87

  empty creditor, 81, 84, 91

  hedging motives, 70

  leverage, 89

  moral hazard, 76

  probability of default, 83, 89

  restructuring clause, 65

  shareholder bargaining power, 86

  Small Bang, 65

  spillovers, 92

  technological innovation, 92

Cross-border prudential policy spillovers, 165

D

Data

  Amadeus, 122

  AnaCredit, 138

A. Bilan et al., *Banking and Financial Markets*, Palgrave Macmillan Studies in Banking and Financial Institutions,
https://doi.org/10.1007/978-3-030-26844-2

Auxmoney, 185
Consolidated Banking Statistics, 138
credit registry, 138
Dealogic, 6
Dealscan, 11
DTCC-TIW, 66, 88
EMIR, 33, 47, 66
Equifax, 6
Home Mortgage Disclosure Act (HMDA), 6
Lending Club, 185
Locational Banking Statistics, 138
macroprudential policies, 141
monetary policy indicator, 140
monetary policy shadow rate, 141
Prosper, 185
supervisory, 33, 42, 47, 138
syndicated loans, 139
synthetic panel data, 145
Debt-Contracting Value of accounting information, 78
Difference-in-differences, 12, 68, 127, 192
Digital footprint, 186
Dynamic panel data models, 143

E
Entrepreneurship, 115
Equity returns
interest rate risk, 53
European Banking Authority, 195
Expected recovery rate, 129
External validity, 139

F
FinTech, 181
lending, 188
robo-advisor, 196
sophisticated investors, 196
Fixed effects, 34, 52, 67, 75, 141, 155, 157
disadvantages, 142
Foreign currency
hedging cost, 164

G
Generalized Method of Moments, 143
Global banking
organizational form, 149
GMM, *see* Generalized Method of Moments

H
Heckman sample selection model, 147
Hedging motives, 41
Home bias, 162
House prices, 116

I
Interbank integration, 144, 146
Interest rate risk
exposure, 43
hedging, 45
loan rate fixation, 37, 50
matching view, 35
measurement; duration gap, 42, 48; income gap, 39, 47
off-balance sheet, 38, 46, 48
on-balance sheet, 38
option risk, 44
repricing risk, 44
traditional view, 35
yield curve risk, 44, 46
Internal validity, 139, 158

L
Liability sensitive, 44
Loan rate fixation, 36

M
Matching, 67
  overlap weighting, 86
  propensity score, 79, 85
Meta-analyse, 158
Monetary policy
  bank lending standards, 14
  Euro OverNight Index Average, 14
Monetary policy transmission
  balance sheet channel, 135, 137
  bank lending channel, 51, 135, 154
  interest rate risk, 51
  international transmission, 154
  inward transmission, 135, 158
  outward transmission, 135, 160
  risk-taking channel, 157
Multivariate analysis, 187

N
Nested decision, *see* Nested logit model
Nested logit model, 72, 152

P
Panel data econometrics, 11
Patents, 125
Probability of default, 187

R
Regression discontinuity, 21

S
Securitization
  asset-backed securities, 5
  conduits, 15
  covered bonds, 26
  monetary policy, 13
  subprime loan, 5
Selection bias, 147, 151
Simultaneity bias, 143
Structural equilibrium model, 121

T
Technological advances, 186
Three-stage Tobit, 147
2SLS-IV, 34, 40, 41, 44, 68, 77, 85
Two-step analysis, 152

U
Unconventional monetary policy, 156, 157
  measurement, 160
Univariate analysis, 187

The manufacturer's authorised representative in the EU is Springer Nature Customer Service Centre GmbH, Europaplatz 3, 69115 Heidelberg, Germany. If you have any concerns regarding our products, please contact ProductSafety@springernature.com

Printed and bound by CPI Group (UK) Ltd, Croydon, CR0 4YY
22/09/2026
02221063-0001